The World of Lawrence

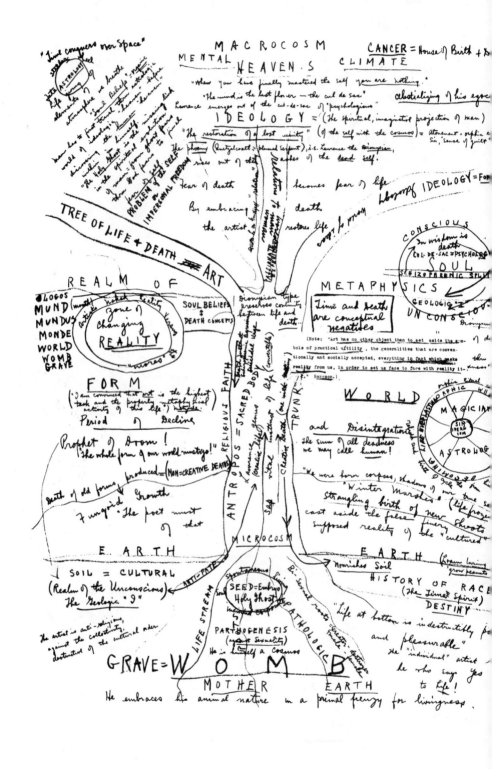

THE WORLD OF
LAWRENCE

A Passionate Appreciation

HENRY MILLER

Edited with an Introduction and Notes
by
Evelyn J. Hinz and John J. Teunissen

CAPRA PRESS
Santa Barbara
1980

ACKNOWLEDGMENTS

The Editors wish to acknowledge grants from the Social Sciences and Humanities Research Council of Canada and the University of Manitoba Grants Committee which enabled them to bring this work to its completion. Their research was much facilitated by the kindness and cooperation of Brooke Whiting and James V. Mink of UCLA Library Special Collections, where the bulk of the Miller manuscripts is housed. They are also very grateful to Elizabeth Kischuk and Douglas Smith for the time and effort they contributed to the project.

Library of Congress Cataloging in Publication Data

Miller, Henry, 1891-
  The world of Lawrence.

  1. Lawrence, David Herbert, 1885-1930. 2. Authors, English—20th century—Biography. I. Title.
PR6023.A93Z6814   823'.912   79-27735
ISBN 0-88496-147-8

CAPRA PRESS
Post Office Box 2068
Santa Barbara, California 93120

CONTENTS

WORLD OF LAWRENCE
(DIVISION OF BOOK)

I. CREATIVE PERSONALITY (including "individual in conflict with mind")

1. **Meaning** = duality of being, conflict, war
   a. Ideal of the Bourgeois = peace, security = because they fear the unrest idealogy
   b. Instead of humanity = because it prevents war (H.H.F.)

I. **Bisexuality** = $\left\{ \begin{array}{l} \text{Wake - World} \\ \text{Woof - Brass} \\ \text{Christ - death} \end{array} \right.$

2. **Type = MYSTIC** (rooted in Mystery) = }
   a. Prophet of doom — apostle of death
   b. Saviour = Resurrection: New Heaven & Earth   Love + Hate   Instead of humanity + providence
   c. Seer = (salvation of Sin (judgement, conquers)   (to attain) ... Cosmos) (apocalyptic vision)

3. Particular humanism = American Artist (self scripture)
   a. Cult of Death = fertility (PHENIX)
   b. Continuity of life & death (PHENIX)

4. **Vision** = New style of man (religion + gallery) = theosophic
   a. Oneness with Cosmos ... Vision-Cosmos-first-vision-man
   b. Godhood of the universe & life ... men live by
   c. Victory thru acceptance of death
   d. ...

5. Pathologic Element   ... nympho...
   a. Value of abnormality (human) = abnormal is the primitive & sacred
   b. Function = invisible pattern of his life + work
   c. Conquest of neurotic self (a neurotic idealogy) = (intuition of neurosis) = death
      a. Productive imagination = unfolding life
      b. * Role of Art = "proper multiplexed task" (disintegration of synthetic death (religious myth involves the tragic sense) — the tragic sense (cover...)
      1. Slavery of War gives men ... a role = (lethargic) (inner task)
         ("of ... to see the eternal ... laughter mask personal titanic ...)
      f. Rainbow made by harmony of proper covenant ... of synthetic ...
      g. Human situation — failure of friend + man — most of alone!

II. TRANSITION

ART
III. DISCOVERY of SELF ... **Ideal**

I. **Potent**
   Subject
   Bi-sexual
   Conflict   Mystic
   Building   Vision (humanism?)
   attainment

   III. (artist) (S)

HIS PHILOSOPHY (Weltanschauung) = Realistic of Conflict and ... experience = inner spiritual transformation thru (passionate experience of the Cosmos ... autonomous ... only Heart vs. Self

Realistic Absolute = total philosophy of spirit
   Soul means head in spirit
   feet ...
   role in man ...
   Western ...
   biological ideas vs. ... Absolute Vitalism
   Cosmic self ... Science
   Permanence of freedom vs. Idea
   Primary ...
   death
   Sacred Body
   Angels
   Art ...

Science
... ...
Absolute God
... ...   Phallic Worship
Warm
Peace
Beauty
Stillness
Absolute Good

No Sign of God Anywhere!
(Western hard on some of death) "the sense of man destroys man" call him "

Eschatology of his experientialism = leads finally to Humanizing process = microcosming of universe

SACRED BODY
(Transition of body) — feminine phenomenon — primal reality

the mystery of Sex = death and transformation
"Passionate curiosity experience = religion of the life worshipper — total instincts

"MASOCHISM
The Son (One force of man)

SACREFILE

May 1912, according to Murry, when he met the woman who was to be his wife "who enters now into the very substance of his work and remains in it to the end" marks the end of the first period of L's life and work, and the beginning of the second. Of these clearly marked period there were four. The first ends with his mother's death; the second begins with his meeting with his wife and ends with the end of the War; the third begins, roughly, with his leaving England in 1919 and ends with his abortive return to England at the end of 1923; the fourth and last period ends with his death, on March 3rd, 1930.

1- mother-trilogy (white Peacock + Trespasser)
2. Rainbow + Women in Love (Aaron)
3. Nights - Savage Pilgrimage (Kangaroo)
4. discovery of Self — wisdom

I

II

III

IV Man above Art = to observe art + create new man!
to life without art = art precedes Religion

V

VI

WOMB = GRAVE
WORLD OF FORM

TRAGIC ART

INTRODUCTION

With the publication of *The World of Lawrence*, Henry Miller's literary career may be said to come full circle. For if things had worked out as planned, instead of being his last major publication this book would have been his first.

The genesis of *The World of Lawrence* dates back to Paris, 1932, when Jack Kahane of the Obelisk Press, who had recently agreed to publish *Tropic of Cancer*, suggested to Miller that it would be politic if prior to the publication of such a shocking novel he were to appear on the literary scene as the author of a short critical study of Lawrence or Joyce. To be associated with these two established writers and to be known as a critic would give him status as a serious thinker—the kind of reputation which had helped Lawrence and Joyce to weather the censors. In addition, as Kahane saw it, it was only logical that Miller should write on Lawrence, since the Lawrencean influence on his ideas was so evident.

As one might expect, Miller's reactions were mixed. That Lawrence was significant in his own literary development was true; moreover, Lawrence had permeated his personal life as well. In the early 1920s, in New York, Lawrence had been the subject of many conversations between Miller and his good friend Emil Schnellock; in the mid-twenties, he had seen the Gudrun-Ursula relationship dramatized in the "lesbian" affairs of his wife, June. In Paris, in April 1931, he had met Walter Lowenfels, who was at the time working on his elegy for D. H. Lawrence. More recently and perhaps most significantly, it was by way of their mutual interest in Lawrence that Miller had met Anaïs Nin, the woman who by now had become his muse, confidante, and patroness.

Furthermore, stimulated by his conversations with Nin, whose *D. H. Lawrence: An Unprofessional Study* had just been published, and outraged by Mabel Dodge Luhan's *Lorenzo in Taos*, Miller had himself already determined to write something on Lawrence. Nor did he envision it as being a short or

11

insubstantial piece. "As for the Lawrence thing" he wrote to
Nin in April 1932, "I am almost afraid to embark on it. I want to
say so much that I am afraid that it will be too long to fit any
magazine or newspaper."

Under different circumstances, therefore, Miller would undoubtedly have welcomed Kahane's suggestion. As it was, he
felt rebellious, partly because of the calculating and spurious
aspect of the idea. Another part of it had to do with the reason
why Kahane thought such a strategy necessary: that Miller was
not sufficiently reputable to stand on his own. And much of it
had to do with the fact that Miller was being asked to borrow
literary stature from two writers who were virtually his own
age. With obvious pride he had written to Nin that during his
meeting with Kahane *Tropic of Cancer* had been described as
the "book of the century," as "magnificent, overwhelming
(epouvantable *etc., etc., etc.*) beside which *Lady Chatterley* and
Ulysses is [sic] lemonade." But to write on Lawrence and Joyce
as advance publicity would put him in the position of follower.
He also explained to Nin that Kahane had said that "Joyce and
Lawrence were sort of 'sneaked over,' but that now the time
had come to do it boldly, etc." If this were the case, however,
then why the need of the "brochure"?

Thus, though he agreed to go along with the plan, upon
returning home he became furious, and wrote out three pages
attacking Kahane. In this "fever," he also determined to write
an additional chapter to *Tropic*, "a gratuitous one, born of [his]
antagonism to Kahane's suggestion" which would "rival, or
excel, the last chapter of *Ulysses*, without being 'imitative'."
But he also plunged into the writing of the brochure with a
vengeance. So that, when a couple of days later Kahane informed him that if the first edition of *Tropic* were to be "private" the brochure would not be necessary, Miller declared
that he was going to go on with it, regardless, "because now it
was *my* affair."

It was now his affair in the sense that he was no longer
thinking in terms of the kind of brief promotional pamphlet
that Kahane had in mind. Rather the work was to be a large-
scale confrontation with Joyce and Lawrence which would
serve to banish them. "I want to say everything you omitted
[from your study of Lawrence] and wished to say," he wrote to
Nin; "I want to exhaust my ideas on these two men, and have

done with them for all time. I don't care how much I write."
Nor was he going to limit himself to these two contemporaries:
"As I said, I want to rid myself once and for all of this
incubus—of all the influences, gods, books, great names, etc.
which throttled me before. I want to free myself by one herculean effort, and in doing so give the finest counterpart to my
creative books. Let them jeer, if they will, at the emotionalism
or lack of form, etc. in the novels. This will give them a piece of
solid meat to bite into—and I hope I give them lockjaw."

With an energy matched only by the scope of his ambitions,
and with a dedication which led him to neglect anything
which did not contribute to the task at hand, Miller began
working on the project. In November 1932, with a mixture of
admiration, chagrin, and understanding, Nin recorded in her
Diary: "Henry has buried himself in his work; he has no time
for June. I fall back into my own work. Henry telephones me.
Mails me the bulk of his work, and I try to follow his ideas, but
what a tremendous arc he is making. D. H. Lawrence, Joyce,
Elie Faure, Dostoevsky, criticism, nudism, his creed, his attitude, Michael Fraenkel, Keyserling. He is asserting himself as
a thinker; he is asserting his seriousness. He is tired of being
considered a mere 'cunt painter,' and experimentalist, a
revolutionary."

That there might be a problem in his "thinking out in all
directions at once" did not at first concern Miller; rather he saw
it as a good sign: "Everything seems to connect. That means
I'm centipetalized, [sic] or something." Also, the original plan
he had devised for the organization of the book was a broad
four-part structure which could accommodate such latitude:
"With these four divisions, five counting introduction, I can
write largely and loosely," he explained to Nin. "There may be
overlapping in these rough divisions. But I think it will iron
itself out as I go along." And when his ideas expanded beyond
the scope of his original scheme, he simply devised another:
"The Brochure keeps expanding—I am drawing up a new
plan—a sort of outline of 10 major divisions. Getting a tremendous grip on it and it's deepening."

Although the brochure was, therefore, quickly becoming "a
veritable slaughterhouse of notes," Miller was not daunted but
exuberant. "All these pages of notes are like the pages of the
brain. I could go mad. But I'm sane as all hell. I feel like a seer,

And a prophet? A scourge." Whatever his writing lacked in terms of immediate coherence it made up for in "Big Macrocosmic Connections." Later there would be time to edit and coordinate; for the present getting his ideas down on paper was the imperative thing: "The notes pile up around me like weeds. I know I'm repeating myself a great deal, but I can't recall any more what I say and I'm afraid of losing a thought."

While generally speaking this period of intensity lasted for two years, in May 1933, its focus shifted dramatically. Whereas from November to May, Lawrence, like Joyce, had to a certain extent become lost in the welter of ideas and writers with whom Miller was concerned, from May onward Lawrence occupied the center of the stage. This happened because in May Miller's attitude toward Lawrence also underwent a profound change.

As we have seen, it was in a mood of defiance that Miller had agreed to Kahane's suggestion that he write on Lawrence and Joyce, and his initial objective was to put them in their place. In March 1933, this continued to be his objective; in a letter to Richard Osborne—who, incidentally, had introduced Miller to Anaïs Nin—Miller explained that he was "knocking the shit out of Joyce." And though, because of the contrast Lawrence presented to Joyce, Miller had come to be somewhat appreciative of the former, as late as March 29, 1933, his concern with Lawrence was also mainly to dispatch him. "I want more and more about Lawrence," he wrote to Nin, "the Murry book and Colin's book and even the Mabel Dodge Luhan one, if you still have it. I'm going to tackle him, while I'm at it, from *every* possible angle—want *all* the facts and interpretations possible. I may never refer to him again in my life. Must wash myself clean of him."

On May 7, 1933, however, he wrote to confess his error: "I feel I have said unkind, unjust things about Lawrence. He is far greater than I ever dreamt . . . . He stands out like a rock. He bides his time. I was practically ignorant of Lawrence when I began this study. Now I appreciate him deeply . . . . I feel humble and chastened. But I am more now than ever I was before." What occasioned this great change was that instead of, or in addition to, the other books he had requested, Nin had sent him Lawrence's short collection of essays entitled *Death of a Porcupine.*

   To appreciate why this collection, and particularly the essay on "The Crown" had such a tremendous impact on Miller, we must bear in mind that up until this time his knowledge of Lawrence had been largely confined to his major novels and to secondary sources. As a result, his image of Lawrence when he began the brochure was that of "a little runt, a nasty devil, a dry, thoroughly English type. I despise his workingman's (no, it was bourgeois) attitude about things—scrubbing floors, cooking, laundering, etc. And his being alone crap! Not sensitiveness, but timidity, lack of guts, lack of humanity." Similarly, "remark the sickly letters Lawrence wrote," he observed to Nin in April 1932—referring to those which appear in Mabel Dodge Luhan's book. "How could he have fallen into the clutches of such a woman? There was something feeble about him—despite his glorious language." In "The Crown," by contrast, he found a man, a profound thinker, and a visionary: "The language is matchless—reminiscent of the best in the Bible. The thought is superior to any of Jesus' sayings, in my opinion. It is like a new Revelation. It is based on Spengler.... And it goes beyond Spengler.... The seed of all Lawrence's writing is here—and more than just seed. It is the mystic at his most mystical. I am in love with it."

   "The Crown," in short, was the kind of manifesto and testament that Miller had for the past eight months been struggling to formulate. Consequently on the one hand he regretted that he had not seen it earlier: "It might have saved me a lot of work. On the other hand, it was terribly good to win through to this and to find the answer to all the enigmas he presents most wonderfully treated." Possibly what is most indicative of Miller's reconciliation with Lawrence, however, is his ability to comment on Lawrence's relative youth when he wrote "The Crown": I am amazed that it was written at such an early age—30 years!"

   That he was now going to make Lawrence his chief concern, and that he was now going to elucidate rather than expose him, did not, as Miller saw it, require that he scrap all that he had written in the previous months. For now that Miller apprehended him correctly, Lawrence was the embodiment of many of the ideas which he had been developing on his own. Almost as much time as he spent writing out his new ideas, therefore, he spent in going over what he had written, writing marginal instructions about the revision or expansion of an idea, and trying to determine where a section should be inserted. Helping him here was Anaïs Nin, and the time and effort she gave to the task is evident from the numerous notations in her hand which are to be found on the typescripts.

Though Miller's new focus meant that Kahane was in a sense going to get a *book* on *Lawrence*, it also meant that he was going to have to wait. In a letter to William Bradley, the agent who had directed him to Kahane, Miller summarizes his situation. His words are too moving to paraphrase, the substance too revelatory to condense:

> *May 30th, 1933*
>
> *Dear Mr. Bradley:*
>   *I realize suddenly that two weeks have elapsed and your letter gone unanswered. I change my mind about showing you the Lawrence book just yet. What good is there in showing it to you now in its imperfect, sadly unfinished, much muddled state? You are obliged to read so much junk, professionally. It can wait. Or I can wait, if you can. I'm seldom in a hurry. I don't mean to say that I want to withhold it until it's absolutely finished and perfect (?), but certainly not yet because I am constantly revising my opinions, or rather constantly deepening my point of view, if there be such a thing as deepening a point of view.*
>   *You must realize that I have given up a hell of a lot of time to this Lawrence devil—first grudgingly, because I had intended to dispatch him en passant, then willingly, and now with fullest delight and admiration for his genius. If I had persisted in my first method of approach (it was mostly all "attack") I would have brought out an interesting and provocative book. As it is, I sincerely believe my book, when finished, will be all that, plus something more. A man like myself, with an earnest purpose (you concede that, I hope!) must have found good reason to tarry so long over this subject of Lawrence. It is what he has given me to ponder on that I want to have permeate the book. I have been see-sawing over various methods of ordering the book—the order, the presentation—that is the most difficult for me. And I want no advice, no help—naturally. I say this probably because I realize so deeply that for me form is so vastly important. But it's got to be my form and not what the jackasses consider form.*
>   *Perhaps you smile a little when you read this, about form.*

Would anybody imagine me to be interested in that? Hardly. But it's so. "From Goethe form . . . from Nietzsche the questioning faculty" said Spengler in his preface to "Decline of the West." And to the French there is probably damned little of what they consider "form" in Spengler's great work. But to any worth-while artist, any man who is above the usual considerations of form, there is something tremendously organic in the conception and execution of this philosophy of doom. And perhaps—who knows how intimately these are related—perhaps what gives form to such works is the very "questioning faculty" he mentions, in paying his tribute to his other influence, Nietzsche.

All of this may seem much beside the point, but it really isn't. In my head I have written the Lawrence book several times over. It is all clear to me now, and the material lies about in the form of notes, some quite elaborately expanded, almost valid as they stand, whole sections very well written out, and heaps more lying tacitly exposed in jagged notes which mean worlds to me, but would be Greek to any one else. I have carried the whole thing around with me for months and I am thoroughly saturated with it. You have only to say Lawrence to me, or stars, or dragon, or evil, or Quetzalcoatl (few mention this ever!)—say most anything and I explode. I can orate from any given point, like a volcano which blasts forth each time from a new crater. That's how it is now. Intensely fascinating. And intensely painful. No suspense quite like that of bringing off the final thing.

The world must be stood on end, defeated, convinced against its will—always, always. The world is always wrong. And I who say this, savagely, fanatically, blindly, obstinately, I know full well what hell there is in store for me with such an attitude, but it is the only attitude, it is true, sincere, just.

I don't know quite why I am saying all this to you—I had intended only to write a brief note of apology and say what ho, about the grand dinner, etc. And here I am, as usual, launching forth on my pet subject. Perhaps it is inspired by a dim apprehension that what appeared in the beginning to look like a good business relationship between us is quite impossible, and that you, no more than Pinker in Lawrence's case, will be able to do much for me—commercially. What you have done already is what I value most and what endears you to me eternally. You put out your hand to me in a critical moment. You did the fine and brave thing of trying to see what it was I was aiming at. That I can never thank you for sufficiently. And so, I imagine, anticipating the strife ahead, we shall have to look forward in the future to a more human and dangerous relationship–simple friendship.

I hope you do not misunderstand my words. I am not trying to make it impossible for you to aid me, but I just fear it will be impossible. I think I shall be even more harried than Lawrence was–because, as I see it, people have not changed, nor is there much likelihood they will. The world grows grayer, drearier, deader. And as it does I grow brighter, gayer, harder. I will not change. I will not compromise. If yesterday I was willing to cut out phrases and lines, paragraphs even, to-morrow I will not change a word, not a word. The word may be trite, cliche, inartistic, wrong even, . . . I will not alter it! I am going to have my say even if it kills me. And what does it matter to me, in the long run, whether I am published now or after my death? I don't give a fuck about posterity–get that straight. Nor about humanity. I care about my own integrity–that means everything to me. There I will not concede an inch, not a millimeter. Sad news for Kahane, perhaps, and all the rest who look forward to feeding on the dead body of the artist. And don't think, either, that I am cutting off my nose to spite my face. I am not! I am in dead, bitter earnest, that's all, and who is Kahane or Knopf or anybody else in this world to tell me what I am to say or what not to say? That's what I want to know. They can squelch me, if they choose. They can deny me, refuse to listen to me. That's their outlook, not mine. I go my way. If I croak, if the fight is too much, tant pis. I am not going to surrender. Take that from me. That's my fundament.

I am so beastly sick of the lily-livered bastards who are feeding the public with the muck and garbage of literature to-day. In defending Lawrence, in championing this corpse, I am waging war against his eternal enemies, my eternal enemies. Never was there an age which a man could be less proud of than this. It is a crime to have been born. And every new child born of this age is a crime against God. Is that going far? That's nothing. I have much worse to say. Perhaps you won't stick when you hear the rest. All right, don't! I am not for balance, or sanity, or therapeutics. I am for a complete fanatical and religious revolution. I don't care how much blood is spilled, nor how many peoples are exterminated. I wouldn't mind if half the earth were depopulated, if there sprang up a plague that strewed the earth with cadav-

ers so that the very heavens stank. *I think it would be a relief
to have a* genuine *stench, a putrescent stench and not just
the stench of* SHIT. *I think, if you will permit me the delicacy,
that Joyce is such a stench. As much as I have championed
Lawrence so much and more will I attack Joyce.*

*I should like by the end of this year to get Joyce and
Lawrence and Proust, and the whole thesis of my brochure
done with, for good and all. Let that be my philosophy. It
was humiliating to me to sit in your office and be requested
to write a little brochure about this man or that man in order
to introduce myself. I didn't want any introduction. I
wanted simply to stand up and let go—be knocked over for it
or lauded for it. But not apologize, not explain myself. I can't
tell you how ignominious that seemed to me. And if, finally,
I appeared to acquiesce, you can see now what manner of
acquiescence it was. Kahane will never accept my Lawrence
book, I feel quite confident of it. Nor the "brochure." Nor the
Joyce, nor the Proust. Nor my "Tropic of Capricorn." I just
know he won't. I feel it in my bones. I feel that at bottom he
doesn't give a damn about me, about what I stand for. He
doesn't know what I stand for. And perhaps it's that that
galls me. But before this year's out it wll be known what I
stand for. And there'll be a sharp alignment—friends and
enemies, mostly the latter, I expect. I am hoping that you
will always remain one of the friends. Even when you dis-
agree with me—mostly then. That is all.*

About the dinner—Jesus, I don't know. That's a practical
*thing, and I'm lost in such matters. I can't invite you to the
royal sort of feast I once anticipated giving you. And why
should you come to Clichy for an ordinary meal? Let things
work themselves out naturally. A dinner isn't so important.
It's more important that you know how I feel about you.
That will stick to your ribs much much longer than the best
meal I could blow you to.*

*After all this emotion the natural thing for you to say
is—"Let me buy the meal!" Please don't. It makes me em-
barassed. I detest being obliged to accept invitations, no
matter how well-meaning. It always makes me feel like
poisoning my host. And I don't want to poison you.*

Cordially,

HVM.

P.S. Seven pages! I don't know how I got this way. Excuse me.

Throughout the summer of 1933 Miller worked on "The World of Lawrence," more than ever like one possessed. "My head's bursting," he wrote to Nin in September; "Never made so many connections, syncopes, ellisions and syntheses in my life." And though he felt on the point of exhaustion—"I have just worn down to a flame in the last two days. I can't go much further than this"—this time he was determined to finish. "Previously everything has been aborted by this or that—by *myself*, I suppose. Now—not even an earthquake could keep me from carrying out my plans." What was driving him now, however, was not merely his respect for Lawrence but his identification with him. "Epoch-making days, I tell you. It's not Lawrence—it's myself I'm making a place for!" In making his study of Lawrence a mode of self-expression he was, of course, moving in the direction of Lawrence in *Studies in Classic American Literature*, and perhaps consciously so since it is in this same context that he mentions the book.

What proved to be the stumbling block, therefore, was not any antagonism between his subject and himself but the question of organization: how to co-ordinate the material he wanted to salvage and the new passages he had written, and how to coordinate the multiple purposes the book was designed to serve?

One of the strategies he considered was to write a "preface" which would explain the genesis of the book and provide an overview. So that the position of this preface should itself be symbolic of the issues involved, Miller also thought of placing it in the midst of the book:

> It may seem unusual to put a preface in the very middle of a book, but a logic which I might call a chronologic logic dictates its appearance here. It was only in the midst of my task that I caught the real clue to my approach; this revelation seems to me important enough to warrant an explanation in the form of a belated preface.
>
> To begin with I must acknowledge that I began my task in a prejudicial mood, rather against Lawrence than for him. I had practically dismissed him from my mind; not that I regarded him as negligible, but convinced rather that he had nothing more to offer me. And so I began a study which was never finished—unless this book be regarded as the outgrowth of it. The hundred or so pages which I had originally planned to write soon passed beyond the mark. When I had written

almost a full-sized book I suddenly realized with alarm and distress that I was slowly sinking into a quagmire, I discovered to my amazement the most abundant and startling contradictions. Finally I began to question my ability to think clearly, if at all. And so the day came when I asked myself very quietly and humbly-what does *Lawrence stand for?*

Now when I had come to this degree of proper humility I promptly forgot my thesis, together with my prejudices and preconceived ideas, and gave myself up to a passionate, whole-hearted study of the man. I read what others had written about him, and I read even more attentively what he had written about himself. It was not long before I discovered that I had never truly understood him. Only now was I beginning to realize the meaning *of his words. In everything which my eye fell upon I began to discover a vast identity of meaning. The whole symbolism of his life and work made itself manifest to me.*

And so, as I planned the form and content of this work, the vast symbolic import of Lawrence remained constant and uppermost in my mind. I saw that as with other men in the past whom he resembled spiritually there was springing up about his name a legend and that this legend was destined to survive. I saw that this legend had its inception in an enigma, the enigma of a creative personality.

One day, when I had been more than usually perplexed as to the shape this work would assume, I picked up a pencil and, almost instinctively began drawing a tree. Now the strange and fascinating thing about this incident is that from the moment I began drawing the tree everything fell into whack–the man, the book, his ideas, the world he found himself in and the world he had created. It was as if I had drawn the tree of life itself, which quite unconsciously I had.

Did I know, when I commenced drawing a tree, that I was falling back upon one of the oldest symbols of man, a symbol which has appeared wherever and whenever man has thought about life and death? No, I am very happy to say I did not. In stumbling upon this eternal symbol I had to repeat a process almost as old as the race itself. I am glad that it happened thus because it made me realize something which heretofore I had only vaguely known–that the oldest symbols of the race are the embodiment of the oldest truths. They are the product of the oldest way of looking at the universe, which is imaginatively. *It is the fictive element in art, I know now absolutely, which sustains the whole grandiose structure of life.*

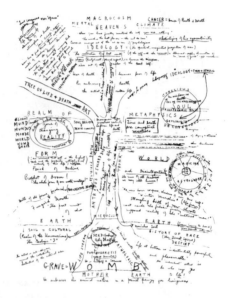

In addition to drawing this "symbolic" tree, Miller also constructed a wall chart entitled "The Tree of Life" as a way of
ordering his thoughts about the Lawrence book. "The great
need I have, with the terrific mass of data in my head," he
explained to Nin, "is to *see* it before my eyes, *to see it in some
order."*

By October 1933, however, his sympathies with Lawrence's
struggles had become so identified with his own frustrations
that he could no longer see clearly or distance himself in any
way from his material. And, as if the suffering caused by the
Lawrence book was not enough, Kahane announced that he
was going to delay the publication of *Tropic of Cancer.*

Exactly when Miller decided to abandon his "World of Lawrence" is difficult to determine. Since Anaïs Nin took a portion
of the book to Rebecca West in April 1934, he was apparently
still involved in the work at that time, and as late as 1941 he
observed that after he finished his current projects and "after
the Lawrence book is finished" he had "nothing more to write"
and would retire. In 1938, however, in the version of "The
Universe of Death" which he published in *Max and the White
Phagocytes*, he explained that he had given up and why. After
emphasizing the significance of Lawrence's vitality and his
creative reaction to death, Miller went on: "The fact remains,

nevertheless, that not even a Lawrence was able to exercise any visible influence upon the world. The times are stronger than the men who are thrown up. We are in a dead-lock. We have a choice, but we are unable to make it. It was the realization of this which impelled me to end my long introduction to *The World of Lawrence*, of which this is the final section, with the title "The Universe of Death." Since, actually, in Miller's plan for the book, this section was scheduled to appear as the third chapter (the organization below), that he should here describe it as the conclusion is symtomatic of his intense despair.

Here and there, in the late 30s and early 40s, Miller also published other fragments from "The World of Lawrence." But the study as a whole has remained in a dormant state until now. Nor was it without considerable thought and some hesitation that Miller finally decided to let it be published. For just as form was one of his major concerns when he was struggling with the work, so when we spoke with him about the book one of his first questions was how the study could be published when it had no concrete or final shape. As we were able to remind him, however, if he had not finished the book he had drawn up a table of contents and provided a synopsis which explained the focus of each chapter and the general direction that he wanted the book to take. Furthermore, we pointed out that one of his central theses throughout his study was that it is vitality not smoothness or consistency that is the mark of greatness, and of the former quality his work lacked nothing.

Since it was such a long time ago that he had written the book, Miller was also worried that the work might have the markings of juvenilia. But when we asked him to read what are now the opening paragraphs his initial response was "Did I write that?" and then, "That was written upstairs, don't you know"—his own very graphic way of explaining that when he was working on the book he had felt inspired, possessed, driven.

In the final analysis, however, it was probably the period of anguish with which the book was associated in his mind that best explains why he had kept it out of sight for so long. "Never did I work so hard and so assiduously, only to end up in utter confusion," he recalled in 1952, when he wrote a brief explanatory preface to "The Universe of Death" for *The Henry Miller Reader.*

Consequently his decision to publish the book becomes a heroic gesture, just as Miller himself begins to emerge as the kind of man he speculated Lawrence might have become had he lived longer. "There is evidence for believing," he wrote of Lawrence, "that had it been given him to enjoy the normal span of life he would have arrived at a state of wisdom, a mystic way of life in which the artist and the human being would have been reconciled."

How different *The World of Lawrence* would have been if Miller had in the 1930s been able to complete the work is impossible to say. It can be said, however, that what follows does measure up to what, in 1933, he described as the only fitting way to pay tribute to a man like Lawrence, a man who "*embraced* everything." "The only way to do justice to a man like that, who gave so much, is to give *another* creation. Not *explain* him—but prove by writing about him that one has caught the flame he tried to pass on."

EJH and JJT
Winnipeg, Canada, 1980.

THE WORLD OF
LAWRENCE
A Passionate Appreciation

CHAPTER I

Personality

A S EVERYONE KNOWS, the body of Lawrence's work forms a huge self-portrait. He looked into the mirror of the world and he saw reflected there the image of his own naked soul. It was not until I had been saturated with his works, and the opinion of others about him, that I came to that intensely human, revelatory self-portrait which *The Letters* gives us. And after reading a hundred pages or so I come upon a photograph of Lawrence at the age of twenty-nine—the year 1914, the most crucial year of his life, and the most fateful year in our lives. I look at the photograph a long time. A very beautiful face, a very wonderful being shining out of those eyes. And almost immediately one is compelled to add—a somewhat feminine face, the face of a Christ, of all those androgynous types of Redeemers which Christ typified. And yet, not an effeminate being! Beauty, tenderness, sensitivity, faith. The man of light who worshipped the darkness, who was attracted as few men have ever been by the power of chaos and mystery.

The photograph holds me spellbound. This is the man, I think to myself, who in only a few more years will develop the features described by his friend Aldington, the features of an aristocrat of life, a face purged of all vulgarity, refined by suffering and struggle, by heaven knows what agonized communings.

I know at what period this comes, this image of a man with soul intact and hope in his breast. "I am rather great on faith just now," he writes to Murry. "I do believe in it . . . One ought to have faith in what one ultimately is, then one can bear at last the hosts of unpleasant things which one is *en route* . . ." He tells of his efforts to write *The Rainbow*. Seven times he began it. And he adds: "I have written quite a thousand pages that I shall burn." It is the spring of 1914. The turning point.

I turn back now to the frontispiece to this volume of letters and look again at the other photograph of Lawrence, the man of middle years with a scraggly beard and sunken, furrowed cheeks, in whose tired eyes there is still that piercing gleam; a man with fever in his bones and a deal of malice, the iron rusted into his soul. Inevitably there comes to mind a third image, the self-portrait which appears as the frontispiece to Murry's *Son of Woman*—what Lawrence saw in the mirror near the end. An astonishingly interesting piece of work, despite its grace and facility. A still more harrowed visage—the artist's portrait of himself. The reality of the mirror, the psychologic reality, not the photographic reality. In this portrait Lawrence has taken care to leave no hollow, no wrinkle, no twist of pain or suffering unnoticed. He has made it painfully muscular—the anatomy of suffering. He is almost a little proud of his self-torture, of all he has endured and survived. It is a bit noble, idealized, a portrait of creative anguish—but perhaps, therefore, more deeply true. It is the definitive portrait which, true to his character, Lawrence had to make. The gesture of the artist who, because he *is* an artist, will tolerate no other image but his own.

Before me lies correspondence covering the span of a lifetime. I can look behind the man's work, behind the criticism and biography, and see what he himself has to reveal of his struggles and temptations, of his own revelations. I look forward eagerly—with trepidation almost—to discovering just when and how it came about that the essentially loving, sincere, genuine man that he was, the *intrinsic* Lawrence, metamorphosed into the portrait we know so well—the bitter man of middle years, with malicious laugh and jeering tongue, the biting waspy tongue reiterating perpetually: *"you know I don't believe in love, you know I don't believe in friendship."*

The more I read the more I come to sympathize, to understand his bitterness, his rancor—to forgive it, I might say, if that did not sound so superfluous. At any rate, I can justify it!

I feel it coming—towards the twenty-ninth year! It crops out already in his letters to Edward Garnett, the older man in whom he sought a friend, a critic, a counsellor. I notice, with peculiar interest, that Lawrence was at first quite humble, quite the willing listener. He looked to the older man for advice, for sympathy, for encouragement. He seems almost to yield implicit obedience. *Until*—until it came to *The Rainbow*. Here is the origin of his rupture—with Garnett, with society, with the whole world. A splendid document, this correspondence concerning *The Rainbow*. So revelatory of the essential Lawrence, the amiable, sincere, tolerant, wise Lawrence, the Lawrence of the 1914 photograph, the Lawrence who is making his entry into the world, the Lawrence who is entering the lists in order to fulfill his destined role.

He is replying to a letter in which Garnett has criticized his work—unjustly, he seems to believe. He had previously warned Garnett that the manuscript in question was very different from *Sons and Lovers*—"written in another language almost." "I have no longer the joy," he writes, "in creating vivid scenes, that I had in *Sons and Lovers* . . . I have to write differently." He dwells at length upon his change in style, in approach, in treatment. "I write with everything vague—plenty of fire underneath, but, like bulbs in the ground, only shadowy flowers that must be beaten and sustained, for another spring . . . *It is my transition state*—but I must write to live, and it must prqduce its flowers, and if they be frail or shadowy, they will be all right if they are true to their hour."

Humble he was, obedient, reverent toward the man to whom he was indebted. *Until the moment when he is sure of himself!* Then, like a cobra he turns and strikes. *Treacherous at the core!* Aye! Treacherous to everyone save himself. At the core a dragon hissing fire. The symbolic, all-powerful dragon which he tells about in *Apocalypse*. When it comes time to destroy, to assert his own value, he is no longer grateful, no longer timid, no longer reverent. He owes allegiance to no one. A traitor to all mankind, to the past especially:

> *You know how willing I am to hear what you have to say, and to take your advice and to act on it when I have taken it. But it is no good unless you will have patience and understand what I want to do. I am not after all a child working erratically. All the time, underneath, there is something deep evolving itself out in me. And it is hard to express a new thing, in sincerity . . . But primarily I am a passionately religious man, and my novels must be written from the depth of my religious experience. That I must keep to, because I can only work like that . . . But you should see the religious, earnest, suffering man in me first, and then the flippant or common things after . . .*

Some of the finest things Lawrence ever wrote belong to this period, in these poignant letters to his friends—Lady Ottoline Morrell, Lady Cynthia Asquith, Edward Garnett, Middleton

Murry, and others. One senses the widening rupture, the steady drift towards the cosmic view of things, the alienation from the purely personal, meaningless relation with people. It is a painful thing to behold, and it is glorious at the same time. It is war—war with friends, society, beliefs, supporters. War with all mankind. It is painful, I repeat, to see this man so desirous of remaining in and of the world, to serve a purpose, and yet steadily, inevitably, by virtue of his very integrity, alienating himself from that world. He wants to "belong," and yet to have his say. He wants to be sincere, truthful, earnest, passionate, religious—and yet not to be hated or misunderstood. You will find this terribly painful period in the lives of all great souls, the period when, fully conscious of their aims, perhaps not certain yet of their power, but aware of their own deep integrity, they long to project their image of the world and make it effective. And it is just because, in this period of transition, they are so utterly sincere, so utterly all of a piece, so genuine, so burning with truth, that they believe in their power to regenerate, to recreate the world.

Throughout this period we perceive, in the letters to Murry, the germ of that discord with his "friend" which grows deeper and deeper with the years until, towards the end, there is a yawning gulf between them. The seed of this discord lies precisely in this matter of integrity. Lawrence, once he had gained an insight into his own being, remains true to himself. A hard, dire consistency, the man moving from within outward, steadily, like a sun piercing its rings of light, the core burning always brighter and brighter, shedding the light rings, the luminous waves of the spirit, in order to reveal the flaming body, the immortal, incorruptible body of man in which the torch of life is concealed. He shames one, Lawrence. His unquenchable, burning spirit, his totality, his ubiquitousness, his aliveness. Lawrence on his deathbed had more life than most men have in their moments of highest ecstasy, if ecstasy there be in the world any more. "We ought to dance with rapture," he said. "That we should be alive in the flesh, and part of the living, incarnate cosmos. I am part of the sun as my eye is part of me."

At the core of him was this God-flame, this wheel of light flashing over the four quarters of the earth, over the heavens, and the waters beneath the earth, this flaming wheel that rolled over Cézanne and Dostoevski and Whitman, that touched the Chaldeans and the Aztecs and the Etruscans, that threw an incandescent light on Plotinus and Nietzsche both, on Lorenzo the Magnificent and on Quetzalcoatl; a flame, scorching and devouring, that reaches to the mystery in all things.

> *Let the Horse laugh. I'm all for a horse that laughs. Though I don't care for him when he merely sniggers.*
> *I'm all for a horse. It's not even the Houyhnhnms. They aren't blue enough for me. It's a turquoise Centaur who laughs, who laughs longest and laughs last. I believe in him. I believe he's there, over the desert in the Southwest. I believe if you'll cajole him with a bit of proper corn, he'll come down to Santa Fe and bite your noses off and then laugh at you again.*
> *Two-legged man is no good. If he's going to stand steady, he must stand on four feet. Like the Centaur.*

This is not sheer, cantankerous misanthropism, as many like to believe. It is not Romanticism. It is not the hollow voice of Rousseau bemoaning a lost Adam. It is the inmost voice of Lawrence speaking. It is not the man with eyes turned backward, searching frantically for a lost Paradise; it is the forward-looking man, the visionary. "Man, as yet, is less than half-grown . . . " he said. "No sign of bud anywhere." It is easy to misinterpret his hatred for humanity. Enemy of mankind he was—but not of man. "It is human destiny," he wrote,

> *since Man fell into consciousness and self-consciousness, that we can only go forward step by step through realization, full, bitter, conscious realization. This is true of all the great terrors and agonies and anguishes of life: sex, and war, and even crime . . . . The small-pox sores are running yet in the spirit of mankind. And we have got to take this putrid spirit to our bosom. There's nothing else for it. Take the foul rotten spirit of mankind, full of the running sores of the war, to our bosom and cleanse it there. Cleanse it not with blind love: ah, no, that won't help. But with bitter and wincing realization. We have to take the disease into our consciousness and let it go through our soul, like some virus. We have got to realize. And then we can surpass.*

Man on his way to ordination! That is the clue to his love and hate. Not an isolated being, not a castrated Christ, not a God remote and absolute, nor even a great spirit, frozen and congealed, but a man *in* the world and *of* it too. Murry has made so much of Lawrence's refusal to hide away from man, to take himself off into the wilderness, to be a spiritual eunuch, a man of God, etc. But that was precisely what Lawrence did not want and would not do, though the four years between his leaving England and his first return, the four years which he characterized as "a savage enough pilgrimage," have something of this flavor of retreat, of alienation, of isolation. It is when we look again at the letters of this transition period that we are able to realize how much Lawrence wanted to belong to the world of men and women. We can see how, in the critical period of his life, when he had taken his stand against the world, he looked about imploringly, supplicatingly, for a friend—just *one* who would stand by and show a spark of faith.

In one of those letters to Garnett about *The Rainbow* he mentions so touchingly the nature of his difficulties with the book. They had been drifting apart, he and Frieda, but now they were together, one again in spirit, and he could put his whole soul into his work. How happy he was to be able to put Frieda and himself in the book!—everything would come out all right, he thought. And then a little later he writes to Murry: *"There isn't a soul cares a damn for me, except Frieda . . . ."* Except *Frieda!* What a lot hangs on this remark! Not enough, then, to have the faith of the woman you love? No. Lawrence is very clear about it. Frieda's faith was *not* enough. There had to be someone else, a man, a *friend.* For the friend represents the world without, and the woman one loves is not the world, however nobly or sincerely she may try to make herself the world.

As an artist he must have sensed early enough that Frieda's judgment was none too good, none too critical. He must also have been touched by her fidelity, as indeed we know he was, and yet he suspected, as we also know, that her fidelity must crack sooner or later, that she would oppose him, not as a wife or lover merely, but as Woman. That is the cruel revelation of these early letters—the deep, inner knowledge that beyond a certain point lay the void, the deep void of utter isolation.

And why was it he felt so good, so atoned, when he had put Frieda in the book? Let me make it clear—Frieda was necessary to him, and Frieda was the only woman in the world for him. *She was Woman,* as he himself said, and how necessary woman was to Lawrence it is scarcely necessary to mention. Frieda was the incarnation of Woman—"complete, but limited," as Mabel Dodge Luhan says. But what a devil's time it was for the artist in Lawrence to come to terms with her, to write faithfully what he had to say and at the same time not omit his wife nor put her in too unlovely a light! For it must have been strong in him, the desire faithfully to record her—not to idealize, not to sentimentalize, and above all, *not to crucify her.* Their life together was a duel. And it was Lawrence who succumbed. But Lawrence died only once in the flesh. Frieda dies a thousand deaths—in his books. If sympathy is to be extended, my sympathy goes toward Frieda, not because she is a woman, but because as a woman merely she was defenseless. As for the living person, Frieda, I do not care a hang. Frieda the woman interests me profoundly. She is the woman who appears throughout (practically) all his books — the mysterious, unknowable foreign woman whom Lawrence loved, if ever a man loved a woman.

One can see how the more Frieda stuck to him when all was failing the more she demanded of him. Not satisfied with giving him her love and encouragement, when she could, she must also have her portrait done. And the more clamorous she grew, the more she bickered and haggled, the more insistent she became, the worse her portrait grew. Even in the first flush of love it is a somewhat strange portrait—a strange beauty he finds in her. When Tom Brangwen goes to marry the strange foreign woman there is much mention of the impression made upon him by her mouth. Three or four times Lawrence stresses it—"her ugly-beautiful mouth . . . . he bent and kissed her heavy, sad, wide mouth, that was kissed, and did not alter . . . . It was ugly-beautiful, and he could not bear it."

In order not to deliver himself up to the avenging furies—also for deeper, unconscious, wholly artistic reasons—Lawrence as he progresses becomes more and more symbolical. In a letter on Marinetti and Futurism he talks for the first time of his leaning towards the "non-human." He wants to get away from personalities. "That which is physic—non-human, in humanity, is more interesting to me than the old-fashioned human element—which causes one to conceive a character in a certain moral scheme and make him consistent." Criticizing the Cubists and Futurists, he says: "They will progress down the purely male or intellectual or scientific line. They will even use their intuition for intellectual and scientific purpose"—a phrase very reminiscent of Nietzsche in his diatribe against Socrates.

*I don't so much care about what woman feels–in the
ordinary usage of the word. That presumes an ego to feel
with. I only care about what the woman is—what she IS–
inhumanly, physiologically, materially–according to the use
of the word: but for me, what she is as a phenomenon (or as
representing some greater, inhuman will) instead of what
she feels according to the human conception. That is where
the futurists are stupid. Instead of looking for the new
human phenomenon, they will only look for the phenomena
of the science of physics to be found in human beings . . . You
mustn't look in my novel for the old stable ego of the character. There is another ego, according to whose action the
individual is unrecognisable, and passes through, as it were,
allotropic states which it needs a deeper sense than any
we've been used to exercise, to discover are states of the
same single radically unchanged element.*

At the same time, however, that he stresses his interest in
this non-human, physiological aspect of men and women, he is
asserting with equal or perhaps greater emphasis the necessity
for men and women to draw closer together because, as he
points out, "the source of all life and knowledge is in man and
woman, and the source of all living is in the interchange and
the meeting and mingling of these two: man-life and woman-
life, man-knowledge and woman-knowledge, man-being and
woman-being."

Lawrence had a gift for portraiture—a cruel gift. But character studies, in the manner of the English novelists or even of the
Russians whom he admired so, was not enough for him; any
more than was the scientific study of disintegrated psychic
states which is so typical of the moderns. Lawrence's
psychologic interest in his characters (chiefly himself, it must
be admitted), for all the seeming smell of the alembic and the
test tube, was based on a feeling for the indissoluble, irreduci-
ble and forever unknowable centrality of the character. He was
seeking a more fundamental, more substantial, psychologic
reality.

By the time we get to the period of *Lady Chatterley's Lover*
there comes a queer avowal, half sincere, half mocking, that
compound of truth, jeer and irony which lay behind so many
of his utterances. A Mr. Lederhandler, from America, writes to
ask if the character of Clifford was not meant to be symbolic.
And Lawrence with characteristic innocence replies, "yes, the

paralysis of Sir Clifford is symbolic—all art is *au fond* symbolic, conscious or unconscious . . . . The wood is of course unconscious symbolism—perhaps even the mines—even Mrs. Bolton."

Even Mrs. Bolton! Aye, he might have added—*even yours truly.* For by now everything had grown symbolic: he had seen life so nakedly, he had looked so deep into the soul and nature of human beings, of beast and plant and tree, that everything, whether he would or not, became symbolic. He had come to the great fundamental reality of things. He was seeing with the naked eye, the inner eye, because the world had put out his weak, sad human eyes. He saw only as an artist. He saw blindly, cruelly, mercilessly. Saw the skeleton beneath the flesh, the chancre in the soul. Out of the quick of corruption he cried for a resurrection—not for himself alone, but for all men. On his dying bed his dream of life is man risen in the flesh. "What man most passionately wants," he writes in *Apolcalypse,* "is his living wholeness and his living unison, not his own isolate salvation of his 'soul.' Man wants his physical fulfilment first and foremost, since now, once and once only, he is in the flesh and potent."

The man Lawrence had been consumed by his own burning flame and the world had plucked the flesh from his ribs and sucked his bones, even before he was put away. Towards the end it was clear what a symbolic figure he was. There was nothing left but the artist, and the artist had already buried himself in his work, had already lain himself down in his own tomb.

It was very likely towards the end, perhaps when he was pondering *The Man Who Died,* that he rose up out of a sick bed and, looking at himself in the mirror, drew with a fine, wavering hand the tortured image of himself which was ironically and justly, to provide the frontispiece to Murry's book. *All symbolic.* All fated, fateful. It was when he had seen enough, more than enough, that he drew the image of himself which his Judas friend was to appropriate for that book of "appreciation" which had to wait until the man who inspired it was dead and could no longer object. *Symbolic.* All symbolic—even down to Mrs. Bolton, and the mines.

Poor Lawrence, I could weep for you when I read your symbolic lines. The humiliation, the insults, the total lack of comprehension. To give yourself so completely to the world and to

get so little back. And yet to have achieved your consummation, to have reached God, as you strove to from the very
beginning. You spoke in *Apocalypse* about the great myth of
the dragon; you described so sensitively, so proudly, the significance of the dragon. You tried to give the world again the
symbolism of the dragon which lashed and coiled inside you.
And you put a little of the dragon into your self-portrait. Once
in a miserable hut with Frieda you said she called you a
scorpion—you had found a scorpion in the spittoon beside the
bed, the spittoon you never used. But Frieda, Frieda "the aristocrat," she liked the spittoon there. It was convenient. She
needed it for her butts as she lay sprawled on the bed. You
slaved away, you wrote the furrows into your cheeks, you
begged for a crust of bread so that Frieda would not go without.
You remarked then that it was funny her calling you a
scorpion—you couldn't imagine biting your own tail. But you
did eventually. You swallowed it whole, you devoured yourself, tail and all, and when you did a third part of the world was
consumed and eaten away and will never be known again.

Wherever I go your words are with me, they obsess me.
Today, standing in the museum looking at the splendid horses
of the Chinese when they were a young and vigorous people, I
thought of your words again, your symbolic words on the
dragon, on the red dragon and the gold which men feared and
worshipped when life ran high and there was blood in men's
veins and not this puling, watery bile, this sickly green lymph,
this ghastly anaemic dirty-white consumptive pallor that covers all things. I think how in the flush of your great love you
looked at your Frieda and you saw in her a Renoir with the head
of a Greek. And I know too what you saw later—the Bertha
Coutts that ate into your soul—how the hard, whorish beak of
the woman you loved carved out your own vulture-like features, made your fine sensitive face twist into a rapacious claw.
I know that when your words ripped and clawed it was with the
hard whore's beak of her who had eaten into your soul, of her
who had become the image of that world which you rejected,
because it had rejected you. The world which wanted to possess you in order to come alive.

I look at the photograph of you in your middle years, the
beard that you had grown to conceal the tortured lines, the hard

malice, the cutting jests, the jeers, the contempt, the derision, the scorn. I look at your weak, tired eyes that once glowed with such tenderness—that blazed forth once again, with surpassing tenderness, in *Lady Chatterley's Lover.* Eyes weak and tired from looking at the world, at people, at fragments of people. Eyes tired because they were constantly searching for some loop-hole, some way out, some means of escape from this mess we are in and in which we will remain forever. The eyes that once lit up when they lighted on a Renoir, trained for an instant on Cézanne, the frightened mouse of a Cézanne looking out of his self-portrait. A failure, like yourself, in the world of men. Your eyes worn out with searching among the tombs of the dead for a sign of life.

I think of Milton blind, of Beethoven deaf, of Renoir painting with his wooden stumps. And you saying towards the end that you would not mind so much if you were to lose your sight— *you did not need your eyes any more.* And, whether the artist does actually lose his sight or hearing or whether he does not, the truth is that as his inward development progresses he does grow more blind, more deaf. He seals up all the outward organs of sense, the *end* organs of touch and sight and hearing, in order to apprehend the truths of life with his spiritual senses.

* * *

And now we come to the man: the "sex-crucified," the "sex-sodden," the "almost sexual weakling," the "spiritually precocious", etc., etc. The man who wanted to make a god of himself, as Frieda said. The man who was not a "gentleman," as Frieda said in one of her rages. The man who was an aristocrat, an aristocrat of the spirit, like Plato, like Jesus, like Buddha.

Let us look at him for a moment in his Chaplinesque role. Let us look at him as a modern Don Quixote tilting against the windmills of white idealism. Let us look at him as the wanderer on the face of the earth. Let us look at him as a "productive neurotic."

He had twenty years of writing. And when one examines not the bulk only, but the quality of his work, when one considers the age in which he wrote—an age so hostile to artistic production, so paralyzing, so devastating!—when one considers these things quite impartially it is only fair to say that he was a giant, an artist worthy of being put alongside Dante or Shakespeare or Goethe. He was a poor and harried man almost until the very end. He was a sick man a good part of the time. He was frail all his life. He was misunderstood, ostracized, rejected. He had an unhappy marriage. He wandered over a good part of the globe. He built his homes with his own hands. He darned his own socks, built his own fires, baked his own bread. He wrote novels, short stories, plays, books of travel and philosophy. He waged war wherever he went. He made enemies. He was loved too, but mostly he was hated. He dug among the Etruscan ruins in search of a civilization he loved; he translated one of the great novels of the age. He wrote some of the most trenchant criticism of American literature ever penned, the essays on Poe, Whitman and Melville being probably unsurpassed in all critical literature. He lived among the Indians and danced with them. He painted and for the collection of his paintings he wrote an introduction in which once again he said the most penetrating things, things about Cézanne particularly which are unsurpassed. He contracted tuberculosis for reasons which he himself has described. After explaining its symbolism, he died of the white sickness against which he had fought all his life. And on his deathbed he wrote several volumes which contain more of life than is contained in all the modern authors now living and combined. He burned so vividly and intensely that he left practically no ash. They are still picking the embers out of the fire.

It seems to me that in twenty years he showed enough activity to prove that he was alive. If, as he said, we were all born corpses, then it is true also that he was the most alive corpse we have ever seen. The only value of an artist is whether he reveals life, he said. He brought life and he revealed life. As they fed on him while he lived, sucked the life out of him, to use his own words, men will go on feeding on him for generations to come. "Only a man of genius could equal his positive achievements," Richard Aldington admits.

It seems to be forgotten, when it comes to looking at the man, that he was first and foremost an artist, and that he was a special kind of artist, one who consumed life, one who had to drain it to the full. He took nothing for granted: he experienced everything for himself. And having tested life for himself, hav-

ing experienced for himself the truth of things, having forged
for himself an iron conscience, he could say with all the vehe-
mence of his positive spirit—"You tell me I am wrong. Who are
you, who is anybody, to tell me I am wrong? I am not wrong!"
And when the tepid admiration of Richard Aldington halts
before the violent extremism of Lawrence, when his mild,
gentle spirit wishes to reprove the living man of genius, he
says: "I fear that Lawrence will expire before the Bull." Well,
Mr. Aldington is wrong. D. H. Lawrence will outlive the British
Empire. He will outlive her as Caesar and Cicero have outlived
Rome. An empire lives only as long as it has living geniuses to
give it their flame—and the great British bull is doing its best to
snuff out its own life! No, the British Empire is almost dead
already. It is not immortal. But the men who gave it life *are*
immortal. That is a matter of fact.

So much for the heroic side of him. He has another side—
pitiable, wretched, pathetic—*ridiculous*. The role he played as
a human being Chaplin has immortalized in every film. It is the
human role, man the homunculus waging his uneven battle
against Fate. Here we see him as a sort of immortal bedbug,
very tiny, very annoying, very smelly, managing by instinctive
cunning to evade the squat, crushing thumb of the torporous
giant Life. It is this side of him that the crowd relishes. They
adore seeing him thumb his nose at the giant, or stick out his
ass, or escape with his breeches coming down, or slip on a
banana peel, the furtive, timid little brushes with danger, with
death. And the spokesmen of the crowd are the intellectuals
who ponder over the imaginative life of the homunculus to
detect the human traces in it, the almost human porcupine
tracks which he left behind as he wriggled out of the giant's
grasp. They come with their microscopic lenses and their
testing and weighing apparatuses and they reconstruct a fine
bedbug activity which brings the mystery nearer to comprehension. They can analyze the lines so finely and the spaces
between the lines that it is possible to inform all and sundry
how on a certain night in June or September D. H. Lawrence the
man and homunculus failed to make proper love to his wife and
so brought on himself a train of misery and woe. They can even
make the bed squeak. They sweat and wrestle with these deeds
and events to give a plausible reality to the man's life when all

the while the man himself has been trying to give another reality, when all the while he has been trying to give an autobiography of his soul.

In his off moments, his very human moments, he was a Chaplinesque figure. Chaplin is the hero of the collectivity—the mob-hero! Lawrence was not a mob-hero, but he had his Chaplin moments. Especially when he was surrounded by his women. Just as Chaplin becomes most ridiculous when he poses as a lover. Woman is the dire test of reality. Woman *is*. Man pretends. Lawrence the artist almost succeeded in becoming God. Lawrence the man gets plates smashed over his head by an irate spouse. Lawrence the artist, or the philosopher, can talk almost as well as Socrates; he can talk about going beyond woman, he can say magnificent things about man's earnest purpose, etc. But in private life his wife leads him around by the apron-string as his mother did before her. She can stand up to him with fire in her eyes and blaze at him: "I'm just as important as you are!" Which we know only too well was a lie. "Why aren't you a gentleman?" This to a man who is searching for God! "You're not an aristocrat!" Meaning that she was, and to prove it she would fling a magazine at his head in public. Of course, if taking one's socks off and darning them in a train is any indication Lawrence was not an aristocrat. His language was a bit coarse at times, perhaps foul would be a better word. And yet this coarse little collier's son, with his Midlands accent and his uncontrollable rages, could write the most magnificent prose, could describe most delicately and imaginatively how the Holy Ghost secreted Himself or Itself in the seed of the dandelion beneath its umbrella of hairs. He wrote a great deal about the Holy Ghost, oddly enough, for a man who was not an aristocrat. He could write about the sacred flame of life and then blow his nose in an old letter. So we are told. Indeed, we are told marvellous things, marvellous little personal details which went to make up the daily humbuggery of a genius's life, by the admiring cows who flocked about him all his life.

And it is my purpose to recount as many of these little items as possible, so that in addition to the heroic figure we shall have the everyday figure, the perpetual bedbug which the mob must smell in order to believe its eyes. For it is part of my purpose to ram D. H. Lawrence, the artist and hero, down the thick gullets of the great collective herd. And in order to do that, I must present the "collective" human side of him. For he was human, too, otherwise he would not have gone up to the mountaintop and died there of the white disease. He contracted his illness in the plains. It was love that killed him, though in explaining this he pretends to give us the case of Edgar Allan Poe. You will notice, parenthetically, that when Lawrence detests a man very violently there is usually a strong affinity between that man and himself. Poe achieves distinction in Lawrence's eyes as an unconscious prophet of doom. Speaking of Poe he says:

> *Love can be terribly obscene.*
>
> *It is love that causes the neuroticism of the day. It is love that is the prime cause of tuberculosis.*
>
> *The nerves that vibrate most intensely in spiritual unisons are the sympathetic ganglia of the breast, of the throat, and the hind brain. Drive this vibration over-intensely, and you weaken the sympathetic tissues of the chest–the lungs–or of the throat, or of the lower brain, the tubercles are given a ripe field.*
>
> *But Poe drove the vibrations beyond any human pitch of endurance.*

Take that last line. Notice again that when Lawrence wishes to pay a man a great tribute or when he wishes to annihilate him—it makes little difference which—he gives you a picture of himself. It seems to me that Edgar Allan Poe in no way deserved that last line. *But Lawrence does!* It is *he* who has driven the vibrations beyond all pitch of human endurance. The Luhan woman puts it baldly enough:

> *It seemed to me that the very thing he fought against in me, he capitulated to in her [Frieda]: the surrender of his will. Why was he forever at her beck and call? If her judgment had been good for him, or if she at least carried him to places that were healthful for him to live in, it would not have been so bad. But the woman had no understanding of ill health and she invariably chose spots that put him down in bed and weakened . . . . his resistance to her. . . . I need not mind if he called me destructive, for he has called her so in every line, in every book he has written, masking his accusation from her as best he could under many guises so she would let it pass.*
>
> *I wonder if she knew what she was doing, or if her instinct guided her to draw him, to her advantage and his*

despite, to the very worst climates and the most de-
pressing surroundings!

Here we have one of those deeply instinctive female truths
which enrich the pages of Lawrence's biography. Trust the
adoring female admirers shamelessly to expose one another.
Mable makes Brett out an idiot; Brett makes Frieda out a slut
and a hussy; Frieda makes them all out to be a pack of intruders.
The Carswell woman writes about him as if he were a saint;
Brett writes about him as if he were a Sir Launcelot—pure,
aloof and tortured; the Luhan woman sees him as a composite
of devil and saint.

Lorenzo in Taos is the sort of book we ought to have on
Christ, as a corrective to the gospels. It is an authentic picture
of what goes on behind the scenes—the private life of a
genius—the mess he creates around him—all that petty, trivial
clap-trap of which he later weaves the fabric of his novels and
poems. It tells us nothing at all about his genius, about what
goes on in his soul; it gives only the raw materials of his life, the
crude stuff of experience which his art refines and to which it
gives significance. As Lawrence said: "out of a pattern of lies art
weaves the truth . . . . Never trust the artist. Trust the tale.
The proper function of the critic is to save the tale from the
artist who created it."

(I am tempted to devote an entire section of this book to
Mabel Dodge Luhan, because she is representative, in a monstrous way, of American femininity, of the male and the
female. Her mind is in her womb and that's a hard, clutching
beak of a thing, like the beaks of the "old rampers" that Mellors
speaks of in *Lady Chatterley;* the *cosmic-orgasmic* mind! The
Taos episode is not just a mere incident in Lawrence's life, but
the dramatic fruition and culmination of a road he had been
long travelling. It puts before us vividly and nakedly the pathos
and the bathos of the life of a genius, of the mystic genius
whom woman always rallies round, vulgarizes, sullies and
degrades. This type of woman, of which America has a bellyful,
is the over-sexed, and the under-sexed both, but sex is the pivot
around which they swing. They don't give a real fuck for the
man's philosophy, only as it affects their tickling or would-
be-tickled cunts. They are the real vultures of the age. The
show becomes a burlesque, their words are priceless. Unbe-

lievable. And the strange thing is that the poor bugger of a genius gets taken in by it, and is obliged to consider them seriously. But in all the low-life gossip, the back-talk, the squabbles, the cosmic love affairs and the alignment of male and female "tubes," one gets a glimpse of the daily life, the daily wash, the painfully real and glamor-less side of the hen-ridden genius. The poor genius is half a woman anyway. He's pissing in his pants all the time—for fear of one thing or another. Mostly for fear they'll castrate him!

The priceless things Luhan says and every item under the sun is worth recording, along with the portraits that poor Lawrence tries to wash out with a "wet thumb." Somehow the portraits are convincing. And they are fine relief to the high-and-mighty philosophy.)

* * *

In this age when everything is so marvellously *mis*understood, interpreted and explained away, it seems to me a delightful piece of irony that the figure who only yesterday was in our midst grows more and more blurred, that he leaves, as indeed every great artist does, only the enigma of himself which haunts and pursues us, mocks our boastful, conceited knowledge of everything, *everything but the future.* Rather than present this phenomenon of Lawrence as a theorem to be demonstrated, I have chosen to regard him from conflicting angles, leaving his personality in that mysterious and inscrutable obscurity which he had the wisdom and the reverence to recognize as all-important. In doing so I feel that I am rendering to Lawrence the only tribute worthwhile, the tribute which genius always exacts of posterity, the revenge, if you like, which the artist always takes for the crime of being misunderstood. The great sin which is committed against the artist—and in this age more than ever—is to *explain* him. For we know in the last analysis, in our hearts, that is, that no interpretation of ours will ever shed light on the mysterious personality of any being, let alone a unique being such as Lawrence. It is only ourselves we are trying to understand.

The critical and biographical material that has already issued out of Lawrence, dead only a few years, is considerable and increases steadily in proportion with the years. Criticism and biography! How symptomatic of the age! And that Lawrence, who was so denigrated, so maligned and condemned during his life-time should be the especial target of the future—what are we to deduce from this? That his importance is only beginning to be understood, that his influence is only beginning to make itself felt, that he really was able to deal death, as he believed, to destroy and create at the same time? Perhaps we should deduce nothing—except that he *was* and that he was unique.

That he should appear as the most singular figure of his age, more important than the whole generation which produced him, is the fact to which I bow, the fact which compels my interest in him. From whatever angle he is approached—attacked usually—whether he be regarded as a psychological problem, an historic event, a failure as artist or prophet or savior, the roots of Lawrence are so firmly lodged in the times that he seems more truly alive now than when he was with us. The conflict of personality which enabled him to expand and express himself is symbolic of the greater conflict which gives this age its character and form. It was magnified and distorted by Lawrence, the individual, whose creativity expressed itself characteristically through the problem of the self.

At a time when the destiny of the individual is merged with the destiny of the mass, the despair that Lawrence voiced, together with the correlative hope of resurrection, was bound to assume the most poignant expression. By identifying himself with the future, as did Leonardo da Vinci, he acknowledged more sincerely and tragically than any man of his day how great was his indebtedness to the past—and how representative he was of the present. He was a nascent personality, the fragment of a man, a torso, if you like. He could neither go forwards nor backwards, nor would he allow himself to drift inertly on the stream that bore him along. He obeyed the demon that was in him, the blind, driving urge which grew out of the conflicting forces within him, of which he has told us in varying ways, varying terms—*the dictates of a man's own conscience.*

"Death is no violation nor ignominy, and can be thought of with sweetness and satisfaction," he said. He conducted his life according to the tragically-apprehended truth. By that knowledge of death his life was quickened. But more important, for us, is that in the knowledge of this truth his death too was quickened. The great symbol that Lawrence chose on the threshold of his career, the symbol which marks his grave and which you will find expressed in manifold ways throughout the body of his work is the Phoenix. Symbol of death and resurrection, symbol of life eternal fixed in the living form.

"The phallic mystic" he is often called, and it is true that the mystery of sex fascinated him almost to the point of obsession. But there was a mystery beyond that which held him even closer, and it is expressed more clearly by two significant phrases of his: *sex is so much more than phallic; death is not the goal.* For him the prime reality, the prime mystery, the glory and the eternity of man was the body, the sacred body. "There never was any universe, any cosmos, of which the first reality was anything but living, incorporate individuals," he says in *Fantasia of the Unconscious.* There was for him only one clue to the universe and that, he said, was the individual soul within the individual being. "At length, for *my* part, I know that life, and life only is the clue to the universe. And that the living individual is the clue to life. And that it always was so, and always will be so."

And just as he refused to die the ordinary, biological hunger-death of the mass which surrounded him, so too Lawrence refused to live that ordinary, biological life which for him represented a continuum of death. Born a creative individual, he interpreted the life about him creatively; he gave it drama by attributing to it the conflict which created his own personality. For the mass, unable to seize imaginatively the elements or forces which gave his life character and outline, there exists no such problem as Lawrence envisaged. Neither life nor death has meaning for them: they are accepted as facts, *dead facts.* The mass live among the dead facts as maggots live in a corpse. For Lawrence the problem expressed itself thus: "Will the bird perish, Shall the bird rise?" Who is to supply this mass with a vicarious life if there be no death? It was the life-instinct itself which he saw in peril.

Like Jesus, Lawrence appears in a time of despair, of hopelessness, when there is a strong suicidal trend, racial and individual. *When the end is clearly in sight!* And like Jesus he finds himself in an emasculated world, a world given up to the economic-biologic drama. "This is a winter," he wrote to Catherine Carswell. "Children and child-bearing do not make spring. It is not in children, the future lies.... It is the truth, the new perceived hope, that makes spring. And let them bring forth that, who can: they are the creators of life."

In any age it is only a few rare individuals, *the truly creative spirits*, who possess seed-bearing possibilities. In our age, so near to exhaustion and sterility, it is the very soil itself which needs fecundating. Out of the dying forms there must emerge a new living rhythm. And whatever hope there lies in the future—a distant future—lies inevitably in the appearance and the death, the continuous rejection and crucifixion, I might say, of these lone, tragic individuals. For in their deaths lie the fertile seeds of the new forms to come. But if their presences pass unnoticed then our dying has no significance. Either we accept our destiny in the reality of the tragic spirit or we rot forever in a state of China, enclosed within the dry, null walls of the womb, as Lawrence put it.

Murry has said that Lawrence strove so to alter the world that an emergent personality such as his own would be forever impossible on this earth. It sounds noble and magnanimous, a tribute to Lawrence, at first glance. For it is true. But as one reads deeper into Murry one discovers how even the perception of a truth—or perhaps just because it was only perception and not experience—can be mangled and falsified.

Murry's interpretation of Lawrence is a pathologic study. We learn from it what we knew to begin with—that the man of genius is abnormal, that abnormality is based on conflict, and that the results are disastrous. But the most important thing about a genius is that he is a creator, and that without conflict, inner and outer, he cannot create. It is *conflict* he thrives on—if he is an artist and not a neurotic. And so when Murry endeavors to give us a portrait of Lawrence, and in so doing whittles away the artist in him, he is guilty of a crime. For to erect a study of genius on the scaffold of pathology is to miss utterly the meaning of art and artist both. It is the fact that he created, and not that he was pathologic, which is vital to us. Even more than *what* he created is the fact *that* he creates, as Otto Rank has pointed out in distinguishing between the "failed artist," whom the neurotic represents, and the creative artist. In every aspect of his being Lawrence was a creative individual. His whole life is a creation. And if, through his "emergent" personality it was only the torso of a man he presented to the world, it was the kind, the quality of that torso which concerns us. Not that he was minus this or that, all the elements which the rest of mankind share abundantly and for no good.

Was Lawrence a neurotic? Most certainly. It is almost silly to pose the question. What distinguishes him, however, from the ordinary neurotic is that he was productive. What genius has not been neurotic? How can there be any question of genius without this question of conflict? How can there be any civilization without this element of disease? Those who are not tainted are worthless, worse than worthless—they are dead. Disease is the germ of life in its most virulent form. Disease springs out of the quick of corruption, and corruption is simply the decay of a living organism. If there be no life there can be no corruption, no decay, no death; disease is the spiritual algebra that equates life with death, that furnishes the continuity between life and death. It is disease we ought to worship. It is only through disease that we know health, that fine balance of the warring forces in us of life and death. Health then should be regarded as the symbol merely of that battle which rages inside us eternal and unknowable; it should represent the equilibrium, not the elimination or the vanquishing or the escape from these warring elements. And that equilibrium is always tentative; in the end the battle comes to an issue, and for all of us the issue is death. *But death is not our concern.* Of death we know nothing—it is the negative reality of life, Lawrence tells us. *The issue is life, more life!* It is agonizing to see how the man went about crying out "More life! More *vivid* life!" only to be told that he was corrupt. Corrupt? Of course he was corrupt. He worshipped corruption. Because it is out of corruption that we shall discover life more abundant. This is the time for corruption to flourish. *We must come to an end,* he kept shouting.

A deathly book, Murry calls *Women in Love.* Deathly? No. *Death-dealing!* Lawrence strove to deal death. A mere economic revolution, a mere political revolution, meant little to him. He put himself above class war, above the Utopia of bread-and-butter freedom. Lawrence wanted the impossible, a new species of man. No patch-work. No plumbing repairs. No compromise. He was fanatical and inexorable. An *absolute,* if you will, but an absolute of life as against an absolute of death. The Lawrence man was struggling to be born. The age would not permit him to be born. What this age desires is neither to die nor to be born. This is the age that accepts life as it is—a *realistic* age. But it is a superfical kind of realism. It is a static realism! Those who pride themselves on the fact that they accept things as they are are the very ones who are killing things as they are, because things never are, things are in movement, in flux continually. He who accepts the present condition is arresting life. And that is our real life of to-day— arrest, permanency, static death.

"The only thing now to be done," wrote Lawrence back in 1916, "is either to go down with the ship, sink with the ship, or, as much as one can, *leave* the ship, and like a castaway live a life apart. As for me, I do not belong to the ship; I will not, if I can help it, sink with it."

And in *The Plumed Serpent,* somewhat later, there comes this significant exchange between his two characters:

> *"You don't think you are wrong, do you?"*
> *"No! I am not wrong. Only maybe I can't hold out."*

Again, in writing to a friend, he reiterates: "You tell me I am wrong. Who are you, who is anybody to say I am wrong? I am *not* wrong." Signed D. H. Lawrence. Signed Jesus Christ. Signed Blake, Emerson, Thoreau, Whitman. Signed Spengler. All who say, "I write not for a few months ahead or for next year, but for the future. What is true cannot be made null by an event . . . . I see further than others . . . . And if no one else has the courage to see and to tell what it is he sees, I mean to do so. I have a *right* to criticism." Who that has ever had any vision, any guts, any integrity, has ever refused to criticize, to judge, to condemn, to set himself up as a value, to inflict his tyranny? In the eyes of a man of spirit, using that word in its fullest sense, the world is always wrong: the very existence of a great being is the proof of it.

Lawrence had three superb qualities: vision, courage, and integrity. Murry, his friend, called him a failure as a man, a sex-crucified man; John Bull dubbed him the sex-sodden genius. He was vituperated against and maligned more than any man of his day. "People are so strangely unwilling to admit the genius of a living artist," says his friend Aldington. "They are insulted by superiority and try to ignore it or to crush it."

Perhaps it was not always so, but today, more than ever, it is true. For today we have the era of the collectivity, the mass, the mob, the blind pigs who are led by the blind. Not until we revert to his precursor, Jesus, do we find a man who detested humanity more than Lawrence. And yet no man had greater hopes for MAN. It was not the defeatism of Jesus that links Lawrence's name to his; it was not the romanticism of Nietzsche that makes one recall the latter as one follows Lawrence's fierce denunciations. Of his contemporaries there are only two men who ought to be compared with him, Spengler and Faure, the former by his picture of world-as-history, and the latter by his picture of man-as-artist.

Doom! Lawrence sees it written over all the universe. Even more forbidding, more devastating, more complete than Spengler sees it. Not just an Occidental culture, not just the Faustian man, the Gothic soul, and so on, *but man everywhere.* "Our day is short and closing fast!" He returns to it eternally. He underlines it in red ink and green, in bile and vitriol. Like the Hebrew prophets, he gnashes his teeth and smears his body with dung. He runs among us naked, exposing the festering sores of the spirit. Despair, anguish—like the last man on earth seeing everything perish. *Doom! Doom!*

When he comes to Herman Melville—one of the few American writers, "a *mystic*," as were the best American writers, says Lawrence—when he comes to describe the symbolic significance of *Moby-Dick* and the great white whale, he writes the finest lines of criticism in all modern literature; they are marvellous, marvellous lines, which should appear in bold type every time that Lawrence's name is mentioned. What has happened since Melville? he asks. *Post-mortem effects.* A living death. Perpetuity. Nullity. The tenacious life of the will, the Faustian spirit, if you like, pushing itself over the precipice, leading on to its own willed destruction, its suicide.

Lawrence had a high opinion of himself. Way back in his career he was saying: "I think I have inside me a sort of answer to the want of today." And later on, talking to some one else, he wrote: "I profoundly believe that a single individual may prove to be of more worth than the whole generation of men in which he lived." And assuming that he had himself in mind, as he very well might, do not let us confound this attitude with conceit. For at the same time and in the same spirit he was able to write to Lady Ottoline Morrell: "Don't think that *I* am important . . . . And don't be sceptical. We are the young. And it is only the young who can know a great cause." And in a letter to Katherine Mansfield about Murry he says most emphatically: "One thing I know, I am tired of this insistence on the *personal* element; personal truth, personal reality. It is very stale and profitless. I want some new non-personal activity . . . . And I want relations which are not purely personal . . . qualities; but relations based upon some unanimous accord in truth or belief, and a harmony of purpose, rather than personality. I am weary of personality . . . . Let us be easy and impersonal, not for ever fingering over our souls, and the souls of our acquaintances, but trying to create . . . a new complete tree of life from the roots that are within us."

A distinction must be made between the glitter of personality and the effulgence of the living spirit. The one is feminine, the other masculine. The flame in man, the strong earnest purpose, the undying will, is the very expression of masculinity, and art *is* masculine or it is nothing. In this connection, I find among the early letters that Lawrence had evinced a characteristic curiosity in a book of Lucka's called *Grenzen der Seele*. He writes to a friend: "The *Grenzeleute* are those who are on the verge of human understanding, and who widen the frontiers of human knowledge all the time—and the frontiers of life . . . . The only person Lucka really reverences at all is the genius, and reverences him the more according to the degree of purity of his genius . . . ."

It was a casual letter, apparently, and that is the end of it. But notice how, a few years later, when he is involved with Magnus, when he is attempting to acquit himself of the one vile act of his life, he renders to Magnus a tribute which that little louse most certainly did not deserve. Never in all his life had Lawrence felt so guilty. He did let Magnus down, there is no getting around it. And he knew it in his soul, and that is why, no doubt, he wrote such a magnificent introduction to the *Memoirs of the Foreign Legion*. He acknowledges his guilt and then tries to absolve himself. It were better had he left off in the true spirit of a murderer, and not tried to absolve himself. But he makes a magnificent statement toward the end, which as I say, should not have been attributed to Magnus, but to him, for it was himself he was condoning. "And so," he says, "though M-----

poisoned himself, and I would not wish him *not* to have poisoned himself: though as far as warm life goes, I don't forgive him; yet, as far as the eternal and unconquerable spirit of man goes, I am with him through eternity. I am grateful to him, he beat out for me boundaries of human experience which I could not have beaten out for myself. The *human* traitor he was. But he was not traitor to the spirit. In the great spirit of human consciousness he was a hero, little, quaking and heroic: a strange, quaking little star."

It is only when we recognize that the man of genius is a monster, a traitor and a criminal, among other things, that we can begin to make distinctions of value. For the more abnormal he is—the more monstrous, the more criminal—the more fecundating is his spirit. It is precisely because Lawrence, like Dostoevski, Blake, Whitman, Jesus, belonged to that order of genius which beats out the boundaries of human experience and widens the frontiers of life, that he has a value for us. Even Murry acknowledges this when in saying that Lawrence was abnormal and his experience abnormal, he adds: "It is the abnormal men from whom we have to learn. They, and they alone, have something of import to teach us. Every man from whom humanity has learned how to make a real step forward into the future has been an abnormal man. He has been abnormal because he belongs to the future, because he was himself the soul of the future. Lawrence was the future; as much of it as we are likely to get in our time." Saying which he promptly forgets what he has written and proceeds to give Lawrence the guillotine. Using Lawrence's life as an explanation of his works, and vice versa, Murry reveals little by little the failure of the man, as husband, as male, as saint, as prophet, as leader, and finally as artist.

Failure! Failure! Complete failure and fiasco. It seems to me as though the discovery of the failure of the artist dates from the discovery of the psychologic method of approach. Everything is failure, because everything is based on a study of failure. It may be convenient, satisfying, and even at times convincing to regard the artist from the standpoint of failure and disease, but it leaves the problem of his appearance, and his art, untouched. It merely adds a new category of scientific lingo to the already boring terminology of the history of aesthetics.

This is an age when the great spirits are taken up only as

illustrations for the text-book of pathology. To read these pompous know-alls is to believe that there never was a psychology but this psychology of dead or diseased tissue. The interest in a great figure, be it Mohammed, Jesus, Napoleon, Tamerlane or Buddha, is not in what the man was, but in what he wasn't. The attitude is negative and evasive. And above all, *false*. Criticism—this kind of criticism—is of no avail. We do not need the critic to discern for us between the true and the false, but to help us to discover what it is that the artist is trying to say. It is of absolutely no consequence to know wherein the man failed, wherein he made mistakes, wherein he contradicted himself. *That* the reader should be able to perceive for himself and be properly silent about. What we want to know, or what we ought to want to know, when we come upon a great figure, is: *what is he seeking to give us?* To point to the weak, human links in his armor is simply to flatter and tickle our own vanity. What mockery that we should seize on the weak, obscure manifestation of the spirit and rend it, rather than go to the source and drink! What irony to inform the artist what is wrong with his work—as if that mattered! The artist speaks out of his inner certainty, and no matter how far astray he may seem to go, no matter how wild, how erratic his words, he is always a thousand times more right, more true, than those who presume to judge him. *If he is an artist!* As for the rest, those who call themselves artists, they do no matter. One should not confound the issue because there are artists and pseudo-artists. If one does not know when he is confronted with a real artist, then it is all hopeless. And that is pretty much how things stand today, with all distinctions fading, with the learned ones talking about Proust, Joyce *and* Lawrence, as though they were all on one platform, one level, and of the same order.

Lawrence's case, as Murry's admirable and treacherous book testifies only too clearly, is precisely of the order which defies the cool, presumptuous, scientific methods of analysis which the modern psychologists exploit. In fragmenting the man, laying bare his conflicts, exploring his experiences, underscoring his shocks and his sufferings, he eats away the living spirit of the man in order to put before us an articulated skeleton of tangible, seizable phenomena. The living dynamism, the unity which is the man and which made him what he was, escapes, eludes forever the probing, useless, scientific instruments. In struggling to grasp the riddle of personality, the inefficacy of the analytical approach becomes especially glaring when it is an artist who is the "object" of study. The fluid, protean nature of the artist defies the rigid touch of science; the reality of his creation, the artist's whole *raison d'être*, is ignored. Because the explanations which the psychologists furnish, and just because they are explanations occupy a separate world from that vital, living world of the imagination which the artist has created. It seems almost like one of Murry's own truisms to say that genius is such by virtue of the fact that it constantly and forever eludes all formulation. The man of genius is he who makes his own laws, his own reality, and it is because they are uniquely his, and that in obedience to them he alienates himself from the rest of men, that he defies the categories of critics, scientists and philosophers.

Truth demands that, in interpreting a man's life, the emphasis should be on the predominant characteristic of his nature, which in the case of Lawrence was the virility of his creative power, a power which certainly overshadowed any sexual or personal insufficiency, assuming that there was such. To analyze Lawrence then according to a formula, to attempt to organize by logic that superb chaos which he was, is to leave out the most important Lawrence—the dreamer and creator. Because of his very physical weakness, and his struggle against it, certain things were revealed to Lawrence which were concealed from other men; but to emphasize this weakness rather than the importance of the revelation is to be untrue to the creative dreams which were as much a part of the man as his human life. Take for example that passage in *The Rainbow* wherein Lawrence describes the union between Anton and Ursula, a passage which Murry's scientific dissection characterizes as a revelation of Lawrence's "animality." We are informed that it is a description of the disintegration which results from this "animality." Murry concludes that Lawrence's own terrible experience of self-immolation in the sexual experience left him unsatisfied because he was too weak to achieve satisfaction. But there may be quite another "explanation" of this violent union between Anton and Ursula. This devastating conflict might also be regarded, not as a mere sexual phenomenon, but as the creator's craving for a climax far bigger than the climaxes which life has to offer. It might well be a creative voraciousness beside which the average man's hunger is insignificant. More life! More hunger! More pain! More experience! And not just quantitative experience, but qualitative experience—intensity of experience.

This overwhelming urge for experience, this fierce, devouring hunger for life, it is true, generally costs the artist his life. His is divided between, at one and at the same time, the desire to live out his deepest impulses and to preserve himself from the destruction which must inevitably ensue. The fear of ultimate physical extinction leads him to immortalize himself through art. His experience of life consequently comes to be regarded by him as both a necessary ailment and an evil, destructive thing. And since it is the sexual life which, as for most of us, provides the greatest measure of experience and suffering, the symbolic, imaginative derivatives of that life endow his art-product with the most cruel and poignant outlines of feeling.

Just as he glorifies life, in order to slay it through his art, so he glorifies woman in order to execrate her, punish her, for the necessitous character of her role, which he himself recognizes only too clearly. It is because his creative instinct is so strong that he is obliged to deny, at least in his art, the tyranny of her power. *Son of Woman* he is, but it is as *Father* that he endows himself for his role in life. Born a mortal he craves immortality; born of woman he appoints himself begetter. Not of her are his children produced, but of HIM who is all. He looks to her for his experience only in order to achieve his final isolation. The sex act is not the consummation or the fulfillment—it is the point of departure. But it is just because his hunger is sharper, his need of experience more exigent, that his thirst for fulfillment, for an isolated union with the universe, emerges with such a painful, discordant clarity.

The fulfillment which Lawrence depicts in *Lady Chatterley's Lover* is not the fulfillment of the artist. It is in *The Rainbow* that we witness this devastating, harrowing soul-struggle. And the struggle has a "disintegrating" character simply because it is an unequal struggle. That which the woman is terrified of, the urgent quest for something beyond her, which makes a real union forever impossible, that is the sole preoccupation of the artist, because it is his problem, his conflct. No mortal woman will ever satisfy the demands of this demon. No mortal man either. That is why love, marriage, friendship, all prove to be insufficient, added tortures to his existence.

God be praised that life can still throw out now and then such an abnormal, diseased, sex-crucified, sex-sodden genius as Lawrence. A fine affair it will be when all the neurotics have been analyzed, when all men have been made "normal" (which is a contradiction in essence), when the lion lies down with the lamb and there is no more struggle, no more conflict, no more pain, only bread and butter for everybody and peace on earth and stinking good-will towards men.

* * *

I trust it is clear by this time that I am not writing a "criticism" of Lawrence. This is an appreciation, passionate and prejudiced, an emotional document, which I consider the only kind of criticism worth while.

CHAPTER II

Soil and Climate

TO APPROACH THE WORLD of Lawrence two things must be steadily borne in mind: first, the nature of his individual temperament, and second, the relation between such a temperament and the times. For Lawrence was both distinctively unique and a figure representative of our time. He stands out among the constellations as a tiny, blazing star; he glows more brilliantly in the measure that we understand our age. Had he not reflected his epoch so thoroughly he would have already been forgotten. As it is, his importance increases with time. It is not that he grows bigger, or that he moves nearer the earth. No, he remains where he was at the beginning: he remains just a little bit above the horizon, like an evening star; but as night comes on—and it is the night which is coming on stronger and stronger—he waxes more brilliant. We understand him better as we go down into the night.

Thus far we have been considering Lawrence from the standpoint of his uniqueness, surveying the various facets of his character which he revealed. What it was about him that caused him to stand out so singularly we may perhaps better understand by studying him against the background of his age, by situating him, as it were, in his particular soil and climate.

In *The Plumed Serpent* Lawrence says of Cipriano: "He was looking into the heart of the world; because the faces of men, and the hearts of men are helpless quicksands. Only in the heart of the cosmos man can look for strength." It was not until I had looked into the heart of the world that I discovered Lawrence. Not until I had looked into the heart of Lawrence that I discovered the world. For the world is like a forest, and so are the hearts of men. One cannot see the trees for the forest, or the forest for the trees. I walked into the heart of the world and I saw this unique tree which Lawrence is. I saw the shining leaves, the queer branches, the stunted trunk. The more I looked the more it seemed to me that this tree was standing upside down. And though the forest was full of trees there was not another like this which I could discover.

At first I could think of nothing but the strangeness of this tree. I lost myself in contemplation of it. Gradually, however, I observed that the trees about were withered, dying. They were old and gnarled, they had shed their leaves. I examined the soil on which I was standing; I saw that the loam was gone, that it was turning to sand. The very climate in which these trees stood desolate and barren seemed to have undergone a tremendous change. I had stumbled into a forest that was dying— the whole forest was dying out.

How then, I asked myself, could this lone tree survive? By what miracle had it shot forth these monstrous roots which dangled in the upper air? What nourished this tree, when all about was death and sterility? Here was a curious phenomenon: a tree manifesting life in the midst of death!

It is said that a tree lives by its leaves. The leaves are the evidence of a tree's livingness. Now the singular thing about this forest is that not only had the other trees ceased putting forth leaves, but there was not even a sign of any new trees springing up. There was only this strange tree whose branches were growing into the ground, whose leaves shone with a peculiar splendor. A mysterious tree which seemed to lead its own existence in defiance of the death around it. By some miracle this tree was still expressing its faith, its desire to live. In some secret way it had achieved the miracle of escaping the general destiny. In the winter of life it had become young again, had undergone a resurrection.

The world is a forest which is continually transforming itself. When one forest dies another is born. The forest dies, but the tree remains. In the spring one sort of tree predominates; in the fall another. Even when the soil is exhausted and the forest threatened with extinction, certain trees persist, certain trees take root and shoot forth strange and splendid leaves. They are the trees which have embraced the mystery of life and death. Whereas the other trees depend upon the nourishment afforded them by the soil, these trees nourish the soil itself by sending their roots into the air above where all the elements of life abide eternally. These other metaphysical trees live a life in defiance of the ordinary laws of nature. They nourish nature.

It is a strange phenomenon, the appearance of this tree, but it is a phenomenon which recurs perpetually. Indeed, it is only when this phenomenon manifests itself that the forest which is

the world and the individual trees which are man commence
to have meaning for us. The endless passing, the endless
change, all that which is beyond comprehension now acquires
a symbolic character. It is not the forest which interests us any
longer, nor even the individual tree, but that which tree and
forest, in their endless coming and going, together signify. It is
the mystery which now engages us. The mystery of perpetual
life manifested always through the individual tree.

As the tree expresses itself through its leaves so man expresses himself through faith. When life is strong, and roots well
nourished, the tree of life which is man has no other impulse
than to send forth its leaves. It is in the winter of life, when the
long sleep lies ahead, that the mystery of life makes itself felt. It
is in the dream of sleep that the dead leaves are gathered up into
the body of the earth and made into a rich and fertilizing
compost. During the fruitful season there was no thought but
to express the life within; but in the winter life has to be
nourished by the dead and fallen leaves. In the winter many are
the trees which die—*forever*. Only the hardy, life-sustaining
trees will see the spring again—those which knew how to
nourish themselves, how to lay by for the long, barren winter.

Finally there comes a period when even spring itself is
threatened, a period when this forest which is perpetually
dying and perpetually being reborn seems scarcely capable of
renewing the cycle. It is the period when the entire forest dies
out, to make way for a new and unknown world of trees. This is
the direst winter of all. A pause of mysterious and dark dura-
tion, when life itself is in question. It is then that we have the
rare bloom, the rare and mysterious blossoming of the sacred
tree of life. It is then that we have the phenomenon of a Lawrence, or a Jesus Christ, or a Lao-Tze, strange, blazing trees of
life which keep alive the remembrance of spring by their talk
of death.

These are the trees which are no longer concerned with their
neighbors, nor even with the forest itself, but with the sacred
mystery of life which the prevailing atmosphere of death inspires. These are the trees which bring forth spring—by standing themselves upside down. These are the trees which have so
lived into death that the dream of life becomes real and expresses itself miraculously. These are the trees which hasten the
death which is inevitable—in order that life may blossom

anew. They sing of death because they have already tasted the new life. They make the world drunk with death; they poison the very air with their song.

There is no knowledge of trees which will enable us to penetrate the mysterious nature of these trees which appear in the winter of life and bring forth spring. Their nature is closed to us, just as life itself is a closed book to us. We know only that they do appear and that their song is always the same. We distinguish them from other trees of the forest by the fact that they bloom out of season. We set them apart because they inspire life. It is only when they have passed away that the significance of their existence is revealed to us. It is only when they have died that their experience can become our experience.

However stately and magnificent the individual tree, however grand and ordered the forest itself may appear at times, the heart of the forest is wild, wild and chaotic. Within the forest there may spring up mighty oaks, giant redwoods, enormous tracts of luxuriant growth with a life seemingly everlasting. Such we might consider China, India, Egypt—vast, fertile tracts studded with magnificent yields. Slow to grow, slow to die. Lingering on in death, feeble ghosts of the past. Throughout great periods profound changes make themselves felt; the forest changing, the trees changing, the leaves themselves changing. The changes so slow that one scarcely heeds the individual tree, but observes only the forest, its form, its physiognomy. Here and there patient, industrious men making note of the changes, recording them for posterity.

These are the patient, industrious ants with nose to the ground who take the facts of life and construct therewith that skeleton of significance which is called history. These are the men of science who note the sequence of cause and effect and give us the supposed laws of life. These are the men, all of them, who wait for the tree or the forest to die in order to reveal the secrets of life. But the individual tree which is man does not live by history or by scientific law. The tree of life is sustained by faith and this faith is expressed by action. No tree yields up its secret when dead and dissected. A tree can express only the mystery of its being, and it is in the expression of the mystery that the forest of life assumes its cast.

There are trees, however, which reveal more than other trees. Trees which manifest the life in them more forcefully, more poetically, than others. These are the trees which, in turning themselves upside down, reveal the very roots of their being. These are the sacred evergreens which defy the seasons, which assert the life eternal by blossoming forth out of a barren soil. They are nourished not by the past, but by the future. They have overstayed their time, and they live outside and beyond their time. They are the violators of all law, all logic. They emerge out of the corpse of life, mysterious and inspiring as maggots. They free the corpse of its death. It is in the performance of this sacred, metaphysical rite that they make manifest the mystery of life. It is their hunger for life eternal which keeps alive faith. Though they are few and almost invisible, though they are buried in the very heart of the forest, they are anchored in the quick of life and their leaves shine forth with a strange and brilliant splendor.

* * *

How well Lawrence understood the complete and fulfilled man, the mortally human man, we see from the portraits of his heroes, and in particular that of Aaron Sisson. *Aaron's Rod* is one of the most important novels Lawrence wrote, although the first three chapters form one of the queerest, most uncertain, stumbling, faltering openings I have ever seen. Commencing with chapter IV, as though conscious of his floundering, Lawrence writes: "Our story will not yet see daylight." And throughout the book, from time to time, he drops these open admissions to the reader. There is a fierce struggle in him to get it off his chest.

The relationship between Aaron, the flute player, and his wife is in fact the story of a struggle in the dark on the part of a man who does not yet know himself, the story of an artist who is strangled by domesticity, by the devouring female, and who is trying to liberate himself.

Consider Aaron's portrait:

> *His father had been a shaft-sinker, earning good money, but had been killed by a fall down the shaft when Aaron was only four years old. The widow had opened a shop; Aaron was her only child. She had done well in her shop. She had wanted Aaron to be a school-teacher. He had served three years apprenticeship, then suddenly thrown it up and gone to the pit.*
>
> *"But why?" said Josephine.*

He had a curious quality of an intelligent, almost sophisti-
cated mind, which had repudiated education. On purpose he
kept the Midland accent in his speech. He understood per-
fectly what a personification was—and an allegory. But he
preferred to be illiterate.

This description of Aaron is that of Lawrence himself, hardly
disguised in the least—except for that curious twist of killing
off the father, a literary revenge. It is the portrait of the young
Lawrence, the nascent artist, man of humble origins, sensitive,
artistic, not yet aware of his destiny. In a sense, one feels that
Aaron's wife might be the unconscious portrait of Lawrence's
mother, the woman whom he recognized as the lover and wife,
the woman who had crippled him as a man, and whom again he
takes revenge upon unconsciously. It is not the portrait of his
earlier loves, nor of Frieda. But it is the fundamental portrait,
for Lawrence, of *all* women—in their role of mother, wife,
destroyer, etc. and Aaron tells Josephine: "I'm damned if I want
to go on being a lover, to her [his wife] or anybody . . . I don't
want to *care*, when care isn't in me." This is superb as the
speech of the artist who can not give himself completely, who
withholds his love for creative purposes. The theme of the book
is not love or friendship between man and man. It is written to
explain to himself the necessity for obeying his own creative
impulse, the Holy Ghost within himself. He is completely
divided. And this is made poignantly clear to him because he is
just recently married and already senses that his allegiance is
not to the woman. The man Aaron to whom he offers himself
in holy communion is his real, uncompromising, lonely,
strange artist self. Complete narcissism, producing the usual
"double" theme.

Josephine, the emancipated woman who loves Paris, who is
free, independent, is made out to be miserably unhappy in her
female freedom. She is the artist type that Lawrence loathed.
Naturally he would make her say: "What I should really like
more than anything would be an end of the world." That is to
say, end of the "female" problem, end of Josephine as problem.

These opening chapters are terribly tedious and unnecessary,
and unconvincing. All cotton-wool. Cheap magazine dia-
logues. Cheap scenes, social affairs, etc. *Why Josephine?* Why
her whole crowd, her milieu? Just to show the hollowness
of the middle-class world? This is typical of Lawrence's

method in most of the novels—typical of his inability to free himself from his hatreds and prejudices and give us a pure work of art. His books are all cluttered up with irrelevant issues. One has to disentangle the story from the emotional issues in which he is perpetually involved, that is, wasted emotional issues.

The story of *Aaron's Rod* is really very slender. Both Dostoevski and Duhamel held it down to the novelette form, where it belongs. Dostoevski, in "The Double," is superb, despite the floundering opening. He keeps boned down, like an athlete, to the central struggle; the whole thing moves like a bad dream, leaving the action stark, hallucinating, fuliginous. Duhamel's "Two Men" likewise—the story is nothing but the situation between the two men. But Lawrence writes like the man he was, torn from his roots, restless, unhappy, a victim of passing impressions, passing hatreds, passing prejudices. And always with a backward, yearning glance—towards England, towards the milieu from which he sprang and from which he was never wholly weaned.

For example, the Jim Bricknell portrait seems as if it were based on the Lawrence-Murry relationship. Jim Bricknell is so obviously the interloper whom Lawrence cannot stand. Murry the cunt-chaser, who has a way with women, who seduces them with his spiritual lingo. Sounds like the same old Huxley caricature of Murry: "I reckon Christ's the finest thing time has ever produced," said he, "and will remain it."

"Don't you think love and sacrifice are the finest things in life?" said Jim over his bacon. Undubitably Murry—and yet one wonders why on earth Lawrence bothered to include the portrait, or the silly, sophomoric discussions on love and sacrifice: "Oh yes," said Jim, "Judas was inevitable. I'm not sure that Judas wasn't the greatest of the disciples—and Jesus knew it. I'm not sure Judas wasn't the disciple Jesus loved." And if that were not enough, Jim adds, "The finest thing the world has produced, or ever will produce—Christ and Judas—"

The question is, was Murry such an imbecile as Jim Bricknell's remarks would lead us to believe him? Or is Lawrence putting it on thick out of revenge, thinking it ver cunning, very diabolical, to make this man who is such a Judas in life, espouse Judas of the Gospel? ("He's a profound figure, is Judas. It's taken two thousand years to begin to understand him.") And Lilly, who is listening to all this, is of course

Lawrence the man, Lawrence the husband—vindictive, jealous, irascible, possessed with biting tongue. So fearful that his friend Jim is going to play him dirty. Really, by his silly, boyish attitude, goading Jim (Murry) to betray him.

More Murry caricatures. About love . . ."I only live when I can fall in love. Otherwise I'm dying by inches." If Murry really talked this way then he was a bigger ass than I give him credit for. It is very doubtful whether Murry ever did utter such words. But in any case, both Murry's attitude and Lawrence's are wrong, absurd, impossible. The one makes life wholly dependent on a woman's love, the other tries to make life independent of her love. Both are untenable ideals. Lawrence, throughout his life, showed himself particularly vulnerable, particularly incapable of functioning without a woman by his side. Furthermore, it is important to note that Bricknell said that he could only live when he could fall in love—stressing the desire, the urge, the potentiality—which after all is not such a distressing symptom as Lawrence would have us believe.

But this does not stand in the way of one of the finest, the most honest bits of writing Lawrence ever pulled off. Jim Bricknell has just given Lilly an unexpected crack in the pit of the stomach. Tanny looks on approvingly. Lilly (Lawrence) contains himself. Then Jim speaks up: "It isn't that I don't like him. I like him better than any man I've ever known, I believe." (*"Judas!"* flashed through Lilly's mind.) Tanny's behavior is very revelatory. One knows that things like this must have happened to Lawrence—and that he knew deep down that he deserved them. Note this queer touch—Jim is repeating his silly remark: "I like the man. Never liked a man more than I like him." And Lawrence, the author, adds: *"The man* stuck safely in Lilly's ears."

Now that we know all about the Murry-Lawrence controversy, we find a certain decent consistency in Murry's behavior. Murry here, in his pseudo-Judas role, is more a Dostoevskian character than Lawrence would care to admit. After all, Murry *did* like Lawrence, adored him, in fact. But he could not swallow Lawrence's philosophy, nor could he ever forgive the insults that had been dealt him by Lawrence's sharp tongue. And being a Judas, and striking his beloved friend, is quite consistent with his "spiritual" role. It is Murry who comes off with the honors in this scene—not Lawrence. But did

Lawrence wish it to appear thus? That is what is often difficult in this book—to detect the obvious as against the unconscious desire. Is Lawrence just devilishly clever? Or is he giving the show away unwittingly? With the terrible inner cleavage that runs through the book, I think it is a case of a little of both. He reveals his true self, wittingly or unwittingly. He *wants* to reveal everything—even though he sets out to conceal, to distort.

The conclusion of this chapter is again significant of Lawrence's inner feelings—his true attitude towards Murry, which as a man, in actual life, he could not adhere to: "But he and his wife never saw Jim again. Lilly never intended to see him: a devil sat in the little man's breast." And Tanny advises immediately after this: "You shouldn't play at little Jesus, coming so near to people, wanting to help them." Tanny's last word. This is remarkable, by way of indicating a grave lapse in the book. In actuality this was Lawrence's fundamental attitude towards Murry. But the story of *Aaron's Rod* does not at all make this evident. Lawrence completely forgot this vital factor. What really impels him to write about Murry in Jim is his hatred and jealousy of him. Not his desire to come close, to help him. He opened the chapter by having Jim confess (and what a big man Lawrence hereby makes of himself!): "I had an inspiration this morning. I suddenly saw that if there was a man in England who could save me, it was you." Jim's remark, so indicative of the nature of the relation between these two historic figures, reveals once again an element in Lawrence's nature which Murry underscores time and again—Lawrence's dishonesty with himself. He wanted to be the savior of mankind, and yet he would not make himself worthy of his role. He could inspire men to look to him for aid and refuge, for enlightenment, for direction, and he could also ignobly let them down. The "devil" which he carried in his breast, as he writes himself (referring to his character, Lilly), was his own meanness, his own littleness. He wanted power, and he was afraid of it, afraid to wield it. He wanted men to come close to him, and then he was unable to stand their presence, their close, vital contact, with all the demands this entailed.

And so, consequently, it was but natural that he created Judases about him. His letters and reminiscences, his novels even, abound in these sorts of references. He feels suspicious, guilty, hunted, persecuted. He brought it upon himself. When he comes up against a Dostoevski, or a Whitman, he lets out a squawk. These were the men who knew the meaning of comradeship, of brotherhood, of democracy, of faith, of power. Lawrence tried to denigrate them. But in doing so he was exposing his own fundamental weakness, his inherent inability to be human, to be natural, to live close to men, with them, for them. The idealism which he fought all his life, and which *is* the poison that he made it out to be, was his own ruin.

In *Aaron's Rod* we find as well the very personal theme of love between the sexes: "'I hate married people who are two in one—stuck together like two jujube lozenges', said Lilly. 'Everybody ought to stand by themselves, in the first place—men and women as well . . . nothing is any good unless each one stands alone, intrinsically.'" But this oft-repeated theme, as introduced here without any development of the love relationship between Lilly and his wife, seems irrelevant. Yet it is Lawrence's big, obsessive theme. He is out to preach, and he has got to work it in somehow. Later, in *The Plumed Serpent*, he modifies this attitude. When the two are really alone in their singleness they must come together in the "Morning Star." Otherwise it's all to no purpose. Murry takes issue on this, with some justice: "Then why not go into the wilderness?" But neither Murry nor Lawrence is right.

In actuality, no man and woman were ever more like two jujube lozenges than Lawrence and his Frieda. They were inseparable. But Lawrence knew that it wasn't a real togetherness—not the Morning Star business. The tragedy of the man's life is, as Murry well points out, that he was terribly dependent on a woman, and because he knew it so well, he was miserable, and created this picture of mutual independence. And because he was afraid of Frieda, too, I imagine, he cloaked his stories in allegory and symbol, married her ideally in the sky, via the Morning Star. The poor devil did his best, no doubt, to convince Frieda that his treachery was really a desire on his part to ennoble her. But Frieda had no illusions. Frieda knew him. And that's why Frieda's barbs had such devastating effect—they were always aimed with deadly accuracy. She knew his soft spots. When she married him she was looking for a lover, for a romantic union. And soon enough she discovered that she had married an egoist, a man incapable of giving her the love which she, as a woman, craved. Her love turned to admiration for his genius, inspired her natural woman's fidelity, loyalty.

She was deceived in him, however, and she never forgave him. When she pokes fun at his philosophy, or criticizes his work, it is always the man she is aiming at, the man who ran out on her. In Bertha Coutts Lawrence has painted her black. In every biography Frieda is painted malevolently. But Frieda deserves justice too. She played a heroic role, against a man who was more than her equal. If Frieda had not been so much the woman she was, Lawrence's philosophy would have fallen to pieces. She gave him, by her living example, the resistance which he needed for creation. If it be true, as he seems to tell us in *Lady Chatterley*, that she clutched at his genitals like a vulture, it is also true that he sucked her dry, used her as an instrument.

What kept them together was a passion in each of them for something which neither could give the other—Frieda wanted him to surrender himself in love and sex, Lawrence wanted Frieda to surrender her woman's role, her nature instinct, her possessiveness. In the artist's usual lying way, his illusive way, Lawrence raised this extraordinary antagonism between them to a magnitude of proportion, invested it with a symbolism, which is not altogether true. Because he hated to be tied to her apron strings, as he had been to his mother's, he declaimed against the jujube lozenge two-in-one business. And he succumbed to it.

So, as Tanny, Frieda finds herself in *Aaron's Rod* alongside poor Murry. According to Lilly, "Tanny's the same. She does nothing really but resist me: my authority, or my influence, or just *me*. At the bottom of her heart she just blindly and persistently opposes me. God knows what it is she opposes: just me myself. She thinks I want her to submit to me. So I do, in a measure natural to our two selves. Somewhere, she ought to submit to me."

This is the first revelatory speech about Frieda, and it is heartbreaking when one knows Lawrence and one cares about him. Murry greedily fastens on this incident—as an admission by Lawrence of his own inadequacy. The leader who cannot even make his own wife obey him. But here Lawrence is deadly accurate. The kind of man, the kind of artist he was, could only have chosen a woman like Frieda. She had all the wild, free, female traits he wanted in a woman. But she had also what every modern woman has—to her ruination—a stubborn will, a desire to play the man's role. (A condition man has brought about himself, to be sure.) Lawrence confuses the issue here. His inability to cope with Tanny/Frieda is based on the fact that he is an artist of a special type, with certain complexes, certain tendencies and defects, a great subjective artist, a narcissist of the first water. It is true, he is not *man* enough for a woman like Frieda. But primarily he is not man enough, not because women have so far usurped man's role, but because as artist, and *dependent on the woman*, he is more keenly sensitive to the external imbalance, the social maladjustment of the artist in the world today. The conflict with woman is only one of the aspects of the artist's fight with the whole outside world. In times of eruption the woman question always comes to the fore—because it is a key-note.

From Aaron's point of view, women "make a criminal of you. Them and their children be cursed. Is my life given me for nothing but to get children, and work for a woman? See them all in hell first—they'd better die while they're children, if childhood's all that's important." And Lilly "quite" agrees: "If childhood is more important than manhood, then why live to be a man at all? Why not remain an infant? . . . Men have got to stand up to the fact that manhood is more than childhood—and then force women to admit it." This is the conversation that Murry exposes for its logical absurdity and in the conclusion of which—Lilly's comment, "And can you find two men to stick together without feeling criminal, and without cringing, and without betraying one another?"—he pretends to find a homosexual twist.

If there is a vital question posed here, it is the old one of *Fantasia*—"It is a man's own religious soul that drives him on beyond woman," etc. But what Lawrence unwittingly reveals through Aaron, his other self, who only apparently is in such perfect agreement with him, is this: that with the end of a culture comes race suicide. Lilly/Lawrence, that is, the poet, the artist, is fighting for a new order of things. *Fighting with ink!* Aaron/Lawrence, that is, the man and husband, simply refuses to go on producing children. *Aaron's Rod,* while apparently dealing with the question of friendship, is really about the death of a race.

Lawrence is simply pointing out a truism—that in the end-periods woman is more nakedly revealed as the enemy of the masculine, civilizing process. Woman allies herself with Nature. "The feminine stands closer to the Cosmic," says Spengler; "It is rooted deeper in the earth and it is immediately involved in the grand cyclic rhythms of Nature." But—just before the moment when this is adequately realized, woman is deified. The great sexual interpretation of all things occurs when the truly religious forces die down. With the sexual theory comes the silent admission, as it were, that death can not be averted. It can only be disguised, sublimated, glorified. It gets aestheticized. And men forget, too, that in this final period, of which Lawrence is so representative, woman must fight man desperately. His symbols are of no use. They are so feeble, so empty, that man is in danger of exterminating the race—*himself.* The polarity is broken down. Homosexuality, promiscuity, bachelorhood, race suicide. Woman saves the day for the race by obeying her own sure instincts.

Certainly women expect men to give them children! They would be strange women if they didn't. It is not a case of pitting children against men, childhood against maturity. Lawrence falsifies. It is the idealist, the savior, the saint speaking again. All these God-seekers aim to destroy the world. Man must not be born of woman, but of God. It is quite true that women emphasize the biologic aspect of life—that is their duty, their business, as it were. And man's business is to emphasize the spiritual—the mature, the rounded, the full life of maturity. But the means to this end is not by justifying sterility. A larger view of life recognizes full well that the great majority are born to lead useless lives. A great spirit is a masculine spirit, a fecundating spirit, one that bids life continue, for good or evil. It creates faith and hope, a will to live.

Lawrence, caught in the whirlpool of the end, tries to resist life. The horror of it is so great to him, sensitive spirit that he is, that he condemns any function of life but the spiritual, the revolutionary, the anarchic. And in doing so he becomes absurd. He credits woman with a purposiveness which she possesses only unconsciously, in obedience to a natural biologic urge. He dramatizes and romanticizes. Women stick together, he says, and men are traitors one to another. This is all rot. It would be more true to say that it is men who stick together and that women stick to the men. Were it true that women are united for a common biologic purpose, to save the race as it were, war would have been eliminated long ago. Women have never yet been able to unite, across the frontiers of race and prejudice, to save their children.

When, in a rotten civilization, deprived of natural male protection, women are obliged to fight for equal rights, for the right to vote, to work, notice how, as soon as they have achieved their ends, they battle for the race. Soviet Russia makes marriage and divorce easy as can be—but the stern foundation underlying the new order is the *rights of children*. The children must be supported, must be educated, must be fed, clothed, sheltered. The State does it. And the State is doing it only because men and women individually, as husband and wife, have failed to do their job. A certain grim bitterness underlies the woman's acceptance of her new role in Russia. She is not so god-damned well pleased with her present status of equality. She is free now to work in the factory, beside the male, she is free also to shoulder a musket when her time comes. And at the same time, she must also perform her duty as a mother. Rather tough on the woman, the new order! She is only a part-time female, as it were. Man has so run things into the ground that woman has to sacrifice her natural instincts in order to save the ship.

"The War Again," the next chapter of *Aaron's Rod*, reads almost like a colloquy which Lawrence, the author, holds with himself. Says Aaron: "Why, you're all the time grinding yourself against something inside you . . . . You're no more than a man who drops into a pub for a drink to liven himself up a bit. Only you give it a lot of names . . . . What have you got, more than me or Jim Bricknell? Only a bigger choice of words, it seems to me." And here Lilly/Lawrence is stumped. The whole "dialogue" is typical of the introspective trend of the artist seeking to justify himself, the artist who can't accept life as it is, who wants to impose his will on it. The authority which he requires, the world no longer gives the artist—since the cult of genius is exploded. There is also indicated here the great craving of the artist for *experience*, for participation in life. He wants, ever so much more than the normal man, to plunge into life, to devour it, but he must do it, as Aaron points out, under guise of doing something lofty. Experience in and by itself is not sufficient.

And a marvellously frank exposure Lawrence makes of himself in the ensuing conversation. Caustic. Spares nothing. Says Aaron: "And you're the idol on the mountain-top, worshipping yourself." To which Lilly responds: "You talk to me like a woman, Aaron." This is a strange remark, unwarranted by what precedes. But in Lawrence's brain is the rankling remembrance always of Frieda's jibes, which always struck home because a woman knows a man's tenderest spots. The man's mission! That was Lawrence's tender spot, his Achilles heel. The artist in him felt that it was always incumbent upon him to fight the woman in order to justify his high purpose. At bottom, of course, woman never concedes to the high purpose. If she seems to give assent, it is only to lull the man into supine abjection, to ensnare him into her own net. Woman wants love—not high purpose. The woman who marries an artist has only half a man—the rest is high purpose!

Lawrence's inner warfare continues. "The two men had an almost uncanny understanding of one another—like brothers . . . . Like brothers, there was a profound hostility between them. But hostility is not antipathy." The remarkable paragraph is an epitome of his whole theme—the eternal duality, the war, the schism, to which there is no solution, except the recognition of it. He wants to say that one aspect of the self is no better than the other, that they complement each other, and only so because they are antagonistic. Not antipathy . . . hostility. If we read these remarks as interpretive of the relationship between two men the significance of them becomes puerile, almost unintelligible. It would be simply a remarkable fatalistic meeting—a dramatic episode, a cheap one.

During the same dialogue between Aaron and Lilly, the latter reminds Aaron of Josephine Ford's remark—"There isn't any such thing as love . . . . Men are simply afraid to be alone." And Aaron replies—"What by that?" Now the quaintness of Aaron's language, the colloquial dialect he drops into at these crucial, awkward points in the narrative, are splendid. One senses that Lawrence feels guilty in dragging in all these irrelevant, random subjects for conversation with a man such as

Aaron, who, he makes quite clear, is so far removed from such discussions as not even to know the terminology, simple as it is, which Lilly employs. But Lawrence is under a tremendous compulsion to solve these problems, and refusing to write the usual introspective novel, he is confronted with the problem of posing and answering these questions in a very ticklish way. He employs his humor, his bitter, naked self-criticism (usually directed against Aaron) to relieve the seriousness of the questions. He is just a little ashamed, we feel, that he should be putting such questions to himself. That is why he can take the fullest liberties of speech (through Aaron), vaunt his sarcasm, his scorn of himself, to his heart's content.

It is a painful spectacle. Lawrence knows himself quite thoroughly. He abhors the noblest side of himself. And yet, he loves himself too. He is so in love with himself that he is unable to enter into any vital relation with another human being. He can only project himself, see himself in others. He really does look upon himself as a god. And finally, in the last works, out of inner necessity, he makes God over, as men always do, into an image of himself. It is this which so enrages Murry. Murry puts it as though Lawrence had to dethrone Jesus in order to establish Lawrence as the supreme force in the world. Murry refuses to recognize that Jesus did the same thing, that *all* the great religious leaders have done it, and will continue to do it. He denies, by his defense of Jesus, the very power that made the latter the force he is—to wit, his *creative instinct*. He does not wish to look upon him as an artist. He wants to differentiate, finely to discriminate between artist and religious man.

This, in turn, enrages Lawrence. Because Lawrence knows that he has as much authority, as much divinity, as Jesus or Buddha, or any of his predecessors. (A theme which Whitman echoes splendidly in his reference to the Bible.) It is a tremendous battle over the question of justification. And so, in the midst of this problem Lawrence suddenly injects the "woman question"—"men are simply afraid to be alone." Why? Because he wants to point out that he is really sufficient unto himself. He has no valid quarrel with love, with woman. It is against dependence he is fighting. And so he can only grant the carnal, sensual love, passion based on fundamental antagonism—not spiritual love. He sees that men have confused the issue. He is right, I believe. Jesus is not talking about love, but about salvation, and salvation is personal, individual, the affair of man with God, not with his brother, or society, or woman.

So Lawrence concludes (through the mouth of Lilly) that men love only because they are afraid to be alone and women love because they are bored if some one doesn't play the fiddle. Love, a pastime! The corollary to Aaron's previous remarks about *earnest purpose*—"only killing time." That is the cardinal fear—the thought of merely killing time! Since, as artist, he is shirking the normal man's enjoyment of life, the pursuit of experience for its own sake, the acceptance of life at face value, he, Lawrence, poet, artist, half-man, must justify his almost criminal violence upon his own nature. He must establish, at any price, a reason for living, for acting as he does, for choosing to act as he does.

Consequently, when Lilly bitingly tells Aaron that he, Aaron, will always be able to get along in the world, since he has his flute (the penis symbolism is quite naked) and his charm (personality), Lilly/Lawrence is really saying to himself: because it is easier for you than most men who have no charm, no talent, no force, to get along, you must make it difficult for yourself, you must *earn* your way, that is, do something noble, something worthwhile, something which the world does not want, which it despises. In this way you will make the world recognize you for what you really are. Of course Lawrence did not know what he *really* was. He wrote his books to discover that.

It is all delightfully involved, painfully intricate, and yet so naked, so sincere, as to be a revelation of the artist's soul. And yet this is glossed over, the whole purpose of *Aaron's Rod*. Says Lilly: "Aaron's rod is putting forth again." Charming remark. As though to say, Lawrence is repeating himself, he is never doing anything but being himself—and all this music, this language, is but dust in your eyes. *I* know it too—but I can't help myself. Thus I am and thus I will be. And when, a moment later, he refers to the "scarlet runners" that came out of Moses' rod, we know what that means—his own blood, the pain, the agony of being one's self.

It is no accident that Leo Frobenius should enter here: "And no sooner had he forgotten Aaron, reading the fantasies of a certain Leo Frobenius, than Aaron must stride in again." A curious allusion. Frobenius who so well expounded the myth of rebirth, the hero-wanderer myth which Lawrence himself so well exemplifies. "Save for my job—*which is to write lies*—Aaron and I are two identical little men in one and the same little boat," says Lilly at this point. Interesting again for the choice of image—"two men in a boat"—i.e., the old sun and the new sun, the difference between them being that the new sun which is to be born "writes lies," keeps up the myth of the world, the myth of power and illusion. And Frobenius still lingers further down the page: "old Africans! and Atlantis! Strange, strange wisdom of the Kabyles! Old, old dark Africa, and the world before the flood!" Intuitively and unconsciously seizing on that prenatal world, the prehistoric, the pre-conscious, the Paradise of the womb—before one has any knowledge of sin, of guilt. Before there is a separation, a thrust-ing forth into life, responsibility. The eternal artist-dream of anarchy, of amoralism, of freedom without punishment. "How jealous Aaron seemed!" Yes, the jealousy of the mass-man, the ordinary man who envies the amoral, the criminal, the free instincts of the artist.

And after the talk, after Frobenius, after the myth and the self-inquisition, this: "He [Lilly] walked quickly down Villiers Street to the river, to see it flowing blackly towards the sea. It had an endless fascination for him: never failed to soothe him and give him a sense of liberty. He liked the night, the dark rain, the river, and even the traffic . . ." He liked them because they suggest movement, direction, goal, perpetuity, mystery. "It was like a fox slipping alert among unsuspecting cattle." That is, wary, alert, conscious—drifting with them, but not of them—stealing among them to plunder, to devour. The artist who drops into the tide of life to nourish himself, to partake of common experience in order to recreate it in song and mystery. But who does it like a thief!

This artist-thief is, above all, an indivualist. We see this in the marvellous discussion between Lilly and Aaron that fol-lows Captain Herbertson's shocking stories of the war. Says Aaron:

> "It was a fact—you can't bust that. You can't bust the fact that it happened."
> "Yes, you can. It never happened. It never happened to me. No more than my dreams happen . . . . It took place in the automatic sphere, like dreams do. But the actual man in

every man was just absent–asleep–or drugged–inert–dream logged. That's it."

"You tell 'em so," said Aaron.

"I do. But it's no good. Because they won't wake up now even–perhaps never. They'll all kill themselves in their sleep."

Here Lawrence expresses superbly my own ideas about the War. It didn't happen to me either! I mean by that that I read about it exactly as I would have read about an earthquake in China, or the destruction of villages in Sicily when Etna erupts. I had no concern in it whatever, except to escape being dragged into it. No man can be made to commit a crime unless he is willing. War will die out, if ever, when men do not care any more about fighting this way. China as a nation, as a people, as individuals, gave up the idea long ago. Certain races in the South Seas also relinquished the idea. Violence, crime—yes, these are permanent elements in human nature. But mechanical, wholesale slaughter—that may well be abolished, stamped out. One has to care, or not care. And it is precisely because we do not care that we will, as Lawrence predicts, kill ourselves in our sleep.

Lilly pithily sums up the idea: "The Germans could have shot my mother or me or what they liked: I wouldn't have joined the *war*. I would like to kill my enemy. But become a bit of that huge obscene machine they called the war, that I never would, no, not if I died ten deaths and had eleven mothers violated. But I would like to kill my enemy: oh yes, more than one enemy. But not as a unit in a vast obscene mechanism. That never; no, never." All this is of a piece with his attitude in *Fantasia* and in the Introduction to the "Magnus Case." It is against war and against pacificism. It is an attempt to keep alive the combative instinct day by day and thus avoid the accumulated unconscious hatreds and vindications which lead to mass war in which the individual has no choice, no direction, no purpose, no grudge, no hope. The attitude of the Chinese on this score was a sound one—if it was necessary to resist an invader, mercenary armies were raised. To fight, as a soldier, was beneath the dignity of an intelligent Chinese. And her history also proves how little it mattered who invaded the country—China always swallowed up her adversaries, converted them into Chinese. It is only those who have nothing to lose who clamor about safety. Real power does not need to manifest itself through brute force.

So, continues Lilly, "All I want is to get *myself* out of their horrible heap: to get out of the swarm. The swarm to me is nightmare and nullity—horrible helpless writhing in a dream . . . . No man is awake and himself." The artist's position to a T. The most precious thing is one's own sacred self—*not* the fatherland, *not* brother and sister, *not* humanity. Exactly the position that Christ took, that every great leader, thinker, lover of man, has taken. *Self-responsibility*. Out of the swarm. Out of nullity, vacuity, nightmare.

When Aaron fails to agree and Lilly tells him to clear out in the morning, comes this, which is also splendid because it defines so passionately and narrowly his view of friendship: "I'm *not* going to pretend to have friends on the face of things. No, and I *don't* have friends who don't fundamentally agree with me. A friend means one who is at one with me in matters of life and death." Again, with his very passion, he cuts through the easy, slippery, opportunistic, lazy, lying, feeble way of friends as the mass understands the word. A noble attitude, now seemingly romantic, old-fashioned, because we are vitiated by indifference, because we are pragmatic and opportunist. We subscribe to abstractions, principles, slogans, ideas, ideals—not to concrete flesh and blood. We talk big and act small. We are so flexible, so elastic, that we can play any tune at all. And the more abstract are our allegiances, the easier it is for us to evade responsibilities.

Lilly goes on, in what I consider one of the finest, the soundest, and the deepest passages Lawrence ever wrote, referring to Captain Herbertson and his kind: "A brave ant is a damned cowardly individual . . . . No life-courage: always death-courage . . . . We simply *will not* face the world as we've made it, and our own souls as we find them, and take the responsibility. We'll *never* get anywhere till we stand up man to man and face *everything* out, and break the old forms, but never let our own pride and courage of life be broken." This is the answer to Lowenfels and Fraenkel, who profess to admire Lawrence so, and who write poems and elegies about him, and pull out the chestnuts that please them, that suit their own philosophy. But this they have never learned—as indeed it cannot be learned. This is handed on only from man to man, like a torch. Yes,

Lawrence is old hat to them now—to many people who profess to be up to the times—they are weary of Lawrence, he can't give them anything more. But to the right person Lawrence will always give something vital and permanent. He stands outside his time. In a passage like this we move from peak to peak and Lawrence can be seen to take his place with the very great. "Never let our own pride and courage of life be broken." There is nothing beyond this that one man can give another, by way of widom.

And, knowing quite well the manner in which his tenderest, bravest, and deepest words would be received by the world, Lawrence puts it down in anticipation, as follows: "He knew perfectly well that Lilly had made a certain call upon his, Aaron's, soul: *a call which he, Aaron, did not intend to obey....* He was not sure whether he felt superior to his *unworldly* enemy or not. He rather felt he did."

Note: "his unworldly enemy!" How well Lawrence knew what awaited him! That he was human enough to squawk when he was hurt is regarded as strange and inconsistent. Droll world . . . .

* * *

A man has no importance except as he represents his time. This, however, is a way of saying a much deeper thing—that his importance lies not in merely representing his time, but in representing an unknown aspect of it which allies his time with the future. As a personality he may reflect either a harmony with the times or a clash—that is relatively unimportant. Unimportant, that is, so far as the world goes. Perhaps fairly enough important for himself. A study of Lawrence, restricted to his personality, or his art-product, has little value for us. Even though he may have been the most important man of his generation, still we might say this. The whole fundamental interest in Lawrence centers upon his appearance as type and the rather obscure relationship of his type to the epoch. He creates in some of us the feeling that there attaches to his appearance at a certain time in our history a significance far greater than is generally suspected. It is relatively easy to trace back his precursors, to place him in the hierarchy of creative figures, and this done, it is also easy to account for his extraordinary power over men.

Similarly, it is comparatively easy to relate our epoch to other periods in the past, and perhaps, though this is not so certain, to explain to ourselves the apparent failure for a man like Lawrence to take hold, as did his precursors. The doubt and the uneasiness which enters into our contemplation of these problems arises precisely because there is the suspicion that with Lawrence there enters into the familiar type, the familiar situation, a new and unknown element, that perhaps he is bound up with our destiny in a quite different way than we are led to imagine. Obviously now I am not thinking of those who have made their peace with him and safely categorized him; nor am I thinking of those who, blinded by his truths, have slavishly identified themselves with him and who rest there. I am thinking, rather, of those who, after making the discovery of Lawrence, realize that he left in them a leaven and that it is this leaven which now relates them to a wholly new world, a wholly new way of life—in short, to a vital future. This leaven, this seed or germ which is created again and again through the great mystics, or perhaps transmitted by them from one to another, is always a source of the wildest hope and the most poignant despair. The realization of its existence brings about the most profound antagonism between man and man. Inevitably a gulf opens up in which not only the great mass of men are swallowed but whole epochs too. The vision always occurs at the moment when we are about to plunge into the abyss. A frenzied dance at the edge and then night. The mystics rise up like semaphores which the engineer is powerless to heed because the speed of the train is beyond control. In that moment between the danger signal and annihilation life reaches its apogee. The moment between the realization of the end and the end there is vertigo, pure vertigo.

The connection between the appearance of the mystic and sheer annihilation has been apprehended, but never, except by succeeding mystics, to the fullest. When a whole world is sliding down to destruction, when it is impossible to put on the brakes, the question that *ought* to be asked is this: what happened to the mystic, to the man who gave the danger signal? Why was he not destroyed too, or was he? In employing the image of engineer, train and semaphore I am simply translating the usual terms of destiny, world or culture, and symbolic figure. Destiny, if applied to the whole world of men and

women, would be meaningless—unless we mean the obvious
thing of birth to death. The world has not yet been annihilated
and, so far as we are concerned, never will be. There is, however, implicit in this analogy, the idea of a common fate versus
an individual fate, of destiny and counter-destiny, or fate and
anti-fate. There is the very important distinction underlying
this parallel of the death of a whole order of men and the
survival of a rare few, perhaps only one.

What dies, *what* survives, is not an individual man or a
whole order of men either—but an idea which they represent,
an idea which has come to be regarded as bound up with the life
force itself, which perhaps, using the language of the mystics, *is
life itself.* An idea that, while life is apparently going on,
perhaps it is not life, but death. Apparent life, apparent death.
The *apparent* is in reality all that we are vitally concerned
with. Since it is we ourselves, by what process we do not know,
who have created the sharp antagonism between real life and
apparent life, real death and apparent death, let us not quibble
about the meaning of *apparent.* We know, all of us, when we
are driven to it, what is meant by this man-made opposition.
We know because we have created for ourselves a reality which
serves as a criterion. It is a valid, human reality, a psychological
reality which, in moments of supreme crisis, is never ques-
tioned. That we can go to sleep on this reality, pretend that it
does not exist, goes without saying. It is, after all, a created
phenomenon. It requires not only consciousness, but volition.
It comes to splendor in something beyond consciousness or
volition, and that is faith. Faith, in the last analysis, is only the
highest corroboration of the life instincts. It runs with destiny
and against it. Both simultaneously. It is nourished, that is to
say, both by life and by death. It disconcerns in both the two
aspects of something beyond, a force unknowable and inde-
scribable, and it is to this power beyond that it yields implicit
obedience.

Any creature, says Lawrence, that attains to its own fullness of being, its own *living* self, becomes unique, a non-
pareil. It has its place in the fourth dimension, the heaven of
existence, and there it is perfect, it is beyond comparison. And
again he says: "Heaven is always there. No achieved consummation is lost. Procreation goes on forever, to support the
achieved revelation. But the torch of revelation itself is handed

on. And this is all important."

The times are always out of joint; war and revolution are always in the offing. And the creative individual is always more out of joint with the times than the ordinary man. For him war or revolution are not enough. Each age imagines that the previous age was more wonderful, more inspiring, more life-giving. In what we consider the best periods in history we find that the highest types of individual were tyrannically persecuted, that the mass of men were miserable and oppressed. If we were to take comfort from the past we would commit suicide.

The struggle to resolve the conflict in which life situates us is usually marked by one of two escapes—either by an effort to make the world over, that is, alter the external pattern, or by the effort to make ourselves over, that is, alter the inner configuration. In the creative individual the resolution of the conflict takes another form: the creation of an imaginary intervening world shaped according to his own needs. There are three solutions always going forward: the social, the religious and the artistic. They are all expressive of a disequilibrium between the individual and his world. They are not solutions, and often they are not even escapes. In each case there is the bitter and humiliating residue of sacrifice: the artist sacrificed to his art, the revolutionary sacrificed to posterity, the saint sacrificed to God. All of them are burdened by a sense of guilt because they have sacrificed life itself to an ideal. And the man who feels even guiltier than any of these is the man who has sacrificed himself to life, that is, the man who recognized no conflict and lived out his animal impulses. Perhaps it is going too far to say that such men existed—we know perhaps of only a few and we have always considered them to be monsters. But there have been times when men were closer to this mode of existence than is commonly supposed. Some have even imagined these periods to be golden periods. Not, however, the men who lived in them!

Even when an age is regarded from its own integral standpoint, one can recognize the snake that was devouring the entrails, the worm that was eating away the quick. The relation of the living organism to an obscure and vital center always provides the sense of dying. The feeling that a people have of soul, or an individual for his soul, is a feeling based on the sense of immortality, undyingness. It arises out of the knowledge of createdness, that what was created is imperishable. The implication is not that something was given, donated, but that something was *won*. And simultaneously there arises the counter-feeling, that what was created, what was won, will perish if the struggle is relinquished. The desire to cherish, to hold what one possesses, is born of the knowledge that it is passing beyond control. One either looks back towards the past, in order to take fuller possession of what is slipping away, or one looks towards the future in the hope of recreating and again participating in a fuller possession. The present is always regarded as a diminishing factor. The present is despised, or else regarded as a mere foothold either on the past or on the future.

Yet everything takes place in the present. There is never anything but the present. The past is a word for something lost; the future is a word for something unattained. Why do we ignore or despise the present? Why do we yearn to be in another place, another time, why do we strive to become something other than we are? Is it because we do not realize that heaven is here and now? The mystic is the man who says that heaven is *here* and *now*. And knowing it, he acts upon it. With the mystic the conflict is broken. He leaves the world exactly as he finds it: he wouldn't alter a blade of grass. He accepts the world, his time, his fellowman, himself. He establishes an entirely new equilibrium which allows him to rest, to be what he is, and to let things be what they are. Everything nourishes him: pain, suffering, joy, wisdom, ignorance, war, peace, the past, the future, the present, all, *all.* He finds himself by a miracle at the dead center of the universe, in perfect accord, in perfect equilibrium. He has no illusions about the world and no illusions about man. He sees with blinding clarity from the inner eye of the world, from the very nexus of time and event. He is one with time, one with the event.

By what miracle does he accomplish this, you ask? Simply by entering the kingdom of heaven, the kingdom of heaven which is within you, as the Bible says. He enters another realm, another dimension, through realization. He asks for nothing beyond his grasp. He stops grasping, and takes possession. *Of himself.* And when this happens he possesses the world. You can ridicule him, you can deny him, you can persecute him, you can crucify him, *but you cannot dispossess him.* He has created for himself a unique and permanent life outside space and time, a transcendental existence which abrogates space and time. He represents the fullest flowering of the life force; he marks off the grand conjunctions. He is the living symbol of that new wheel of life which is always hoped for and always denied. He is the symbol of life because he has made the supreme identification with life.

Naturally no man ever lived who answered this description. But the legendary figures whom man has created do follow these outlines. There is a definite type of man who corresponds to our imagination; we might say that it is our imagination which has created the type. What does our imagination not create? The world about us, is that not a direct product of our imagination? And ourselves, are we not the products of our own imaginations? Let us call for a description of the world, let us call for a description of ourselves—will it not correspond to every available imagination? If now we sit down to write the history of yesterday, no, not even yesterday, of the last five minutes, let us say, will any two histories be alike? And yet we will all recognize the world, recognize ourselves, recognize the past five minutes. Even so we recognize in the legendary the actual. Let us say, rather, that we recognize the germ of truth.

When we speak of the fictive, the imaginary world of the artist, do we mean an unreal world? Was ever anything the least unreal created? Was there ever anything but reality? Does not this fictive, this imaginary world of the artist seem indeed *more* real to us—more real than what?—more real than reality? Let us not be absurd. What is called reality, in common sense language, is simply the imaginative picture of the most unimaginative. Reality is there always, like an ocean in which we swim, only some of us are capable of inhabiting more depths, greater depths. The artist creates nothing, except new relationships. He swims about more, he explores further, and consequently he sees differently.

When a man sees too differently from his fellowmen he is feared and then hated. This applies to a Napoleon, a Christ, a

Tamerlane, a Caligula, a lunatic, a gangster, or an artist. Vision is not a static thing. One acts according to how one sees. Imagination, which is the vision, is always father to the deed. It were better, says the man in the street, to see eye to eye. Much safer. But man is powerless to adjust his vision. Even when he puts on glasses he does not alter the vision. The glasses may help him to adjust himself to the world, to the particular stratum in which for the moment he is swimming, but the moment he throws the glasses aside he sees with the old vision. Vision is unalterable: it is the most delicate, the most precious organ of the body. When the body languishes the vision decays. Each man looks out on the world with his own eye, and to each man the world is different. Each man builds up a reality which is for him the world and which *is* the world. He creates it for himself by his own power of vision.

* * *

Whenever Lawrence's name comes up there is sure to arise a discussion as to the relative merits of *Sons and Lovers* and *Lady Chatterley's Lover;* these two works, the one representing the youthful Lawrence and the other representing the mature man, are contrasted as if they exemplified antagonistic elements in his nature. Those who prefer the former regard his later works as a decline in thought and creation, not a decline merely, but a progressive deterioration, with *Lady Chatterley's Lover* touching the abyss. Very few of those who admire the latter work are inclined to see in it anything like an approach to artistic perfection, yet they persist in regarding it as perhaps the most important creative expression of the man.

Superficially there is a great gulf between the two works, but it is no more profound a division than that which characterizes the passage from youth to maturity; in the works of every creative individual there should be, and usually is, this divergence, sometimes so strongly marked that between the early and the late works there is scarcely anything to bind them except the author's name. At best we are able to detect in the artist's early works the seeds of the future man, and this not so much by the individuality of his expression as by the transparency of his influences. The origins of the man and the germs of future conflict lie clearly exposed in the works of youth. Henceforth we witness the struggle of the artist to free himself from the discordant elements of his being, to establish the superiority of certain values, revealed to him during some crisis in his life—the arrival at artistic maturity—and to reject other values which had been of tremendous importance to him during his period of incubation. In the case of a great artist, such as Goethe, the whole conflict and development is summarized in one work which covers a life-time. The work represents the man's life, and when it is completed he dies. Proust is another example.

In the case of Lawrence one feels very doubtful that he might have gone much beyond *Lady Chatterley's Lover.* The restricted life he led, his deliberate isolation from all the stimulating currents of art, his intensely personal vision, all this led to an inevitable withering at the roots.

Had he continued in the vein of *Sons and Lovers* Lawrence would undoubtedly have become a popular artist, the sort especially which the Anglo-Saxon world would have been proud to acclaim as its own. The high poetic feeling for Nature, which so many of the English poets share, and which characterizes *Sons and Lovers,* represents in Lawrence the vast and compelling power of tradition; there runs through it that peculiar feeling for death so noticeable in all the poets of Nature.

Lawrence emerged from this adolescent union with Nature to die a bigger death. Under the spell of Idea he allowed a whole world of past to die in him; he killed the poet in himself in order to become the evangel of a new order. He sought to identify himself, and the world, with a greater cosmos. After *Sons and Lovers* he appears on the horizon of his unknown world as an archangel flourishing a glittering sword. His tongue becomes sharp, his words are bitterness; like all the redeemers of mankind he becomes filled with hatred. He searches frantically for symbols of destruction; he admits of no solutions other than his own.

As a thinker he may be confused, as an artist he may reveal the most woeful shortcomings, as a man he may be a failure, but as scourge and avenger he moves forward—with terrifying consistency.

CHAPTER III

The Universe of Death

"Unless from us the future takes place, we are death only!"

IN THE CASE of Lawrence I see a man fighting to come clean of the womb, fighting to be born alive, to express himself, his personality—but never realizing that personality because he was not given a clean birth. This prenatal struggle is profoundly interesting: it symbolizes man's eternal interest in genesis. Even though never quite born, however, the Lawrence personality is mysteriously alive and engaging. There is a perpetual thumping and shrieking in the womb, like a fight in a glass cage between two cobras who finally strangle each other.

The difference in caliber between Lawrence and his contemporaries is enormous. We have only to think of men like Proust, Joyce, Pound and Eliot, the most prominent figures of our time, to mark the quality of difference. In the case of Pound, for example, we have an artist who is strangled by the umbilical cord. He is born perfect—that is, *dead!* No problems, no conflicts, except technical ones. For him, to come alive is to retrace his uterine life. His poems reveal the spade work of the cultured individual buried alive under the crust of civilization. A poet digging for the true sources, digging up obscure things—relics, fossils, bringing to light forgotten names, talking *about* the fecundating spirit, but unable to lay hands on it, his gorgeous spew of words resembling that other spew of waste matter by which the foetus was once nourished, but which every live womb ejects when the child is delivered. In Pound we have a case of no-personality, or not-yet-personality—the reminiscent ego, birth and death in the womb. An interesting phenomenon in itself, but of no value, not contributive to life.

"Every soul has religion," says Spengler, "which is only another word for its existence. All living forms in which it expresses itself—all arts, doctrines, customs, all metaphysical and mathematical form-worlds, all ornament, every column and verse and idea—are ultimately religious, and must be so.

85

But from the setting-in of Civilization they cannot be so any longer. As the essence of every Culture is religion, so—and consequently—the essence of every Civilization is irreligion—the two words are synonymous."

"It is this extinction of living inner religiousness," says Spengler, again,

> which gradually tells upon even the most insignificant element in a man's being, that becomes phenomenal in the historical world-picture at the turn from the Culture to the Civilization, the Climacteric of the Culture, as I have already called it, the time of change in which a mankind loses its spiritual fruitfulness for ever, and building takes the place of begetting. Unfruitfulness—understanding the word in all its direct seriousness— marks the brain-man of the megalopolis, as the sign of fulfilled destiny, and it is one of the most impressive facts of historical symbolism that the change manifests itself not only in the extinction of great art, of great courtesy, of great formal thought, of the great style in all things, but also quite carnally in the childlessness and "race-suicide" of the civilized and rootless strata, a phenomenon not peculiar to ourselves but already observed and deplored—and of course not remedied—in Imperial Rome and Imperial China.

It required about a century, after the great *Climacteric* had been reached, for the full import of this doctrine to be promulgated—through the independent researches of Petrie and of Spengler. But Nietzsche had divined it all, in that great work written at the threshold of his career: *The Birth of Tragedy.* "I appended hopes," writes Nietzsche in a postscript to this book, "where there was no ground for hope." It is a magnificent echo of that profound despair which animated the work of all the great spirits of the nineteenth century, a century of madmen, of renegades, iconoclasts, mystics, a profound despair which belied the cheap surface optimism that prevailed during that century, based as it was on the delusions of the scientific-minded spirits.

Now it is realized, in full, that we have entered upon the final stage of arteriosclerosis, with all the anarchy and chaos prevailing in politics pointing fatally to the preparation for a nightmare of biologic life, another Dark Age in which the soul of man lies like a seed in the earth, those few shallow feet of earth which compose our history, and which, when it is sown with the relics of the past, with that rich compost of dead things, will blossom forth again in new forms. Spiritually we have entered the Empire of Neurosis, all that was heretofore regarded as soul-substance now being examined scientifically, classified according to pathology, the entire history of mental therapy a thinly disguised admission of the decay of the soul. The rise of psychoanalysis, for example, is but a symptom of the fact that, unknown to ourselves, we are paving the way to an acceptance of the death which is on us, the stress of Reality being nothing more than a scientific conversion of the idea of Destiny.

Now it may be realized that the disintegration of the ego is only part and parcel of that larger disintegration going on. Those who, like Keyserling, seek to indicate the ever-imminent possibility of a break with the brief historical cycle in which man is imprisoned, offer us at bottom scarcely any more hope than a Spengler. It is precisely the problem of man's *psychological maturity* which underlies the whole historical record of man. It is this far-distant future of man, which the mystics and saviors of mankind have described time and again, which recedes further and further, which is glimpsed in periods of extreme desperation, but never attained. It is wisdom, indeed, which man never accepts. It would almost seem, from the nature of things, as if it were man's destiny to live toward a wisdom forever beyond his grasp. *More*—that the desire to attain this goal constitutes, perhaps, a far greater menace than the pursuit of religion or idealism.

This coming "era of the Holy Ghost" is an imaginary, unhistorical epoch created by the artist in man when he has arrived at the brink. At the moment when Lawrence was dreaming of a new order of things—the moment when Spengler was decreeing its impossibility—Proust was putting the finishing touches to that tomb of art in which he buried himself. It was the moment when Joyce, through Stephen Dedalus, was declaring—"History is the nightmare from which I am trying to awake!" In these three great artists of our time we have the whole symbolic drama of death, dissolution and rebirth: Proust burying himself in the womb, a symbol of schizophrenic regression; Joyce giving way, through his night language, to the dissolvent forces of Nature; Lawrence, with his symbol of the

Phoenix, proclaiming the power of resurrection, of life eternal, worshipping neither the past nor the future, neither man nor god nor art, but turning his face resolutely toward the Sun, the source of all hope and inspiration, the only symbol of life that man may honestly worship.

This is the period when the dynamic atheism of the world cities gives expression to its religious longing through the mysticism of the forward spirits. The period when, of necessity, all values are transvalued, when what is practised as art is, beyond all doubt, impotence and falsehood. Art, arriving at its final goal (from body ornament to psychologism) lives only in the memory of the past, if at all. Here lies the great importance of the metaphor, which Proust emphasized: the recapture through Time of the whole past. And Joyce, by his destruction of language, a prime symbol, expresses for us our inmost desire—to finish off the whole cultural process. We want death, the death of everything, and we preserve merely enough of language (i.e., *communication*) to deliver our own funeral oration.

The emphasis which the psychologists have given to the role of the Unconscious (the obverse of the Soul) is the effort of the intellectual man to account for the artistic process. When Proust says that we have only to translate what is there (in our hearts), he reveals the whole case; creation cannot be underwritten by a word like "translate." It is defeatism, surrender to destiny. This emphasis on the Unconscious (dominant in the work of Proust, Joyce *and* Lawrence) reveals, moreover, the fact that man, in his finished state, recognizes with conscious mind that he has attained the limits, that to rediscover the sources of his inspiration, the mantic quality of language, the magic of primitive life, he must return to the dark, obscure regions of the soul. But as he is no longer able to interpret things spiritually, he elaborates a scientific lingo—the current ideology of analysis—to explain the secret.

The theory of the Unconscious, with its transmogrified language of Faustian dynamism, its great emphasis on the incestuous wish, is the ideology of a dying race whose language and symbology are now converted into the religio-scientific lingo of electro-dynamics. The complete domination and exploitation of life by science, the language of the soul borrowed from the physical sciences, the worship of utilitarian forces, the high place given to work, the emphasis on world-peace, the pursuit of self-knowledge through art, the reduction of all criticism to analysis, the artist and his art-product studied as form and symptom of disease, the emphasis on adjustment, on the need to face reality, the desire to solve insoluble problems, the desire to deny, to escape problem and conflict, all this together with the rebellion of the post-war writers, commencing with Dada and ending in Surrealism, all this is but the representation of the mind's abortive efforts to recapture what the soul alone is capable of grasping. The great exploration of the personality which is going on is but the imitation, or the reflection, of that other external exploration—paleontology, archaeology, geology. Finally the "I" is conceived of in geological terms, and the grand study of the personality resolves itself into the futile study of the fossil layers of the brain!

For just as the soul of man is walled up in the megalopolis, so the personality is found to be walled up in the fossilized brain. Instead of the grand irrational fear which has characterized man's life-history, and which the artist has never ceased to exploit, that fear which lies behind the expression of all Culture, we have now a *fear of life*, creating that empire of neurosis to which we are becoming more and more acclimated. For the function of the psychologist, who is the priest of life today, comes more and more to resolve itself to this—that, instead of aiding man to go crazy under the crazy system by which we live, instead of urging man to revolt, to upset the system, or at least to alter the external pattern, all his efforts tend rather toward adjusting him to an impossible condition of things. With the result that what was once regarded as disease becomes the norm. The picture of disease becomes, through the ideology of the psychologist-priest, the picture of reality. And so all art now appears as compensatory, substitutive, *as means of escape*, to use the psychologic parlance of the day. And indeed, so it is! The study of the neurotic—the artists representing the supreme example of neuroticism—leads to the discovery of the preponderance of the *incest motif*, or the desire for death and rebirth. Significant language! In this age of skepticism there can appear, it would seem, no aspect of the eternal religiousness of man except this negative one, this flowing backward toward the womb, the fount, the matrix of life. More and more, in the reigning language of art, woman is reinstated under the symbol of destruction.

Coincident with this growing fear of life is the growing terror of reality, for reality now takes on the guise of death, and it is this death for which he is destined that man is trying to ignore. And with this slackening of the life impulse, expressing itself in every form of suicide, there is the correspondent loss of the fear of death; with the diminution of this urge for immortality, or its effective weakening, at least, it gradually begins to appear that the artist has no longer any *raison d'être*. He comes, by a long and devious route, to the discovery of the self, a cross-road at which he may elect either to create a new religion or develop a new personality.

It is at this point, the most crucial point in our history, when pausing, reflecting, criticizing, appraising, when we are perforce obliged to interpret everything genetically, that the significant character of our souls must decide the choice. There is a unanimous opinion in every field that we have arrived at the end, at the bankruptcy of the soul, and yet vague, mystical hopes, lies, illusions, romantic deceptions abound. The force of Will, the dynamic character of our culture, tends to nourish the life illusion—but it is obvious that—soulless, rootless, mythless—we can neither create a new religion nor develop a new personality. The great personalities lie behind us. And the study of the self, by which it is hoped to arrive at a clue, a way out of the impasse, leads nowhere, unless to a feeling of futility.

For the study of the self is the admission that we are dead: it is the intellect triumphing over the soul. And the dead cannot resuscitate themselves—*they can only be resurrected*! What was great in us will be revived—later. It is only thus that we retain the illusion of being imperishable. The study of the Western soul yields the unanimous verdict that there is no more development, granted the structure and function of our peculiar organism. The complete discredit of idealism, which has characterized our whole history, shows that the only possible hope lies in the cultivation of wisdom, a metaphysical attitude that is situated beyond striving and willing, in a superidealism whereby ideas are related to living, an active, mobile, flexible idealism of which we seem, indeed, to be thoroughly incapable. In fact, the very constitution of our mentality seems to preclude such a possibility; the very

language we employ—and how important is language!—
being against us.

Though the Chinese have proved themselves infinitely wiser
than any Western peoples, the history of man nevertheless
shows one thing clearly—the inability of man to profit by
wisdom, to act according to wisdom. That is reserved to the
few, always and everywhere. It cannot be indoctrinated. Out of
wisdom springs the tragic sense of life, which the Greeks, in
their heyday, possessed. But there is no evidence to support the
view that our destiny lies in the direction of increasing wisdom. Everything, indeed, points to the opposite conclusion. "I
appended hopes," said Nietzsche, "where there was no ground
for hope!" That, it seems to me, is *the* most tragic remark made
by any man throughout the entire course of Western history.

* * *

So far as the creative individual goes, life and death are of
equal value: it is all a question of counterpoint. What is of vital
concern, however, is how and where one meets life—or death.
Life can be more deadly than death, and death on the other hand
can open up the road to life. It is against the moribund flux in
which we are now drifting that Lawrence appears brilliantly
alive. Proust and Joyce, needless to say, appear more representative: they reflect the times. We see in them no revolt: it is
surrender, suicide, and the more poignant since it springs from
creative sources.

It is through examining, then, these two contemporaries of
Lawrence that we come to see the process all too clearly. In
Proust the full flower of psychologism—confession, self-
analysis, arrest of living, making of art the final justification
but thereby divorcing art from life, an intestine conflict in
which the artist is immolated. The great retrospective curve
back towards the womb: suspension in death, living death, for
the purposes of dissection. Pause to question, but no questions
forthcoming, the faculty having atrophied. A worship of art for
its own sake—not for man. Art, in other words, regarded as a
means of salvation, as a redemption from suffering, as a com-
pensation for the terror of living. *Art a substitute for life.* The
literature of flight, of escape, of a neurosis so brilliant that it
almost makes one doubt the efficacy of health. Until one casts

a glance at that "neurosis of health" of which Nietzsche sings in *The Birth of Tragedy*.

In Joyce the soul-deterioration may be traced even more definitely, for if Proust may be said to have provided the tomb of art, in Joyce we can witness the full process of decomposition. *Ulysses* is a paean to "the late-city man," a thanatopsis inspired by the ugly tomb in which the soul of the civilized man lies embalmed. The most astoundingly varied and subtle means of art are herein exploited to glorify the dead city. The story of *Ulysses* is the story of a lost hero recounting a lost myth; frustrated and forlorn the Janus-faced hero wanders through the labyrinth of the deserted temple, seeking the holy place but never finding it. Cursing and vilifying the mother who bore him, deifying her as a whore, bashing his brains out with idle conundrums, such is the modern Ulysses. Through the mystery-throngs he weaves his way, a hero lost in a crowd, a poet rejected and despised, a prophet wailing and cursing, covering his body with dung, examining his own excrement, parading his obscenity, lost, lost, a crumbling brain, a dissecting instrument endeavoring to reconstruct the soul. Through his chaos and obscenity, his obsessions and complexes, his perpetual, frantic search for God, Joyce reveals the desperate plight of the modern man who, lashing about in his steel and concrete cage, admits finally that there is no way out.

In these two exponents of modernity we see the flowering of the Hamlet-Faust myth, that unscotchable snake in the entrails which, for the Greeks was represented by the Oedipus myth, and for the whole Aryan race by the myth of Prometheus. In Joyce not only is the withered Homeric myth reduced to ashes, but even the Hamlet myth, which had come to supreme expression in Shakespeare, even this vital myth, I say, is pulverized. In Joyce we see the incapacity of the modern man even to doubt: it is the simulacrum of doubt, not its substance, that he gives us. With Proust there is a higher appreciation of doubt, of the inability to act. Proust is more capable of presenting the metaphysical aspect of things, partly because of a tradition so firmly anchored in the Mediterranean culture, and partly because his own schizoid temperament enabled him to examine objectively the evolution of a vital problem from its metaphysical to its psychological aspect. The progression from nerves to insanity, from a tragic confrontation of the duality in man to a pathologic split in the personality, is mirrored in the transition from Proust to Joyce. Where Proust held himself suspended over life in a cataleptic trance—weighing, dissecting, and eventually corroded by the very skepticism he had employed—Joyce has already plunged into the abyss. In Proust there is still a questioning of values; with Joyce there is a denial of all values. With Proust the schizophrenic aspect of his work is not so much the cause as the result of his world-view. With Joyce there is no world-view. Man returns to the primordial elements; he is washed away in a cosmological flux. Parts of him may be thrown up on foreign shores, in alien climes, in some future time; but the whole man, the vital, spiritual ensemble, is dissolved. This is the dissolution of the body and soul, a sort of cellular immortality in which life survives only chemically.

Proust, in his classic retreat from life, is the very symbol of the modern artist—the sick giant who locks himself up in a cork-lined cell to take his brains apart. He is the incarnation of that last and fatal disease: *the disease of the mind.* In *Ulysses,* Joyce gives us the complete identification of the artist with the tomb in which he buries himself. *Ulysses* has been spoken of as being "something solid like a city." Not so much a solid city, it seems to me, as a dead world-city. Just as there is, beneath the hollow dynamism of the city, an appalling weariness, a monotony, a fatigue insuperable, so in the works of Proust and Joyce the same qualities manifest themselves. A perpetual stretching of time and space, an obedience to the law of inertia, as if to atone, or compensate, for the lack of a higher urge. Joyce takes Dublin with its worn-out types; Proust takes the microscopic world of the Faubourg St. Germain, symbol of a dead past. The one wears us out because he spreads himself over such an enormous artificial canvas; the other wears us out by magnifying his thumb-nail fossil beyond all sensory recognition. The one uses the city as a universe, the other as an atom. The curtain never falls. Meanwhile the world of living men and women is huddling in the wings clamoring for the stage.

In these epics everything is of equal prominence, equal value, whether spiritual or material, organic or inorganic, live or abstract. The array and content of these works suggests to the mind the interior of a junkshop. The effort to parallel space, to devour it, to install oneself in the time process—the very nature of the task is forbidding. The mind runs wild. We have sterility, onanism, logomachy. And—the more colossal the scope of the work the more monstrous the failure!

Compared to these dead moons how comforting the little works which stick out like brilliant stars! Rimbaud, for example! His *Illuminations* outweighs a shelf of Proust, Joyce, Pound, Eliot. Times there are, to be sure, when the colossal work compels admiration, when, as with Bach or Dante, it is ordered by an inner plan, by the organic mechanism of faith. Here the work of art assumes the form and dimensions of a cathedral, a veritable tree of life. But with our latter-day exponents of head-culture the great monuments are lying on their sides, they stretch away like huge petrified forests, and the landscape itself becomes *nature-morte*.

Though we do, as Edmund Wilson says, "possess Dublin seen, heard, smelt and felt, brooded over, imagined, remembered," it is, in a profound sense, no possession at all: it is possession through the dead ends of the brain. As a naturalistic canvas *Ulysses* makes its appeal to the sense of smell only; it gives off a sublime mortuary odor. It is not the reality of nature here, still less the reality of the five senses. *It is the sick reality of the mind*. And so, if we possess Dublin at all, it is only as a shade wandering through an excavated Troy or Knossus; the historical past juts out in geological strata.

In referring to *Work in Progress*, Louis Gillet, an admirer of Joyce, says: "In such manner are the themes of this strange symphony generated. Men are, today as at the beginning of the world, mere playthings for the forces of nature. They convert their impressions into myths, incorporating fragments of recollections and scraps of reality suspended in their memory. A legend is thus shaped, a sort of timeless history composed of the residues of all histories, something that we could call (borrowing a title from J. S. Bach) Cantata for All Times."

A noble ring to these words, but absolutely false. This is not how legends are made! The men who are capable of creating an "extra-temporal history" are not the men who create legends. The two are not coeval in time and space. The legend is the soul emerging into form, a singing soul which not only carries hope, but which contains a promise and a fulfillment. In "timeless history," on the other hand, we have a flat expanse, a muddy residue, a sink without limits, without depths, without light and shadow—an abyss into which the soul is plunged and swallowed up. It marks the end of the great trajectory: the tapeworm of history devours itself. If this be legend, it is legend that will never survive, and most certainly never be sung. Already, almost coincidentally with their appearance, we have, as a result of *Ulysses* and *Work in Progress*, nothing but dry analyses, archaeological burrowings, geological surveys, laboratory tests of the word. The commentators, to be sure, have only begun to chew into Joyce. The Germans will finish him! They will make Joyce palatable, understandable, clear as Shakespeare, better than Joyce, better than Shakespeare. Wait! The mystagogues are coming!

As Gillet has well said—*Work in Progress* represents "a panorama of all floating reminiscences, vain desires and stray impulses which swarm in our unbound, dozing soul and constitute the dim existence of thought." But who is interested in this language of night? *Ulysses* was obscure enough. But *Work in Progress*...? Of Proust at least we may say that his myopia served to render his work exciting, stimulating: it was like seeing the world through the eyes of a horse, or a fly. Joyce's deformity of vision, on the other hand, is depressing, crippling, dwarfing: it is a defect of the soul, and not an artistic, metaphysical device. Joyce is growing more blind everyday—blind in the pineal eye. For passion he substitutes books; for men and women rivers and trees—or wraiths. Life to Joyce, as one of his admirers says, is a mere tautology. Precisely. We have here the clue to the whole symbolism of defeat. And, whether he is interested in history or not, Joyce is the history of our time, of this age which is sliding into darkness. Joyce is the blind Milton of our day. But whereas Milton glorified Satan, Joyce, because his vision has atrophied, merely surrenders to the powers of darkness. Milton was a rebel, a demonic force, a voice that made itself heard. Milton blind, like Beethoven deaf, only grew in power and eloquence; the inner eye, the inner ear, became more attuned to the cosmic rhythm. Joyce on the other hand, is a blind and deaf soul: his voice rings out over a waste land and the reverberations are nothing but echoes of a lost soul. Joyce is the lost soul of this soulless world; his interest is not in life, in men and deeds, not in history, not in God, but in the dead dust of books. He is the high priest of the lifeless literature of to-day. He writes a hieratic script which not even his admirers and disciples can decipher. He is burying himself under an obelisk for whose script there will be no key.

It is interesting to observe in the works of Proust and Joyce, and of Lawrence as well, how the milieu from which they sprang determined the choice of the protagonist as well as the nature of the disease against which they fought. Joyce, springing from the priest class, makes Bloom, his "average" man or double, the supreme object of ridicule. Proust, springing from the cultured middle-class, though himself living only on the fringe of society, *tolerated,* as it were, makes Charlus, his king figure, a bitter object of ridicule. And Lawrence, springing from the common classes, makes the type Mellors, who appears in a variety of ideal roles, but usually as the man of the soil, his hope of the future—treating him, however, no less unsparingly. All three have idealized in the person of the hero those qualities which they felt themselves to lack supremely.

Joyce, deriving from the medieval scholar, with the blood of the priest in him, is consumed by his inability to participate in the ordinary, everyday life of human beings. He creates Bloom, the shadow of Odysseus, Bloom the eternal Jew, the symbol of the outcast Irish race whose tragic story is so close to the author's heart. Bloom is the projected wanderer of Joyce's inner restlessness, of his dissatisfaction with the world. He is the man who is misunderstood and despised by the world, rejected by the world because he himself rejected the world. It is not so strange as at first blush it may seem that, searching for a counterpart to Daedalus, Joyce chose a Jew; instinctively he selected a type which has always given proof of its ability to arouse the passions and prejudices of the world.

In giving us Dublin Joyce gave us the scholar-priest's picture of the world as is. Dirty Dublin! Worse even than London, or Paris. The worst of all possible worlds! In this dirty sink of the world-as-is we have Bloom, the fictive image of the man in the street, crass, sensual, inquisitive but unimaginative—the educated nincompoop hypnotized by the abracadabra of scientific jargon. Molly Bloom, the Dublin slut, is an even more successful image of the common run. Molly Bloom is an archetype of the eternal feminine. She is the rejected mother whom the scholar and priest in Joyce had to liquidate. She is the veridic whore of creation. By comparison, Bloom is a comic figure. Like the ordinary man, he is a medal without a reverse. And like the ordinary man, he is most ludicrous when he is being made *cocu*. It is the most persisitent, the most fundamental image of himself which the "average" man retains in this woman's world of today where his importance is so negligible.

Charlus, on the other hand, is a colossal figure, and Proust has handled him in colossal fashion. As symbol of the dying world of caste, ideals, manners, Charlus was selected, whether with thought or not, from the forefront of the enemy's ranks. Proust, we know, was outside that world which he has so minutely described. As a pushing little Jew, he fought or wormed his way inside—and with disastrous results. Always shy, timid, awkward, embarrassed. Always a bit ridiculous. A sort of cultivated Chaplin! And, characteristically, this world which he so ardently desired to join he ended by despising. It is a repetition of the Jew's eternal fight with an alien world. A perpetual effort to become part of this hostile world and then, because of inability to become assimilated, rejecting it or destroying it. But if it is typical of the mechanism of the Jew, it is no less typical of the artist. And, true artist that he was, thoroughly sincere, Proust chose the best example of that alien world for his hero, Charlus. Did he not, in part, become like that hero himself later on, in his unnatural effort to become assimilated? For Charlus, though he had his counterpart in reality quite as famous as the fictive creation, Charlus is, nevertheless, the image of the later Proust. He is, indeed, the image of the whole world of esthetes who have now incorporated under the banner of homosexualism.

The beautiful figure of the grandmother, and of the mother, the sane, touching, moral atmosphere of the household, so pure and integrated, so thoroughly Jewish, stands opposed to the glamorous, the romantic, alien world of the Gentile which attracts and corrodes. It stands out in sharp contrast to the milieu from which Joyce sprang. Where Joyce leaned on the Catholic Church and its traditional masters of exegesis, thoroughly vitiated by the arid intellectualism of his caste, we have in Proust the austere atmosphere of the Jewish home contaminated by a hostile culture, the most strongly rooted culture left in the Western world—French Hellenism. There is an uneasiness, a maladjustment, a war in the spiritual realm which, projected in the novel, continued throughout his life. Proust was touched only superficially by French culture. His art is eminently un-French. We have only to think of his devout admiration for Ruskin. Ruskin! of all men!

And so, in describing the decay of his little world, this microcosm which was for him *the* world, in depicting the disintegration of his hero, Charlus, Proust sets before us the collapse of the outer and the inner world. The battleground of love, which began normally enough with Gilberte, becomes transferred, as in the world to-day, to that plane of depolarized love wherein the sexes fuse, the world where doubt and jealousy, thrown out of their normal axes, play diabolical roles. Whereas in Joyce's world a thoroughly normal obscenity slops over into a slimy, glaucous fluid in which life sticks, in Proust's world vice, perversion, loss of sex break out like a pox and corrode everything.

In their analysis and portrayal of disintegration both Proust and Joyce are unequalled, except perhaps by Dostoevski and Petronius. They are both objective in their treatment—technically classic, though romantic at heart. They are naturalists who present the world as they find it, and say nothing about the causes, nor derive from their findings any conclusions. They are defeatists, men who escape from a cruel, hideous, loathsome reality into ART. After writing the last volume, with its memorable treatise on art, Proust goes back to his death-bed to revise the pages on Albertine. This episode is the core and climax of his great work. It forms the arch of that Inferno into which the mature Proust descended. For if, retiring ever deeper into the labyrinth, Proust had cast a glance back at that world which he left behind, he must have seen there in the figure of woman that image of himself in which all life was mirrored. It was an image which tantalized him, an image which lied to him from every reflection, because he had penetrated to an underworld in which there was nothing but shadows and distortions. The world he had walked out on was the masculine world in process of dissolution. With Albertine as the clue, with this single thread in his hand which, despite all the anguish and sorrow of knowledge he refuses to let slip, he feels his way along the hollows of the nerves, through a vast, subterranean world of remembered sensations in which he hears the pumping of the heart but knows not whence it comes, or what it is.

It has been said that *Hamlet* is the incarnation of doubt, and *Othello* the incarnation of jealousy, and so they may be, but the episode of Albertine, reached after an interval of several centuries of deterioration, seems to me a dramaturgic study of doubt and jealousy so infinitely more vast and complex than either *Hamlet* or *Othello* that the Shakespearean dramas, by comparison, resemble the feeble sketches which later are to assume the dimensions of a great fresco. This tremendous convulsion of doubt and jealousy which dominates the book is the reflection of that supreme struggle with Fate which characterizes our entire European history. Today we see about us Hamlets and Othellos by the thousand—such Hamlets, such Othellos, as Shakespeare never dreamed of, such as would make him sweat with pride could he turn over in his grave. This theme of doubt and jealousy, to seize upon its most salient aspects only, is in reality just the reverberation of a much greater theme, a theme more complex, more ramified, which has become heightened, or muddied, if you like, in the interval of time between Shakespeare and Proust. Jealousy is the little symbol of that struggle with Fate which is revealed through doubt. The poison of doubt, of introspection, of conscience, of idealism, overflowing into the arena of sex, develops the marvellous bacillus of jealousy which, to be sure, will ever exist, but which in the past, when life ran high, was held in place and served its proper role and function. Doubt and jealousy are those points of resistance on which the great whet their strength, from which they rear their towering structures, their masculine world. When doubt and jealousy run amok it is because the body has been defeated, because the spirit languishes and the soul becomes unloosed. Then it is that the germs work their havoc and men no longer know whether they are devils or angels, nor whether women are to be shunned or worshipped, nor whether homosexuality is a vice or a blessing. Alternating between the most ferocious display of cruelty and the most supine acquiescence we have conflicts, revolutions, holocausts—*over trifles, over nothing*. The last war, for example. The loss of sex polarity is part and parcel of the larger disintegration, the reflex of the soul's death, and coincident with the disappearance of great men, great deeds, great causes, great wars.

Herein lies the importance of Proust's epic work, for here in the Albertine episode we have the problem of love and jealousy depicted in Gargantuan fashion, the malady becomes all-inclusive, turning in on itself through the inversion of sex. The great Shakespearean dramas were but the announcement of a disease which had just begun to run its staggering course; in Shakespeare's time it had not yet eaten into every layer of life, it could still be made the subject of heroic drama. There was man and there was the disease, and the conflict was the material for drama. But now the toxin is in the blood. For such as us, who have been eaten away by the virus, the great dramatic themes of Shakespeare are but swashbuckling oratory and pasteboard sets. Their impression is nil.We have become inoculated. And it is in Proust that we can sense the deterioration of the heroic, the cessation of conflict, the surrender, the thing become itself.

I repeat that we have in our midst today greater Hamlets, greater Othellos, than Shakespeare ever dreamed of. We have now the ripe fruit of the seeds planted by the masters of old. Like some marvellous unicellular organism in endless process of exfoliation these types reveal to us all the varieties of body cells which formerly entered into the making of blood, bone, muscle, hair, teeth, nails. We have now the monstrous flower whose roots were watered by the Christian myth. We are living amidst the ruins of a world in collapse amidst the husks which must rot away to make new loam.

This formidable picture of the world-as-disease which Proust and Joyce have given us is indeed less a picture than a microscopic study which, because we see it magnified, prevents us from recognizing it as the world of every day in which we are swimming. Just as the art of pscyhoanalysis could not have arisen until society was sick enough to call for this peculiar form of therapy, so we could not have had a faithful image of our time until there arose in our midst monsters so ridden with the disease that their works resemble the disease itself.

Seizing upon the malodorous quality of Proust's work Edmund Wilson, the American critic, is moved to doubt the authenticity of the narrative. "When Albertine finally leaves him," he writes, "the emotional life of the book becomes progressively asphyxiated by the infernal fumes which Charlus has brought with him—until such a large percentage of the characters have tragically, gruesomely, irrevocably turned out to be homosexual that we begin for the first time to find the story a little incredible." Of course it is incredible—from a realistic point of view! It is incredible, as are all authentic revelations of life, because it is too true. We have modulated into a higher realm of reality. It is not the author whom we should take to task, but life. The Baron de Charlus, like Albertine again, is precisely the illuminating figure on which to rivet attention. Charlus is Proust's supreme creation, his "hero," if his work can be said to have a hero. To call the Baron's behavior, or those of his satellites and imitators, *incredible*, is to deny the validity of Proust's whole edifice. Into the character of Charlus (derived from many accurately studied prototypes) Proust poured all that he knew of the subject of perversion, and that subject dominates the entire work—justly. Do we not know that he originally contemplated labelling the whole work by the title given to the cornerstone of his work—*Sodom and Gomorrah*? Sodom and Gomorrah! Do I not detect here a little of the smell of Ruskin?

At any rate, it is indisputable that Charlus is his grand effort. Like Stavrogin for Dostoevski, Charlus is the supreme test. Like Stavrogin also, observe how the figure of Charlus permeates and dominates the atmosphere when off scene, how the poison of his being shoots its virus into the other characters, the other scenes, the other dramas, so that from the moment of his entry, or even before, the atmosphere is saturated with his noxious gases. In analyzing Charlus, in ridiculing and pillorying him Proust, like Dostoevski, was endeavoring to expose himself, perhaps to understand himself.

When in *The Captive*, Marcel and Albertine are discussing Dostoevski, Marcel feebly endeavoring to give a satisfactory response to Albertine's questions, how little did Proust realize, I wonder, that in creating the Baron de Charlus he was giving her the answer which then he seemed incapable of. The discussion, it may be recalled, centered upon Dostoevski's propensities for depicting the ugly, the sordid, particularly his prepossession for the subject of crime. Albertine had remarked that crime was an obsession with Dostoevski, and Marcel, after venturing some rather weak responses about the multiple nature of genius, dismisses the subject with something to the effect that *that* side of Dostoevski really interested him, but little, that in truth he found himself incapable of understanding it.

When it came to the delineation of Charlus, Proust nevertheless showed himself capable of performing a prodigious work of creative imagination. Charlus seems so removed from Proust's actual experience of life that people often wonder where he gathered the elements for his creation. Where? In his own soul! Dostoevski was not a criminal, not a murderer, Dostoevski did not live the life of Stavrogin. But Dostoevski was obsessed with the *idea* of a Stavrogin. He had to create him in order to live out his other life, his life as a creator. Little matter that he may have known a Stavrogin in the course of his manifold experiences. Little matter that Proust had under his eye the actual figure of Charlus. The originals, if not discarded, were certainly radically recast, transformed in the light of inner truth, inner vision. In both Dostoevski and Proust there existed a Stavrogin, a Charlus, far more real than the actual figures. For Dostoevski the character of Stavrogin was bound up with the search for God. Stavrogin was the ideal image of himself which Dostoevski jealously preserved. More than that—Stavrogin was the god in him, the fullest portrait of God which Dostoevski could create.

Between Stavrogin and Charlus, however, there is an enormous gulf. It is the difference between Dostoevski and Proust, or if you like the difference between the man of God whose hero is himself and the modern man for whom not even God can be a hero. All of Dostoevski's work is pregnant with conflict, *heroic* conflict. In an essay on *Aristocracy* Lawrence writes—"Being alive constitutes an aristocracy which there is no getting beyond. He who is most alive, intrinsically, is King, whether men admit it or not....More life! More *vivid* life! Not more safe cabbages, or meaningless masses of people....all creation contributes, and must contribute, to this: towards the achieving of a vaster, vivider cycle of life. That is the goal of living. He who gets nearer the sun is leader, the aristocrat of aristocrats. Or he who, like Dostoevski, gets nearest the moon of our not-being."

Proust, early in life, relinquished this conflict. As did Joyce. Their art is based on submission, on surrender to the stagnant flux. The Absolute remains outside their works, dominates them, destroys them, just as in life idealism dominates and destroys the ordinary man. But Dostoevski, confronted by even greater powers of frustration, boldly sets himself to grapple with the mystery; he crucified himself for this purpose. And so, wherever in his works there is chaos and confusion, it is a rich chaos, a meaningful confusion; it is positive, vital, soul-infected. It is the aura of the beyond, of the unattainable, that sheds its luster over his scenes and characters—not a dead, dire obscurity. Needless to say, with Proust and Joyce there is an obscurity of another order. With the former we enter the twilight zone of the mind, a realm shot through with dazzling splendors, but always the pale lucidity, the insufferable, obsessional lucidity of the mind. With Joyce we have the night mind, a profusion even more incredible, more dazzling than with Proust, as though the last intervening barriers of the soul had been broken down. But again, *a mind*!

Whereas with Dostoevski, though the mind is always there, always effective and powerfully operative, it is nevertheless a mind constantly held in leash, subordinated to the demands of the soul. It works as mind should work—that is, as machinery, and not as generative power. With Proust and Joyce the mind resembles a machine set in motion by a human hand and then abandoned. It runs on perpetually, or will, until another human hand stops it. Does anybody believe that for either of these men death could be anything but an accidental interruption? When did death occur for them? Technically one of them is still alive. But were they not both dead before they commenced to write?

It is in Joyce that one observes that peculiar failing of the modern artist—the inability to communicate with his audience. Not a wholly new phenomenon, admitted, but always a significant one. Endowed with a Rabelaisian ability for word invention, embittered by the domination of a church for which his intellect had no use, harassed by the lack of understanding on the part of family and friends, obsessed by the parental image against which he vainly rebels, Joyce has been seeking escape in the erection of a fortress composed of meaningless verbiage. His language is a ferocious masturbation carried on in fourteen tongues. It is a dervish dance executed on the periphery of meaning, an orgasm not of blood and semen, but of dead slag from the burnt-out crater of the mind. The Revolution of the Word which his work seems to have inspired in his disciples is the logical outcome of this sterile dance of death.

Joyce's exploration of the night world, his obsession with myth, dream, legend, all the processes of the unconscious mind, his tearing apart of the very instrument itself and the creating of his own world of fantasy, is very much akin to Proust's dilemma. Ultra-civilized products, both, we find them rejecting all question of soul; we find them skeptical of science itself, though bearing witness through their works to an unadmitted allegiance to the principle of causality, which is the very cornerstone of science. Proust, imagining himself to be making of his life a book, of his suffering a poem, exhibits through his microscopic and caustic analysis of man and society the plight of the modern artist for whom there is no faith, no meaning, no life. His work is the most triumphant monument to disillusionment that has ever been erected.

At the root of it was his inability, confessed and repeatedly glorified, to cope with reality—the constant plaint of the modern man. As a matter of fact, his life was a living death, and it is for this reason that his case interests us. For, intensely aware of his predicament, he has given us a record of the age in which he found himself imprisoned. Proust has said that the idea of death kept him company as incessantly as the idea of his own identity. That idea relates, as we know, to that night when, as he says himself, he had "obtained from my parents the initial abdication." That night which dates "the decline in my health and my will power" also dates his death. Thenceforth he is incapable of living in the world—of accepting the world. From that night on he is dead to the world, except for those brief intermittent flashes which not only illuminate the dense fog which is his work but which made his work possible. By a miracle, familiar enough now to the psychiatrist, he stepped beyond the threshold of death. His work, like his life, was a biological continuum punctuated by the meaningless interruption of statistical death.

And so it is no surprise when, standing on the two uneven flagstones and re-experiencing to the ultimate degree those sensational truths which had assailed him several times during the course of his life, he proceeds with a clarity and subtlety unrivalled to develop those thoughts which contain his final and highest views of life and art—magnificent pages dedicated to a lost cause. Here, when he speaks of the artist's instincts, his necessity to obey the small, inner voice, to eschew realism and simply to "*translate*" what is there ever surging upward, ever struggling for expression, here we realize with devastating intensity that for him, Proust, life was not a living, but a feasting upon sunken treasures, a life of retrospect; we realize that for him what joy remained was nothing but the joy of the archeologist in rediscovering the relics and ruins of the past, of musing among these buried treasures and re-imagining the life that had once given form to these dead things. And yet, sad as it is to contemplate the grandeur and nobility of these pages, moving as it is to observe that a great work had been built up out of suffering and disease, it is also tonic to realize that in these same passages there had been dealt the death-blow to that school of realism which, pretending to be dead, had resuscitated itself under the guise of psychologism. After all Proust was concerned with a view of life; his work has meaning and content, his characters do live, however distorted they are made to seem by his laboratory method of dissection and analysis. Proust was pre-eminently a man of the nineteenth century, with all the tastes, the ideology, and the respect for the powers of the conscious mind which dominated the men of that epoch. His work now seems like the labor of a man who has revealed to us the absolute limits of such a mind.

The breakdown which, in the realm of painting, gave rise to the school of Impressionism is evident also in Proust's literary method. The process of examining the medium itself, of subjecting the external world to microscopic analysis, thereby creating a new perspective and hence the illusion of a new world, has its counterpart in Proust's technique. Weary of realism and naturalism, as were the painters, or rather finding the existent picture of reality unsatisfying, *unreal*, owing to the exploration of the physicists, Proust strove, through the elaborate diffraction of incident and character, to displace the psychologic realism of the day. His attitude is coincident with the emergence of the new analytical psychology. Throughout those veritably ecstatic passages in the last volume of his work—the passages on the function of art and the role of the artist—Proust finally achieves a clarity of vision which presages the finish of his own method and the birth of a wholly new kind of artist. Just as the physicists, in their exploration of the material nature of the universe, arrived at the brink of a new and mysterious realm, so Proust pushing his powers of analysis to the utmost limits, arrived at that frontier between dream and reality which henceforth will be the domain of the truly creative artists.

It is when we come to Joyce, who succeeds Proust by a short interval, that we notice the change in the psychologic atmosphere. Joyce, who in his early work gives us a romantic confessional account of the "I," suddenly moves over into a new domain. Though smaller in scope the canvas which Joyce employs gives the illusion of being even more vast than Proust's; we lose ourselves in it, not as with Proust, in dream fashion, but as one loses oneself in a strange city. Despite all the analysis, Proust's world is still a world of nature, of monstrous yet live fauna and flora. With Joyce we enter the inorganic world—the kingdom of minerals, of fossil and ruin, of dead dodos. The difference in technique is more than remarkable—it is significant of a wholly new order of sensation. We are done now with the nineteenth-century sensibility of Proust; it is no longer through the nerves that we receive our impressions, no longer a personal and subconscious memory ejecting its images. As we read *Ulysses* we have the impression that the mind has become a recording machine: we are aware of a double world as we move with the author through the great labyrinth of the city. It is a perpetual day dream in which the mind of the sick scholar runs amok.

And, just as Proust's animus was directed against that little society which had first snubbed him, so with Joyce the satire and the bitterness is directed towards the philistine world of which he remains the eternal enemy. Joyce is not a realist, nor even a psychologist; he makes no attempt to build up character—his are caricatures of humanity only, *types* which enable him to vent his satire, his hatred, to lampoon, to vilify. For at bottom there is in Joyce a profound hatred for humanity—the scholar's hatred. One realizes that he has the neurotic's fear of entering the living world, the world of men and women in which he is powerless to function. He is in revolt not against institutions, but against mankind. Man to him is pitiable, ridiculous, grotesque. And even more so are man's ideas—not that he is without understanding of them, but that they have no validity for him; they are ideas which would connect him with a world from which he has divorced himself. His is a medieval mind born too late: he has the tastes of the recluse, the morals of the anchorite, with all the masturbative machinery which such a life entrains.

A Romantic who wished to embrace life realistically, an idealist whose ideals were bankrupt, he was faced with a dilemma which he was incapable of resolving. There was only one way out—to plunge into the collective realm of fantasy. As he spun out the fabric of his dreams he also unloaded the poison that had accumulated in his system. *Ulysses* is like a vomit spilled by a delicate child whose stomach has been overloaded with sweetmeats."So rich was its delivery, its pent-up outpouring so vehement," says Wyndham Lewis, "that it will remain eternally cathartic, a monument like a record diarrhoea." Despite the maze of facts, phenomena and incident detailed, there is no grasp of life, no picture of life. There is neither an organic conception, nor a vital sense of life. We are confronted with the machinery of the mind turned loose upon a dead abstraction, *the city*, itself the product of abstractions.

It is in comparing this city-world—vague, diffuse, amorphous—with that narrower, but more integrated and still perfumed, if wholly decadent, world of Proust's that we realize the change which has come over the world in but a few years. The things men discussed in that artificial world of the Faubourg St. Germain no longer bear resemblance to that which passes for conversation in the streets and pubs and brothels of Dublin. That fragrance which emanates from the pages of Proust, what is it but the fragrance of a dying world, the last faint perfume of things running to seed?

When, via *Ulysses*, we penetrate Dublin and there detect the flora and fauna stratified in the memory of a highly civilized, highly sensitive being such as Joyce, we realize that the absence of fragrance, the deodorization, is the result of death. What seem to be alive and walking, loving, talking, drinking are not people, but ghosts. The drama is one of liquefaction; it is not even static, as in Proust's case. Analysis is no longer possible because the organism is defunct. Instead of the examination of a dying, though still intact, organism, as with Proust, we find ourselves inspecting cell life, wasted organs, diseased membranes. A study in etiology, such as the Egyptologists give us in their post-mortems of post-mortems; a description of life via the mummy. The great Homeric figure of Ulysses, shrunk to the insignificant shadow now of Bloom, now of Dedalus, wanders through the dead and forsaken world of the big city; the anaemic, distorted and dessicated reflections of what were once epic events which Joyce is said to have plotted out in his famous ground-plan remain but simulacra, the shadow and tomb of ideas, events, people.

When one day the final interpretation of *Ulysses* is given us by the "anatomists of the soul" we shall have the most astounding revelations about the significance of this work. Then indeed we shall know the full meaning of this "record diarrhoea." Perhaps then we shall see that not Homer but *defeat* forms the real ground-plan, the invisible pattern of Joyce's work.

Is it wittingly or unwittingly that in the famous section of questions and answers Joyce reveals the empty soul quality of the modern man, this wretch who is reduced to a bundle of tricks, this encyclopedic ape who displays the most amazing technical facility? *Is Joyce this man who can imitate any style—even the text-book and the encyclopedia?* This form of humor, in which Rabelais also indulged, is the specific remedy which the intellectual employs to defeat the moral man: it is the dissolvent with which he destroys a whole world of meaning. With the Dadaists and the Surrealists the powerful stress on humor was part of a conscious and deliberate attitude toward breaking down the old ideologies. We see the same phenomenon in Swift and Cervantes.

But observe the difference between the humor of Rabelais, with whom the author of *Ulysses* is so frequently and unjustly compared, and Joyce. Mark the difference between that formidable Surrealist, Jonathan Swift, and the feeble iconoclasts who today call themselves Surrealists! Rabelais' humor was still healthy; it had a stomachic quality, it was inspired by the Holy Bottle. Whereas with our contemporaries it is all in the head, above the eyes—a vicious, envious, mean, malign, humorless mirth. Today they are laughing out of desperation, out of despair. Humor? Hardly. A reflexive muscular twitch rather—more gruesome than mirth-provoking. A sort of onanistic laughter....In those marvellous passages where Joyce marries his rich excretory images to his sad mirth there is a poignant, wistful undercurrent which smells of reverence and idolatry. Reminiscent, too reminiscent, of those devout medieval louts who knelt before the Pope to be annointed with dung.

In this same chapter of riddle and conundrum there is a profound despair, the despair of a man who is giving the works to the last myth—*Science.* That disintegration of the ego which was sounded in *Ulysses,* and is now being carried to the extreme limits in *Work in Progress*, does it not correspond faithfully to the outer, world-disintegration? Do we not have here the finest example of that phenomenon touched on before—*schizophrenia?* The dissolution of the macrocosm goes hand in hand with the dissolution of the soul. With Joyce the Homeric figure goes over into its opposite: we see him splitting off into multitudes of characters, heroes, legendary figures, into trunks, arms, legs, into river, tree and rock and beast. Working down and down and down into the now stratified layers of the collective being, groping and groping for his lost soul, struggling like a heroic worm to re-enter the womb. What did he mean, Joyce, when on the eve of *Ulysses* he wrote through Stephen Dedalus that he wanted "to forge in the smithy of [his] soul the uncreated conscience of [his] race?" When he cried out—"No, mother. Let me be and let me live!"—was that a cry of anguish from a soul imprisoned in the womb? That opening picture of the bright morning sun, the image of navel and scrotum, followed by the harrowing scene with the mother—everywhere and throughout the mother image. "I love everything that flows," he says to one of his admirers, and in his new book there are hundreds of rivers, including his own native Liffey. What a thirst! What a longing for the waters of life! If only he could be cast up again on a distant shore, in another clime, under different constellations! Sightless bard . . . lost soul . . . eternal wanderer. What longing, groping, seeking, searching for an all-merciful bosom, for the night in which to drown his restless, fruitless spirit! Like the sun itself which, in the course of a day, rises from the sea and disappears again, so

Ulysses takes its cosmic stance, rising with a curse and falling with a sigh. But like a sun that is up-to-date the split-hero of *Ulysses* wanders, not over the waters of life and death, but through the eternal, monotonous, mournful, empty, lugubrious streets of the big city—dirty Dublin, the sink of the world.

If the *Odyssey* was a remembrance of great deeds *Ulysses* is a forgetting. That black, restless, never-ending flow of words in which the twin-soul of Joyce is swept along like a clot of waste matter passing through the drains, this stupendous deluge of pus and excrement which washes through the book languidly seeking an outlet, at last gets choked and, rising like a tidal wave, blots out the whole shadowy world in which this shadowy epic was conceived. The penultimate section, which is the work of a learned desperado, is like the dynamiting of a dam. The dam, in the unconscious symbology of Joyce, is the last barrier of tradition and culture which must give way if man is to come into his own. Each idiotic question is a hole drilled by a madman and charged with dynamite; each idiotic answer is the detonation of a devastating explosion. Joyce, the mad baboon, herein gives the works to the patient ant-like industry of man which has accumulated about him like an iron ring of dead learning.

When the last vestige has been blown up comes the flood. The final section is a free fantasia such as has never been seen before in all literature. It is a transcription of the deluge—except that there is no ark. The stagnant cesspool of the cultural drama which comes again and again to nought in the world-city, this drama which was personified by the great whore of Babylon, is echoed in the timeless reverie of Molly Bloom whose ears are stuffed by the lapping of the black waters of death. The very image of Woman, Molly Bloom bulks large and enduring. Beside her the others are reduced to pygmies. Molly Bloom is water, tree, and earth. She is mystery. She is the devourer, the ocean of night in which the lost hero finally plunges, and with him the world.

There is something about Molly Bloom, as she lies a-dreaming on her dirty,crummy bed, which carries us back to primordial images. She is the quintessence of the great whore which is Woman, of Babylon the vessel of abominations. Floating unresisting, eternal, all-contained, she is like the sea itself.

Like the sea she is receptive, fecund, voracious, insatiable. She begets and she destroys; she nourishes and she devastates. With Molly Bloom, *con anonyme,* woman is restored to prime significance—as womb and matrix of life. She is the image of Nature itself, as opposed to the illusory world which man, because of his insufficiency, vainly endeavors to displace.

And so, with a final, triumphant vengeance, with suicidal glee, all the threads which were dropped throughout the book are gathered up; the pale, dimunitive hero, reduced to an intestinal worm and carried like a tickling little phallus in the great body of the female, returns to the womb of Nature, shorn of everything but the last symbol. In the long retrospective arc which is drawn we have the whole trajectory of man's flight from unknown to unknown. The rainbow of history fades out. The great dissolution is accomplished. After that closing picture of Molly Bloom a-dreaming on her dirty bed we can say, as in Revelation—*And there shall be no more curse!* Henceforth no sin, no guilt, no fear, no repression, no longing, no pain of separation. The end is accomplished—man returns to the womb.

* * *

The phrase in my head which keeps repeating obsessively is: *no creative men in the world today! Not one!* No oceans, like Shakespeare and Dante, to swim in. Inland seas there may be; great lakes even. But no oceans! Not even a great river—an Amazon, or a Mississippi! Certainly no new oceans. There are, on the other hand, great critics emerging—monstrous, fascinating beings, hideous freaks of nature. Like those rank, perverse plants in the tropics which drain the sun and soil of vitality, men who give themselves up to the examination of life, and of art. Critics, biographers, historians, philosophers, psycho-analysts, statisticians. *All one!*

When I regard the truly formidable, the horrible, monstrous activity of these types, the lust with which they slay and devour, I realize that even such "failures" as Rimbaud, Nietzsche, Dostoevski, Van Gogh, Proust, Cézanne, etc., are no longer capable of being spawned. Even as "failures" there was about these men a magnificence! At least they were trying to *do* something. At least they were trying to *utter* something!

There was in them the germ of greatness. Not the flower, perhaps—but the germ of something. Whereas today, in this nightmare sterilized of all pain and struggle and beauty, not even a germ can manifest itself. *Not one MAN in the world today!* Not one! And the world needs a *man!*

In a study of American literature recently, Ludwig Lewisohn parades before our eyes a sick and learned pageant of the eunuchs, cripples, perverts, who embellished the arts in America. The two biggest figures which America produced, Emerson and Whitman—the one, according to Lewisohn, a eunuch, the other an invert—have left America unaffected. But even these "cripples" said things which, if America had had a soul, might have created a genuine spiritual revolution. The seed died. There was not even the possibility of germination. *The long night had already settled in*—the great works were still-born. And if, now, we succeed in expressing ourselves at all it is only in fragments, only as fragments. We are incomplete. We are lapsing into a long silence in order to be born again—born whole. Those who force themselves to be heard are those who are born out of time. *Monsters that are born prematurely!*

I say that today we are like maggots flourishing in the body of a corpse—that now we are feasting on the corpse of life. But soon the corpse will be devoured—and then we shall be obliged to turn upon one another, devour one another. And that will be the end of *our* tapeworm of history!

Especially when I consider the efforts of the great critics about me today do I have the sensation of observing the work of maggots. Maggots stealing into the dead body of life and feasting there gloatingly. I see them already turning on one another, not just to strike or to paralyze, but turning on one another with eyes bulging and jaws dripping. Turning to rend and devour one another. And so I can understand, for instance, why a cadaver like Joyce, which has not even turned cold, a cadaver in which the cells are still sprouting, must seem to these worms like a particularly juicy morsel. It is not only that he is still warm, that he is sprouting even in death, but it is the *size* of him that whets their appetite. For with each death their world grows larger; with each fresh corpse that is seized upon the philosophy of time-space increases in size and importance. Joyce is one of the recently dead kings of time-and-space, a bigger than usual corpse, a more succulent one. He provides an eschatological banquet of the first order. Here, for aeons of bacteriological time, the microbes can feast to the full.

And all this was presaged in Shakespeare, in the sick mind of a sick Hamlet. Now all the characters have been killed off, and the drama goes on among the worms. Four centuries after Shakespeare, the great genius of the biological world appears, a Hamlet who is lost, swamped in the miasma of prevailing doubt and disintegration. He gives us a work of unilateral dimension, a prodigious, monumental piece of labor on the flat, a drama without action except the scissors-like motion of the mandibles, a poem with a peristaltic rhythm, a complete world with index, maps, charts, photographs, and addenda, but a world without light or shadow, a world made up of worked-out soil; so that all the genius, all the labor, all the inventiveness, all the digging and all the tunnelling, all the metaphor, all the reminiscence, all the longing and all the spade work is not worth as much as a penny's worth of manure. A world of rubber goods and platinum, a debris of the past. A world without even pus . . . .

So much has been said about the revival of a mantic personality, about a possible renascence of art through tapping the unconscious leaven of the mind—in all of which there is a ring of truth were it not also unfortunately the death knell which is sounding. True it is that in the vast reservoir of the Unconscious there lie the materials for life, for art, for faith, layer upon layer of racial experience, an ineradicable record of five hundred thousand years, more perhaps, with its triumphs and defeats, its deaths and regenerations. Unfathomable treasures lie buried there—and wild, unfathomable hopes. It is the *hopes* that lie buried there that may one day give the lie to history. It is the instincts that lie crushed and thwarted which may upset our ant-like industry, our ape-like mimicry. There may be thousands and thousands of years yet of history— and then a complete break, a new, wild life beyond our craziest dreams. It is this fanatical surge of hope, rising like the antiphony to utter despair, which is to be detected in all Orphic revivals, which after all, are only recrudescences of mysticism.

It is out of a profound disgust that heroic madness springs, and not one among the great mystics of the past, the *Surrealists*, we might well call them, but was inspired thus. The movement which today calls itself Surrealist is a contradiction: there is no Surrealism, there are only Surrea*lists*. And about whom these have been there can be no real dispute. They were the wild men, the fanatics, the impossible ones, the men who were out of step with their times, the men who were lopsided, diseased, visionary, hallucinated. The mantic personalities, yes! In their language there was always dream and madness, more dream perhaps than madness.

In Swift and Rabelais, for example, one smells the "dithyrambic chorus;" it is that note of sublime comedy which gives us the illusion of the demonic; in returning to pre-conscious images, to the instinctive, magical source, the sacral quality of life itself, there is the true effort of man to restore the prime symbols which are vitiated through culture, and particularly by the "language" aspect of culture, since the whole process of language is one of further and further deviation from the roots. It is this demonism that Nietzsche describes when he speaks of "the metaphysical comfort—with which...every true tragedy leaves us—that life is at the bottom of things, despite all the changes of appearances, indestructibly powerful and pleasurable . . . . This comfort," he says, "appears in an incarnate clarity in the chorus of satyrs, the chorus of natural beings who live ineradicably, as it were, behind all civilization and remain eternally the same."

In Proust there is no demonic quality. This man who had the vision to perceive the great value of the unconscious processes and who himself resuscitated, through image and metaphor, the heroic myths of the past, this man never uttered a phrase that was not strictly intelligible, that had not been filtered through the screen of the mind. Complex, fluid, evanescent, limpid though his writing was, nevertheless Proust remains always transparent; that opacity of thought which the blood alone bequeaths is missing. There was no goat, no satyr in his make-up; he was a *marble* faun, if faun at all. What a significant exclamation he uttered when he said that Ruskin had gone to his head a little. *To his head!* Never to the solar plexus! Never to the seat of the soul, to liver and entrails. Ruskin . . . . Archaeology . . . . The spade of a spade.

And this madness of which Proust was incapable we today

are even more incapable. There is no genuine madness among the artists today. There is only neuroticism. Intelligence, alas, does not yield madness. At the most it yields despair—or nerves. Little wonder that the Surrealists envy the schizophrenics, the paranoiacs, the assassin, the sexually depraved. It is an envy, a longing, based on deficiency. No wonder they are in revolt against that view which Aristotle voiced: *art as catharsis*. When very justly they attempt to resurrect crime, it is only the effort to purify the muddy springs of action. But the pathetic aspect of this, the give-away, as it were, is the acknowledgedly *therapeutic* value of crime. However, favorable, from a Surrealistic point of view, or a psychoanalytic point of view, may be the mounting wave of crime, the fact is that men are growing less and less criminal.

Crime is in the air—but it is not in the heart. We are living in the midst of crime, and we have become immune to it. The great crimes are committed in the heart—by the pure at heart! Compared with Tamerlane or Capone, Christ was a criminal of the first water. Compared with Huxley's or Faulkner's crime annals, the exploits which Dostoevski recorded seem positively holy. Jesus, Dostoevski, Villon, Napoleon—these men gave expression to their criminal instincts directly. But all the ravings of the Surrealists and all the atrocities of the American underworld are nothing but the pale, automatic refllection of an instinct turned in upon itself, luxuriating in a waste land.

If only yesterday we were terrified by the thought of insanity, today we no longer recognize it as such, or else we regard it as deliverance. The significant plaint of the artist now is that he has not the freedom to go mad, nor even the opportunity. How like the language of the insanities is this new Orphic revival, this dream language which the ultra-moderns vainly endeavor to exploit! It is not madness, in the Dionysian sense, but the expression of frustration, a phantasmagoria of wish and longing, completely saturated with the dead flora and fauna of psychiatry. A middle realm, a no-man's land, over which there reigns a nightmare of destruction. There is neither the possibility of going forward to death, nor the possibility of return to pick up the fight again. There is only an everlasting torment in which the quaking soul is shattered. In this Purgatory more ignominious than life, more horrible than death, all the symbols in which life's values lie implicitly concealed are burned away, burned to utter ashes and clinkers.

The artists who have escaped death, who have overstayed their time, these living ghosts which we are today, all of us, find ourselves utterly powerless to communicate our anguish. Formerly the artist made himself understood by the very virture of his madness. Perhaps not "understood" precisely, but what is better, he found it possible to spread his contagion. With insanity the norm, the artist finds no mode of communication. He has completely lost his *raison d'être*. Confusedly he tries to point out that this madness is not madness at all, nor this sanity, sanity. There is no means of expressing an anguish which has already penetrated the whole organism, which screeches from the roots of the hair and the raw tips of the nerves.

It is this utter break-down of values, this chaos, this confusion which is signalized chiefly by the great critics who, now more than ever, find themselves unable to differentiate between style, form, school, ism, etc., *and* the various orders of insanity. The whole vast literature, for example, which has grown up around the name of Joyce attests the failing powers of the very minds to which Joyce is appealing. Joyce, who employs a dead language, is, by the irony of things, being hailed as a life-bringer. This remarkable man, whose activity can be likened only to that of a powerful, unisolated microbe, has done more than any man of our time to hasten the process of dissolution, The astounding luxuriance of his language is not a sign of new life, not the exuberance of vitality, but rather the manifestation of a cancer which is ravaging our souls. He proliferates with such virulence that the body of our literature offers not a single point of resistance. There is not even the sign of an antitoxin making its appearance.

* * *

It was near the end of his life that Lawrence set down these memorable words:

We, dear reader, you and I, we were born corpses, and we are corpses. I doubt if there is ever one of us who has even known so much as an apple, a whole apple . . . . Shadows of everything, of the whole world, shadows even of ourselves. We are inside the tomb, and the tomb is wide and shadowy like hell, even if sky-blue by optimistic paint, so we think it is all the world. But our world is a wide tomb full of ghosts, replicas. We are all spectres, we have not been able to touch even so much as an apple. Spectres we are to one another. Spectre you are to me, spectre I am to you. Shadow you are even to yourself. And by shadow I mean idea, concept, the abstracted reality, the ego. We are not solid. We don't live in the flesh. Our instincts and intuitions are dead, we live wound round with the winding-sheet of abstraction. And the touch of anything solid hurts us. For our instincts and intuitions, which are our feelers of touch and knowing through touch, they are dead, amputated. We walk and talk and eat and copulate and laugh and evacuate wrapped in our winding-sheets, all the time wrapped in our winding-sheets.

Now this is not a despair produced by defeat, nor is it the language of a dying man who has been finally disillusioned; it is, on the contrary, the reiteration of a conviction which seized him early in life and which runs like a refrain through all his works. It was the motivating impulse of his life—the knowledge and conviction of the death that is on us.

As the poet the idea quickens him, leads him, as in *New Heaven and Earth* to the utmost limits of realization; here he accepts the idea of death and, with the true artist's vision of its meaning and purpose, reaches to a profound Orphic conception, one with the great mystics of every time and place. But it remains a momentary vision, a momentary wisdom which he grasps again and again, and then forsakes. He is, in his most lucid moments, the prophet, the seer, the visionary; in his moments of frenzied exaltation he is indeed a savior. But he cannot sustain the role; he comes down from the heights, he grows confused, he preaches, groans, wails, laments, his voice grows hysterical, it screeches, it rasps. A very human, very frail voice: the voice of anguish, of a man crucified. It is the voice of a savior who cries out in anguish against the despair and the doubt prevailing: *not death, but life! life everlasting!*

CHAPTER IV

Resurrection

*I was a lover, I kissed the woman I loved
and God of horror, I was kissing also myself.*

IN LAWRENCE'S novels one is almost baffled by the fierce antagonisms, the hatred of woman, which he displays. One is almost equally baffled by his search for a more perfect relationship with man, one based on love and yet not homosexual. The conflict, it is said by those who endeavor to interpret his works by his life—that is according to the tenets of modern psychology—had its origin in the man's obsessive love for his mother. Oedipus complex! The story of *Sons and Lovers* is regarded as the depiction of the tragic influence of the mother. And so it is! But it is the end of it! He comes through!

In *The White Peacock*, where he voices his hatred for civilization, "the painted fungus of rottenness," his hatred (symbolically expressed) is for the woman, she who is the vulture soiling her perch—the very incarnation then of Civilization. It is the "sin of idealism" which causes him suffering and pain. Civilization is the enthronement and perpetuation of this female idolatry (the *Magna Mater*), of this false spiritual glorification of Woman.

In *Sons and Lovers* he records his release from the "Empire of the Mothers"—he has deepened his picture by the realization of the sinister, tyrannical role of the mother whom he loved so passionately. Henceforth his image (symbol) of the world is the womb, the mother's womb from which he has himself escaped, but to which and in which he sees the rest of mankind still bound, unable to be born, let alone to cut the umbilical cord. The world then is the world of form and ideology, which is so old, so enfeebled, that the walls of the womb are dry and the muscles inflexible—so that the child can not be ejected. In "The Crown" (where he has condensed and crystallized his ideas on this subject) he represents, therefore, our life as something going on in the dead womb and all our struggles as being ineffectual—a dual conflict—back towards the primal powers of darkness, or forward towards the light. Being born, then, becomes an act of creation, an achievement, a fulfillment. And this is brought about only through a realization of the mysterious nature of birth: its profound relation to death.

The Rainbow and *Women in Love* have for their theme the relation between man and woman—the former showing the disintegrative powers of curruption and the latter the creative powers. *Sex and death*—the dominant motif. Lawrence sees the falsity of the current spiritual ideology, the Sexual interpretation of life. The "phallic mystic" is the man who sees beyond this regressive, disintegrative view. He is reestablishing the male, generative, spiritual principle. In combating the current "spiritual" he is asserting the supremacy of the creative instinct which is pre-sexual, parthenogenetic.

His hope is to save the world. Art has been only a means to enable him to promulgate his ideas. In Frieda he had hoped to find his sanction. But Frieda is thoroughly a woman, does not understand, and fights him, cripples him. In desperation he seeks a man, a friend, a loyalty and support. Murry, the man he turned to, is equally incapable of understanding him. This conflict produces another book—*Aaron's Rod*—wherein Lawrence voices the need for leadership, for authority. Friendship is impossible because he has no equals. Henceforth, more and more sure of his value, his superiority, he demands only *disciples*. And Murry, who represents for him the incarnation and apotheosis of the inferior, non-comprehending humanity which lives eternally in the present, becomes the symbol of all humanity—the Judas type—that rests in compromises. His hatred of humanity is his hatred of Murry who refuses to follow him, who betrays him. Forced into isolation he makes himself god. He achieves his individual, private union with the cosmos.

Paul's affair with Miriam, recorded in *Sons and Lovers*, reveals the knowledge and the effect upon Lawrence of his mother's great love. Miriam was not wholly to blame—Paul was aware of that—but she was partly to blame because her love was only a reflection of the mother-love against which he was struggling. He went to Miriam to be liberated, but Miriam was incapable of liberating him. The alternating love and hatred which he bore towards his mother he transferred to Miriam, and later Lawrence transferred it to the whole white world poisoned at the fount by this obscene idealism, this tenacious mother love.

In "Virgin Youth" he writes: "Dark, ruddy pillar, forgive me! I/Am helplessly bound/To the rock of virginity...Thy tower impinges/On nothingness." At the very threshold of sexual life he saw himself a prisoner of life, a victim. The man who twenty years later will address his own penis and glorify it began by feeling ashamed of his virginity, his impotence. He realized at the very start that he was handicapped, that he could not establish a vital contact with the world of living men and women. The problem which beset him was that of finding release from the prison of self, of making an entry into the world, into others.

It was only with his mother's death that he acquired a feeling of liberation. "I am myself at last!" he exclaims. The shock of his mother's death brought about an illumination; it enabled him to discover his own true self, to discover his power and uniqueness. From this point on the quality and the character of his work are marked by a radical change. The earlier Lawrence seems henceforth distinctly embryonic. The earlier Lawrence belongs to the past, to tradition, to the cultural world against which he was to savagely set his face.

Until his mother died and left him free to battle with the world he could find no escape through the sexual experience. The affair with Jessie, instead of liberating his powers, only crippled him further, left him in despair. The death of his mother, while in a sense a liberating thing, nevertheless left him a permanent cripple. He had not affected his own liberation, through pain and struggle, through understanding—he had simply been released from the prison in which she confined him during her life. He makes his entry into the world a divided being. He is marked by the shackles of her binding love. It is the realization of this which provides the motivating force of his future behavior, which furnishes the traction of hate and revolt against the world. Unable to bring himself to the world as a whole man he turns upon the world to destroy it, to wipe out that condition of living which had made him what he was. His emotional, affective self was blighted at the roots. He felt that he had been sterilized, that his feeling had been atrophied. He saw the whole world of men and women experiencing the same blighting process, from birth on.

He saw that it was impossible to achieve liberation, wholeness, through the sexual adventure. Revolt! Only revolt!

It seems to me that *Women in Love* amplified what was a narrower theme in *The Rainbow*. The latter comes after his mother's death and after his marraige to Frieda. It is Frieda's first appearance in his novels. Having broken the incestuous bond of the mother, so to speak, through *Sons and Lovers*, he now finds through wedlock the corruptive, disintegrating aspect of the ideal-love mode with Frieda, the tyrannical power of woman coupled with the comforting annihilation of her big womb and her draughts of death and forgetfulness.

In *Women in Love* he visualizes the death and corruption of our present life. He pits himself against this world of death by transferring to Hermione all the sterile, evil, death-like qualities of the world he knows. The struggle to attain a unity within himself, the conflict which he wages with his own self, is projected and universalized. His own crippled self, his impotent manhood, he represents through the Lesbian character of Hermione. It is the expression of the fundamental schism in himself, of that warfare between his masculine nature—which is gradually being converted into the spiritual—and his feminine nature—which he is powerless to utilize creatively because he transfers it to the woman he loves. His love of his wife, a love which is a continual torture to him, is nothing more than a love of self. Woman as a person, as the object of love, since he is powerless to give himself, to attach himself to her, he makes a force for evil, the devil which combats his spiritual, masculine nature.

In describing the corruptness of the world during this period, he says of himself: "I detest what I am outwardly. I *loathe* myself as a human being." This is the despair of a man who craves a full life, a free life, the despair of a man who realizes that he is chained forever to the rock of idealism. More, there is the realization also that in wearing away his chains he will bring about a liberation which he himself will never enjoy. His powerful descriptions of the great carrion birds and the hyenas, these are in reality but descriptions of his own incorrigible, devouring self, the gnawing Absolute that claws at his vitals. It is the drama of vicarious freedom, the old Promethean drama. He wants the world to hate him, he says, because he can't bear the thought that it might love him. It is the feeling of guilt which comes upon the man who presumes to combat the gods, who perhaps does not realize yet that he is himself a god.

In *The Rainbow* this conflict between his human and his divine self comes to a resolution. The very title is significant of his will to bridge the two extremes of his duality. The mystic unity which he caught, which enabled him to visualize the two halves of himself, becomes the basic criterion for all his future dichotomies. Henceforth his characters are constructed from the standpoint of possession or non-possession of this essential unity. "Nothing," he says, "can stop me now, not I myself."

With the outbreak of the war, an almost fatal blow was directed towards this new unity. The war was a reality and the most crucial test for the idealist type Lawrence represents. For a man of this type the horrible reality of the war had to be rendered into a greater significance than was provided by political or economic interpretations.

Anaïs Nin has rightly pointed out that Somers, of *Kangaroo,* is another of Lawrence's self-portraits, this time of the artist as "devil-creator," as a kind of human bomb. In Lawrence's words: "Well, all right then, if I *am* finally a sort of human bomb, black inside, and primed, I hope the hour and the place will come for my going off: for my exploding with the maximum amount of havoc. *Some* men have to be bombs, to explode and make breaches in the walls that shut life in. Blind, havoc-working bombs too. Then so be it." This is interesting because *Kangaroo* is written around Lawrence's ejection from Cornwall by the military: Lawrence, regarding himself as a savior of mankind, universalizes this personal and unimportant experience (one that was very petty and absurd, really, in comparison to other forms of torture imposed by the war-devils); he comes down from his lofty isolation, as must all fanatics and saints and prophets, when confronted with tangible realities. He then becomes rebel, revolutionist, the advocator of violence.

One forgets too often how much violence there was in Jesus—and always over petty matters. It is of the essence of world-savers to stumble over trifles. Where the broad, ironic, realistic man of the world, accustomed to judge human nature in its due proportions (not idealistically or too imaginatively) dismisses these trifling incidents with a shrug of the shoulders, the *Redeemer* (Lawrence, Jesus, et al) must needs make a great issue of them. Really the issue never lies here. These incidents are made vastly symbolic. This is the peculiar feature of such minds: they possess the faculty of magnifying everything so as to incorporate events and incidents into their cosmic ideologies.

They alternate, in the world of reality, between *comic* (absurd, pathetic) figures, and *tragic* (sublime, heroic) figures. They are never *just men*—that is, never *real*. They *should* always be despised, persecuted, harassed and crucified. They *must!* The world would be insufferable with them at the helm. The true man of action, or even of thought, knows how to take them. Pontius Pilate (Murry, Bennett, Wells, etc.) hands them over to the mob. What is truth? they ask. Interesting speculation—insoluble. A Daniel come to judgment? O.K. Then be judged! The conflict is always between the One and the Many. The penalty of being God is alienation. One should not ask to enjoy the privilege of godhood and at the same time ask to be spared the sufferings of misunderstanding. The gods exist to be dethroned, to be destroyed. God persists only because He is in every man: He is that impossible Absolute which every man creates in order to hide his great irrational fear of death. What is built upon that illusion must crumble and be rebuilt—so we have gods appearing and disappearing *ad infinitum*.

"The walls that shut life in," then, are those walls which the masses represent, the walls of inertia. In order for the God to function, to exist, even, there must be attraction and repulsion—there must be the violence (love and hatred) to nourish the illusion. The eternal life that Lawrence seeks to preserve is Lawrence's eternal life—his private eternality, his value, which the masses ignore. And the war, with its denial of individual values, is a blow at his divine right, his sacredness. It dramatizes his nullity, and that is why he must talk of exploding. The great explosion going on at the front is nothing to him in comparison with this private explosion he wishes to see. The war is enlisting the annihilation only of nations, only of armies, only of a few millions of persons. He would have the whole world in arms, one against the other. For *his* sake! In this he shares the madness of all saints—Buddha, Mahomet, Jesus. No compromise. No other God but *me*! A perfect case!

Thus the war was a cruel test for Lawrence. He could not see it as a reality, only as a nightmare. It was for him merely another aspect, a violent aspect, of that nullity and death to which he saw life reduced everywhere. In the World War he saw that "nightmare of reality" which the poet sees constantly in our daily peacetime life, that nightmare which is symbolized by the machine, a nightmare which has shattered the individual soul, which gave man, not the courage, but the wholehearted wish to go to war, not as a hero, not for a personal, comprehensible triumph, but for a wholesale slaughter, an extinction, in the schizophrenic regression, in the return to the womb of nature. This crawling back into the earth and reabsorption again in Nature takes away from war its old meanings—conflict, triumph, fecundation through sorrow and agony—and gives it a new one: escape from the nightmare of reality, from the machine in suicide. This is how Lawrence speaks of the men lined up with him for the physical examination required for induction: "They are all so brave, to suffer, but none of them brave enough, to reject suffering. They are all so noble, to accept sorrow and hurt, but they can none of them demand happiness. Their manliness all lies in accepting calmly this death, this loss of their integrity. They must stand by their fellow man: that is the motto."

His conflict with reality now becomes sharper, more stern, more grandiose. Rather than acknowledge himself the victim of a process which he refuses to recognize, he decides to triumph over life by sheer force of will. He must destroy the *fact*. He must dominate on another plane. Once he realizes this, once he realizes that he is the instrument of destiny, all issues become clear to him, and he earns his artistic release, his spiritual freedom. He now appoints himself a savior of man.

In this period of *The Rainbow* and *Women in Love* (during which he also wrote "The Crown" and *Twilight in Italy*), came Lawrence's realization of the self-discovery of the Holy Ghost, of his role and mission in life. He at last has the "truth" in his hands, the "illumination" that will save the world! This is clearly borne out in the letters of the period to Asquith, Morrell, Garnett and others. Indeed, Catherine Carswell tells us that after *The Rainbow* Lawrence envisaged only one more work (*Women in Love*), a sequel that would make really one work, and then devoting himself to active life in the world with man, creating a new world.

*   *   *

The savior is a dual type who, unable to conquer his personal division, arranges the world in terms of it. Unable to save himself he tries to save the world. The savior type is the essentially religious man who has an unusual portion of femininity in his character which comes to represent his spiritual nature. The savior and the artist type are fundamentally one and the same, which is why the prophetic and healing character of the artist is always remarked upon, and always a source of discussion. This type must of necessity fight its greatest conflict in the sexual field. Woman, like nature, represents for him the harsh enigma of reality, and it is reality with which his religious nature is always locked in combat. His creativity works upon reality. In other words, his abnormal mixture of male and female represents his abnormal sense of reality. Most profoundly this type realizes that the essential characteristic of life is flux—flux because his intense creativity is the dominant thing. His artistic goal is to recreate his personality. His language is always one "of identification with the universe," a doubly significant thing: first in the effort at unity, abolutism; secondly in the effort to posit himself as universe, as God. The whole evolution of the man is an effort to arrive at godhood. When as Son he offers himself as sacrifice it is to become one with the Father. Son and Father are really Man and God.

The question of fulfillment is the all important one. In Lawrence's evolution we see the trend toward fulfillment characteristic of this type: first an attempt at fulfillment through sex, which proves a failure; second, the attempt through friendship, also a failure. Always isolation. The failures revealed to him the necessity for lordship, for authority. In the experiment with friendship he learns that what he really wanted was not a friend—what he wanted was to establish himself as leader. He wanted to justify his role of savior. The very adoption of such a role points only to his alienation from mankind, to his non-human characteristic. In the end he must either find God, or appoint himself God.

In *The Plumed Serpent* he posits his dark god in the form of Quetzalcoatl, feathered snake, symbol of the eternal duality in

man's nature, a duality which he deifies. This method of conquering one's duality is the essence of great creativity. It gives
to what can become insanity a religious cast. Lawrence skirts
insanity.

But before Lawrence can find his god (unity) he must give to
man a soul. In accord with the age he finds the soul in the
unconscious processes. He recognized strongly that he was
permanently maimed—born a divided being, born a corpse! In
Women in Love he visualizes the death and corruption of
life—the real soul life, religious unified life of man. He pits
himself against the world as it is—the world in death—by
transferring to Hermione all the sterile, evil, death-like qualities of the outside world. It is significant that this force, this
antagonistic element in himself, should be represented
through Woman—through a Lesbian type of woman. What the
world suffers from, in other words, is its loss of polarity. Nature
and Spirit—these antagonists preserve the religious element of
man's nature. Break them and you have death, corruption,
sterility. He finally sees the world as soulless.

Woman is always given a dual role, as a force of good or of
evil. According to the state of soul in which man finds himself
the woman question always appears with the soul question.
The animal side of his nature he attributes to woman. His
masculinity he makes the spiritual side. In reality it is this
strong element of femininity which has given him his religious
cast. And we know from Jung on the *anima* that his creative
genius is the result of his abnormal sexuality. If he were sternly
realistic he would recognize the bisexual character of his
makeup. This he refuses to do. It is this conflict, like all the
other conflicts, which nourishes his creativity.

His futile search for a more satisfactory relation with man
than is embraced under the traditional conception of friendship
is based on his desire to give to men the element of femininity
which is so strong in him. This is erroneously regarded as a
homosexual tendency. It is that when acknowledged, but because it is not the goal of this type to resolve his sexual conflict
realistically it becomes therefore the same mystical quest for
relationship with man as all his other quests for relationship—with woman and the universe and god. That is to say the
core of the mystic resides in the recognition of the obscure and
mysterious nature of his personality. The mystic is the oppo-

site to the scientist. Hence the warfare between religion and atheism. The mystic wishes to preserve the obscurities; the other to explain them away. The axis of the mystic is the schism. He glorifies the duality by making it the polarity which gives life significance. Conflict which is his own problem he raises to religious proportions. The psychologist wants to have man face and accept reality. The religious man makes reality obscure and mysterious, hence unconquerable, unknowable.

He does this because the very conflict which gives him life and creativity he wishes to impose upon the world as the true and only reality, the stress being on the fecundating aspects of the conflict, not on the solution. The man of genius is he who does not adapt himself to reality but adapts reality to himself. The function then of the artist is to microcosmize the universe. The two processes, microscomizing and macrocosmizing, go on eternally. The whole aim of culture is to arrest the flux in which life is fundamentally apprehended. The symbols of culture represent the macrocosmizing process. Having laid out the universe, given it a significance, man's tendency is to destroy it again and to recreate it, wherefore the artist represents the dual aspect of creator, he who gives birth and he who destroys. But the important thing is the effort toward a new significance, his own significance.

The value of the artist is that he refuses to find a solution and instead revives the fundamental problems. The passionate infusion of his personality revitalizes the problems and renews our enthusiasm, out taste for struggle, therefore our interest in life.

Therefore when the artist creates his world it is natural that he should take up the empty vessels, the inanimate, exhausted things and by giving them a negative, evil aspect create a conception of the opposite, reviving the necessary antagonism.

And here, it seems to me that in *Aaron's Rod* Lawrence deserves the highest recognition. Here he has been, like Dostoevski (and he resembles him greatly in this because like the latter he is a completely divided being) able to objectify for us the two halves of himself, to oppose them in the most diabolically sincere and truthful manner. Lawrence puts back, in the person of Aaron Sisson, all those elements which Shakespeare had withdrawn from man in the character of Hamlet. Hamlet is the man whose will has become paralyzed by ego. Aaron Sisson is the man who achieves freedom of movement and thought by renouncing his petty, imperious ego. Aaron Sisson, unlike Lawrence, does not hold himself up as an ideal, does not try to alter people or the world. But he will not allow others to alter him! Aaron Sisson proclaims in his own personality the majesty of his unique being. He neither accommodates himself to the world nor asks it to accommodate itself to him.

Such a type is indubitably an ideal, for the world has never seen such a man. This is what Lawrence would like himself to be. And though, in the person of Lilly (as I have said, his other self, his truer self), he seems to point to the possession of something beyond what Aaron holds, in reality he makes his antagonist the heroic force by virtue of his ability to resist the snares and enchantments of the ideal. Aaron is a loyal, steadfast, loving friend, the essence of humanness. Lilly is loyal only to his Holy Ghost, that is, to his conscience. For him friendship, in the ultimate sense, has no significance. What he wants of Aaron is fidelity. He wants him to obey him, trust in his leadership. It is the inhuman principle at work, the remote, detached love of all mankind which refuses to reach out in human sympathy.

In Lawrence, this steady drift away from the human does not end with the mere denial of the value of friendship! When he has finally retreated into that "proud, isolate self," disentangled himself from persons and people, rid his consciousness of the domination of humanity, he is able to turn beyond them, and he goes out with a new sense of wholeness to his dark God, Quetzalcoatl. But his dark God inspires horror too. The woman, Kate, voices this feeling. And so, utterly, devastatingly sincere and consistent, through Cipriano he replies: "Why not? . . . Horror is real. Why not a bit of horror, as you say, among all the rest? . . . Get used to it that there must be a bit of fear, and a bit of horror in your life."

For Lawrence this is a sort of brave echo to his own timidity, for he is the man who, by his great love of man, of life, his great desire to participate and not to be set apart and aloof from others, has had to accept finally the full horror of life also. It is his deep tenderness which made him susceptible to pain, to stupidity, to the apathy and dullness, the morbidity of the life he saw about him. He has had to recognize finally that what he feared he must learn to embrace, and he embraces it in the figure of Quetzalcoatl who personifies all the cruelty, horror and terror of life. Quetzalcoatl demands human sacrifices. He swims in the blood of the slain. And Lawrence, who had been so horrified, so maimed by the cruel reality of the war—"this thing must not be, it was foul, as long as I am a man it shall not be, it shall not!"—this Lawrence finally comes to embrace the very incarnation of cruelty in his dark God. He sees that his fundamental human self is rooted in this cruelty, this eternal killing and sacrifice. The ideals which he had inherited had blinded him for a while to his real animal nature; they had tried to assert the supremacy of the one nature over the other. Now, in the bird-serpent, he restores this cruel element to its natural place in the human being. He not only restores it and justifies it, he raises it to supreme importance by deifying. It is again his idealistic nature at work, that driving quest for the Absolute which never lets him be.

Here, moreover, like Freud, who opened up the Unconscious in order to liberate man's suppressed animal nature, Lawrence has plumbed his deepest being in order to seek his own salvation. His whole dark world and his dark God are the dramatic and artistic expressions of the libido and the Unconscious to which Freud and his followers have introduced us. But whereas the psychologists have sought in their theories to find a panacea for human ills, if not a remedy by the eradication of suffering at least a remedy by the *explanation* of their origins, trusting to the belief that when we know the cause of a thing and can name it we shall be cured of our suffering, Lawrence, on the other hand, refuses to name, refuses to explain, refuses the grace of salvation by either sublimation or abandonment of responsibility.

Lawrence, instead of avoiding the religious issue, accepts it unqualifiedly. He seeks to reestablish the sacred character of life, to re-enthrone God, to make God the only issue. All that is important to him in surveying human activity is the question: how much of God is there in it? He detests the psychologists' explanations because they would rid man of the God-element. The trauma of birth, the shocks of infantile experience—instead of regarding these as morbid symptoms which explain the religious interpretations of human behavior and thereby nullify the God-element—instead of this he beseeches man to abandon himself to his fate, to assert his power over fate in his abandonment to it. Out of the fight with the octopus of life, the dragon of degenerate or incomplete existence, one must win this soft bloom of living. This is the living quality in Lawrence, this is the instinct which enabled him to create his world. When he admires the life-wisdom of the Egyptians and the Etruscans and the Greeks he is admiring the creative spirit in them which, while permitting them to accept the horror and cruelty of life, also gave them the power to struggle against, to combat their fate. The struggle is the creative thing in life. Immortality is a question of character. Immortality, he would say, is a by-product of the struggle, not the thing to be sought in itself. The fear of death which brings about a fear of life is overcome by the surrender to one's fate, but it is not a supine, fatalistic acquiescence, it is rather the complete fulfillment and obedience to one's instincts no matter where they lead.

Lawrence has no fear of where they will lead—even if that place be called destruction. The real fear, the real horror, he discovers, is in the frozen immortality of a life dedicated to ideals, a life that seeks to be protected by its ideals, the life of the tortoise whose blood is congealed, the life of the civilized man whose inner, sacred core is so hedged in and protected by the crusts of dead ideals that he cannot feel, cannot respond to the currents of life. That is why, in "The Crown," he can say "Whatever single act is performed by any man now, in this condition, is an act of reduction, disintegration." He means by "act" the expression of a being asserting his will, his instincts. He means further, that the deep, unconscious wish of the individual today is to die. *He must discover a means of dying.* By rediscovering his animal nature, by giving expression once again to his primal instincts, he will destroy the old being that was hidden away under the carapace of ideals. He must not go on in this hideous biological immortality. He must learn to die in his corruption in order to be reborn, to enjoy a new spirit and a new body and a new life!

This teaching of obedience to the deepest instincts is profoundly solipsistic. Writing to the Luhan woman, he says: "I believe in actual, sacred, inspired authority: divine right of natural kings: I believe in the divine right of natural aristocracy, the right, the sacred duty to wield undisputed authority. Naturally I find myself in diametric opposition to every American—and everybody else, besides Americans—whom I come across. Nevertheless, there it stands." D. H. Lawrence, Inc. He is so damned sincere and serious that he never sees how ridiculous these assertions sound. "To wield undisputed authority"! And the poor bugger can't even make his own wife obey him, except by bully-ragging her, threatening her, grumbling, whining, and making her absolutely miserable. (Please remember the important distinction here, when I attack the man, between the validity of his ideas, in their accuracy and value, and his own inadequacy to absorb and live out his own philosophy.)

No, Frieda, the woman, rightly resented "this superiority and death" stuff, as she calls it. Since he could never make her feel, never convinced her by his own attitude towards her, of this power which he wanted men to wield. There was the rub! Frieda was the bitter stone of reality, whatever her limitations may have been. And that is why these Saviors never have wives! (Murry is quite right here. To play the Savior one must be a eunuch! One must marry God, the Spirit, etc., because the wives give the Saviors away, expose their vital, inner weakness, their divided self, their bisexual nature.) Frieda really broke his back. By returning in the end (as the "Escaped Cock") to a resurrection in the flesh, in order to live out a man's full life, sexually perfect and otherwise, Lawrence pays his tribute unconsciously and unwittingly to the Frieda whom he denied in life. It is not to criticize him I say this, but to point out the limitations of the type, the Savior type.

And there is always this oscillation between the sublime, heroic figure and the Chaplin. When society chooses to recognize him as an enemy and to fight him he is capable of being truly heroic. But society seldom pays any attention to him— they don't know what it is he is fighting against. In this manner the Age, by its inability to recognize a worthy antagonist in its midst, reduces a man like Lawrence in actual life to a pathetic, ridiculous figure who appears to be tilting at windmills. The age degrades him—it is not that it refuses the gage of combat, but it does not even see a *cause* for combat in Lawrence. This is the irony of the artist's fight, his sad fight to impose his reality on the world. It comes out more especially in his opposition to Woman. Woman is the stubborn workaday reality against which he continually stubs his toe. And his wife, Frieda, is the personification of this everyday reality. She is always against his ideology, against his books, against his attitudes and behavior. She finds it ridiculous, exaggerated, monomaniacal.

Consequently, it seems significant to me that although, with all the power that was in him, Lawrence strove to put woman back in her rightful place—a most un-modern view!—it is the women who are coming forward to champion him. Even the fatuous Luhan woman who, in giving us a portrait of Lawrence has succeeded in giving us an even more vivid portrait of herself, and a most abominable one, even this spiritual fraud, I say, divined what Lawrence was aiming at: "He was the Son—the second person of the Trinity—but (God help all women!) though we tried to overcome and possess him, yet secretly we always wanted him to be the Father! ... Everything conspired against him. The women who loved him seemed to be impelled to hold him back, even while they themselves most greatly needed his attainment." And when she forgets herself and is annoyed by his masculine obstinacy she says: "He was entombed in his recalcitrant body."

But at any rate, they loved him, these women—they adored him and worshipped him. And they adored him and worshipped him not just because he inspired them with his great purposive faith or because he went beyond them into his own dark futurity, they prostrated themselves before him also, perhaps primarily, because he revealed them to themselves in their nakedness. The masculine world, on the other hand, deeply and shamefully feminized, is more inclined to distrust and despise Lawrence's ideas. The masculine world, lulled to quiescence in the scorpion's nest, prefers the most fantastic cures to the simple, naked, horrible truth with which Lawrence confronts it.

Why is the Oedipal so dominant in Lawrence's work—and not only in Lawrence but in so many men of genius, noticeably the moderns? Because it is the central theme in the artist's conflict with life, the root-pattern of his struggle to emancipate himself, to raise himself to fatherhood—that is, to restore the great religious motive of life.

In rejecting his father, Lawrence rejected his own manhood, his human limitations and human responsibilities. He became a victim of his mother's love through the pursuit of the ideal, and the failure and the horror of this, when he realizes it, towards the end of *Sons and Lovers*, causes him to revolt, and to turn in hate upon woman, upon the mother image especially. When free of her tyranny, when he found his dark gods (in his father's image), he found himself—the Kingdom of Heaven within. Henceforth he worships what he was uniquely, not what he shares in common with others, their false ideals. This search for God and fatherhood is only the expression of the search for one's true self, one's own value, one's final and complete authority, whereby one owes allegiance to none. This is the meaning of "going beyond the woman." Because as son and lover he is bound to the woman. They are roads to death through sex. The other is death through the spirit—recognition of the blind, driving force of will in man which would lead him to more perilous and more illusory ends.

The woman, says Lawrence, has not the courage to give up her hopeless insistence on love and her endless demand for love, demand of being loved. She has not the greatness of soul to relinquish her own self-assertion, and believe in the man who believes in himself and in his own soul's efforts—if there *are* any such men nowadays, which is very doubtful.

Lawrence was one of such men, a possessor of that contagious, magic nature, that masculine-spiritual force (symbol of creativity) which has always attracted women (so powerfully), to the figure of Christ, despite Christ's obvious sexlessness. They feel, no doubt, that the sexuality is there, but converted (or sublimated) to higher powers. The Savior's attitude towards women—that is, one of indifference to their sex—permits the florescence in woman of her own "masculine-spiritual" element, which every age of sexuality (the antique world especially, India also) has stamped out. In other words, the deepest desire of woman is to have the man make her aware of his superiority of vision and purpose. She knows also that the recognition and insistence upon the mere "biological" forces in her will lead to death, the extinction of race and culture. She herself is incapable of assuming this cultural role. She can only nourish it. The tragedy of the "Antique" collapse was the surrender to the female element, that is to the "biological" principle.

At the same time what Lawrence means to say, if I understand him rightly, is that man, in fulfilling his biologic function through sex, does not establish a sufficient importance for woman. Though the biologic function is what she demands of him, through the rigorous laws of her being, in reality she, as well as he, needs the illusion of a greater purpose. The building of a masculine world—all that is implied by the word *Culture*—is a necessity *imposed on the man by the woman* in order to sustain an illusion. Deep down woman feels a large indifference toward man; she tolerates him in order that she may enjoy a larger life herself. At bottom he is almost unnecessary. She created him, did she not? At least, that is the myth which man-made science has handed down. If we read into the myth of the evolution of sex its deepest import then we can understand woman's role, her activity, her ceaseless war and depredation—*and we can stand it!* The eternal battle with woman sharpens our resistance, develops our strength, enlarges the scope of our cultural achievements: through her and for her we build our grandiose structures, our illusions, our myths, our legends, religions, philosophies.

But when this polarity breaks down, as it has today, when instead of a true blood-polarity as the basis of sexual union we have "companions," "Women who think like us," then beware! Lawrence's abuse, if you notice, goes out equally to the man and the woman. He is not a misogynist. Nor is he a misanthropist. "This was the world of the monks, the rim of pallor between night and day"—that is what he railed against and fought against with tooth and nail. The sickly, ideal love-world of depolarized sex! The world based upon a fusion of the sexes, instead of upon antagonism. Right he was in saying: "not for a second do they [our mothers] allow us to escape from their ideal benevolence. . . . Always the *will*, the will, the love-will, the ideal will, directed from the ideal mind. Always this stone, this scorpion of maternal nourishment."

It is that great Christian ideal of love, that spiritual perversion which has triumphed over the animal nature of man, that has ushered in the bodily disintegration now so painfully visible. We have made woman our equal and now we are indoctrinated with her ideas, our whole idealistic corpus of thought is saturated with the female principle. The perversion of the great maternal instinct in woman, the one fundamental and eternal alliance between the sexes, has resulted in woman's expressing her deeper, inimical, all-sufficient role of creator. Man's inability to throw off the yoke of swaddling clothes and apron-string has brought about an open scorn and contempt upon the part of woman, a genuine usurpation of his role in life. The great leaders of today, before making a decisive move, must first consult their wives or their mistresses. An artist, like Proust, must wait until his mother dies before he can set about the great task of his life. Joyce drags us through the dreariest pages to attack an outworn institution like the Catholic church, which is really his mother. The mother stands for church and wife and spiritual love. The result, in the case of Proust, is his love for an invert; in the case of Joyce it is the glorification of the eternal whore in woman. In the case of Lawrence it is the search for a mythical man who is not a pervert. The Oedipal! The root-malady, the pain, the torture, the horror from which springs their art.

*   *   *

"I don't want my Fate or Providence to treat me well. I am essentially a fighter." It was towards the end of his life that Lawrence wrote this, but at the very threshold of his career he was already saying: "We have to hate our immediate predecessors to get free of their authority."

The men to whom he owed everything, the great spirits on whom he fed and nourished himself, whom he had to reject in order to assert his own power, his own vision, were they not like himself men who went to the source? Were they not all animated by that same idea which Lawrence voiced over and over again—that the sun itself will never become sterile, nor the earth barren? Were they not, all of them, in their search for God, for that clue which is missing inside men, victims of the Holy Ghost?

Who *were* his predecessors? To *whom*, time and again, before ridiculing and exposing them, did he acknowledge his indebtedness? Jesus certainly, and Nietzsche, and Whitman and Dostoevski. All the poets of life, the mystics, who in denouncing civilization contributed most heavily to the lie of civilization.

For Lawrence was an intellectual savage. I do not label him so pejoratively, as is customary today when a true anarchist appears in our midst. Only the most forward spirits, only those who have pushed the life force to fullest flower, only those who are supremely *aware* are capable of realizing the immediacy of past and future. "You've got to know, and know everything," said Lawrence in criticizing Dostoevski, "before you 'transcend' into the 'unknown'."

Lawrence was tremendously influenced by Dostoevski. Of all his forerunners, Christ included, it was Dostoevski whom he had most difficulty in shaking off, in surpassing, in "transcending." Lawrence had always looked upon the sun as the source of life, and the moon as the symbol of non-being. Life and death— like a mariner he kept before him constantly these two poles. "He who gets nearer the sun," he said, "is leader, the aristocrat of aristocrats. Or he who, like Dostoevski, gets nearest the moon of our not-being." With the in-betweens he had no concern.

He saw man as a seasonal phenomenon, a moon that waxes and wanes, a seed that emerges out of primal darkness to return again therein. Life, brief, transitory, eternally fixed between the two poles of being and non-being. Without the clue, without the revelation, no life, but being sacrified to existence. Immortality he interpreted as this futile wish for endless existence. To him this living death was the Purgatory in which man ceaselessly struggles. Speaking of Melville he said: "He was born for Purgatory. Some souls are purgatorial by destiny." This Purgatory he regarded as the twilight of the womb which the white man hungers for eternally and out of which he erects his "ideal" philosophy, his heaven and hell, his salvation and hereafter, his treadmill of guilt and punishment.

What Lawrence detected in Dostoevski, in *all* his predecessors, I might say, though in Dostoevski supremely, was man's attempt to forestall the death process. To transcend death it is first necessary to relinquish the notion of a personal, immortal ego. But this, he felt, was impossible as long as men clung to an abosolute God. The clue which he felt was missing in men and which, among other things, he called the Holy Ghost, was the non-human, cosmic view of life. He regarded the lives of men about him as wasted in a sort of eternal twilight of the womb, their energies frustrated in a vain struggle to break the walls that shut them in. This everlasting struggle, this conflict with the self which Dostoevski apotheosized, Lawrence characterized as a disintegrative process, a struggle of the mind which ends only in the complete disintegration of the personality, the worship of the mind as a thing in itself, as end and aim. And yet he realized that in this struggle to approach the moon of our

non-being, as he called it, Dostoevski had brought to an end a
great epoch of the human mind. As a sun-worshipper, however,
Lawrence could not but regard this struggle as obscene, as
perverse and death-loving. "Why pin ourselves down on a
paradisal ideal?" he said. "It is only ourselves we torture." One
must go on! Gauguin, Melville, Whitman, Dostoevski, Jesus,
great or little flames, he saw them as renegades. One cannot go
back, he insisted. "It is one's destiny inside one." The renegade
hates life itself. He wants the death of life.

It has always seemed strange to me how quickly and readily
(whenever China is brought up) the white peoples grasp this
phenomenon of automatic living death, which Lawrence
speaks about so eloquently. When China is mentioned at once
everything becomes clear. When you press a white man hard
enough, when at last he admits the superiority of Chinese
thought, of Chinese art, of Chinese culture, still, even then, his
last words are bound to be—"but the Chinese are *dead!*"
"*Whereas . . . .*"he would like to add—but we know what it is
he would like to add.

For us China will always be that imaginary realm of non-
being which we have miraculously escaped. We make this
imaginative hurdle, no doubt, because in very truth China,
everything Chinese, is the extreme opposite of all that we feel,
think, do, believe. Life *there* might just as well be a lunar life, so
far as we are concerned. China, I repeat, seems indeed the
antithesis of all that we regard the human world to be.

There are two Chinas always: the real one, which we make
no effort to comprehend or come to grips with, *and* the imaginary one which we conveniently set up as a straw image in
order, by overthrowing it, that we may flatter our own petty
vanity. Somewhere between these false absolutes China has its
real being. Somewhere there is the *eternal* China whose image
we see through our distorted lens as an immortal cadaver
sprouting new hair and nails.

Strange as it may seem today to say, the aim of life is to live,
and to live means to be aware, joyously, drunkenly, serenely,
divinely *aware*. In this state of god-like awareness one sings; in
this realm the world exists as poem. No why or wherefore, no
direction, no goal, no striving, no evolving. Like the enigmatic
Chinese, one is rapt by the ever-changing spectacle of passing
phenomena. This is the sublime, the amoral state of the artist,

he who lives only in the moment, the visionary moment of utter, far-seeing lucidity. Such clear, icy sanity that it seems like madness. By the force and power of the artist's vision the static, synthetic whole which is called the world is destroyed. The artist gives back to us a vital, singing universe, alive in all its parts.

In his individual works—and this is more particularly true of the Dionysian type—the artist seems fragmented. But each individual work is a complete representation of his momentary wholeness. He lives and dies in each work. His works are a succession of births and deaths, a spiritual progression, a quickening that mocks the slow, torpid life-death, or death-life, of the mass about. Through his inexhaustible roles he records the changeless ego, through the poem the eternal *how* of things. He is like the *ouroboros*, the snake that swallows its own tail. He consumes himself, and in devouring himself he completes the picture of the world. He is the circle without beginning or end. His is a constant, ceaseless hunger, a desire for union, for oneness, for completion.

This is the only spiritual dynamic he recognizes. To put it another way, his goal is to rival the dung-beetle which evacuates in the same measure and the same rhythm as it devours. He eats his way into the ball of dung, which is life, in perfect bliss. The whole organism sings of digestion—a state of "adjustment" beyond any described by the psychologists. The misery which we create for ourselves appears to him to result solely from an inability to unload the food which we have ingested. We have indigestion, and we build up a picture of the world-as-disease: this is the spiritual picture of the world. The genuine and very real belly-ache meanwhile is subtly modulated into a language of imaginary pains and aches for which there is no remedy except death. What is not fully experienced—that is, ingested and excreted—passes off into the poison of knowledge. To "know oneself" becomes the all-important: a false and endless pursuit, a tail-chasing.

For the artist there is nothing but the present, the eternal here and now, the expanding infinite moment which is flame and song. And when he succeeds in establishing this criterion of passionate experience (which is what Lawrence meant by obeying the Holy Ghost) then, and only then, is he asserting his humanness. Then only does he live out his pattern as MAN.

Obedient to every urge—without distinction of morality, ethics, laws, custom. He lays himself open to all influences— everything nourishes him. Everything is gravy to him, includ- ing what he does not understand—*particularly* what he does not understand. He lives it out in the dung-beetle's world, in the incomprehensible world of China, the final reality.

This final reality which the artist comes to recognize in his maturity, this China which the psychologists situate some- where between the conscious and the unconsciuos, is that symbolic paradise of the womb, that pre-natal security and immortality and union with nature from which he must wrest his freedom. Each time he is spiritually born he dreams of the impossible, the miraculous; he dreams he can break the wheel of life and death, avoid the struggle and the drama, the pain and the suffering of life. His poem is the legend wherein he buries himself, wherein he relates of the mysteries of birth and death—*his* reality, *his* experience. He buries himself in his tomb of poem in order to achieve that immortality which is denied him as a physical being.

China is a projection into the spiritual domain of this biologic condition of non-being. To be is to have mortal shape, mortal conditions, to struggle, to evolve. Paradise is, like the dream of the Buddhists, a Nirvana where there is no more personality and hence no conflict. It is the expression of man's wish to triumph over reality, over becoming. The artist's dream of the impossible, the miraculous, is simply the resul- tant of his inability to adapt himself to reality. He creates, therefore, a reality of his own—in the poem—a reality which is suitable to him, a reality in which he can live out his uncon- scious desires, wishes, dreams. The poem is the dream made flesh, in a two-fold sense: as work of art, and as life itself, which is a work of art. When man becomes fully conscious of his powers, his role, his destiny, he is an artist and he ceases his struggle with reality. *He becomes a traitor to the human race.* He creates war because he has become permanently out of step with the rest of humanity. He sits on the doorstep of his mother's womb with his race memories and his incestuous longings and he refuses to budge. He lives out his dream of Paradise. He transmutes his real experience of life into spiritual equations. He scorns the ordinary alphabet which yields at most only a grammer of thought, and adopts the symbol, the metaphor, the ideograph. *He writes Chinese.* He creates an impossible world out of an incomprehensible language, a lie that enchants and enslaves men. It is not that he is incapable of living. On the contrary, his zest for life is so powerful, so voracious, that it forces him to kill himself over and over. He dies many times in order to live innumerable lives. In this way he wreaks his revenge upon life and works his power over men. He creates the legend of himself, the lie wherein he established himself as hero and god, the lie wherein he triumphs over life.

* * *

Yes, Lawrence was treacherous at the core because he knew no loyalty except to his inner flame. He is forever telling others (Murry especially), "Don't think you are doing something for me. I don't want that. Move for yourself alone. Decide for yourself, in your backbone. I don't want any pact. I won't have anything of that sort." Human beings are usually faithful to ideals, not to one another. Lawrence despises the ideal and ideas about the ideal. He will have no sovereignty but his own livingness. This, alas, is a curse—as well as a great virtue. He is enraged by the tolerance, the indifference of the men about him. They have no passion, no fixed sense of values. They exploit their ideals for selfish, personal desires which they mask to themselves. Man, says Lawrence, unlike other beasts, is false to his pattern, to himself. He does not obey his human instincts—he betrays them, degrades them. This means that the live human personality must be treacherous to humanity, and faithful only to the man in himself. Man is always above, always greater than the abstract, collective society, than this abstract collective wraith called the man in the street, a statistical figure which adds up to zero, which is intangible and non-existent. There is no humanity: there are only men. Man's sole problem is God, not humanity, not society, not solidarity, not anything else.

The God problem! Whether one's aspirations are towards the angels or the worms, whether to fly in dizzy orbits around the Glory seat of Self, or to batten on the Culture Corpse forever.

Art will undoubtedly disappear with this new type who is to succeed our Homo Sapiens, or Post-man of 25,000 years standing. The rise and fall of our great Cultures (marking our meager history of 1,000 years) is the record of western man's failure and repeated efforts to rise into a new cycle of being. That history lies recorded in the *History of Art;* our history is nothing but that, the History of Art, of changing soul concepts, from the body ornament of primitive man to the psychologism of today. This next era, as Lawrence says, will be the era of the Holy Ghost. We have been striving repeatedly to break through the shell, to be born, to sever the umbilical cord of history whereby we pay our acknowledgement to the animal kingdom from which we emerged. It is this thralldom of Fear (represented by all our totems and taboos which lie beneath the lying ideological mask of culture) which we are struggling to free ourselves from. Soul/God/Immortality. A vicious circle in which we are caught. The discovery of the Self means the elimination of this crystallized fear. Rank tells us that Art conserves the irrational phenomena of Fear. But the creative personality will get beyond this and destroy art itself.

The Dionysian type which Lawrence was makes its appearance only when the genetic (world as history) philosophy appears, announcing to us the end of a culture. It is at this point that the artist's vision (arising as Anti-Fate, out of a frenzy of despair, out of a sharp sense of death, out of the deepest realization of "Form & Symbol," out of the highest individual truth) appears as counter-active and combative, challenger to the picture of destiny given by the decapitated head of the thinkers. The artist voices once again what the few rare spirits have always voiced: the possibility of the miracle, i.e. of the "new" man, the *real* human type who will put an end to the culture cycle of history.

He can do so because he is himself the very symbol and incarnation of the tree of MAN, the tree of life and death. He restores to death its high meaning: "Death is neither here nor there. Death is a temporal, relative fact." Otherwise were the continuity lost; death would lose its meaning. This is the highest spiritual truth; and it is fecundating because life and death appear as insoluble, mysterious phenomena of the same tree, the *individual.* By anchoring himself thus in the very heart of mystery and accepting it, he nourishes both impulses—of life *and* of death—because both are imperative, and to try to conquer over one at the expense of the other (which is what religion, spirituality does with its emphasis on "Immortality") is destruction of the miracle of the tree of life, or man himself. That is why Lawrence talks of "resurrection." That is what he means when he tells us that the souls of the dead persist and inhabit the living. That is his "mysticism."

The apparent contradictions in Lawrence's utterances on this subject can be resolved only by what the woman, Luhan, calls his treacherous core, what Lawrence called being true to and obeying his Holy Ghost. He speaks of this as a sacred pact, a loyalty to death with his fellow man. In *Aaron's Rod* he says, "I will not have a friend who is not one with me in matters of life and death," and we know that he did not have such a relationship. All this reechoes in the perplexity which has always hung about Christ's words: "I come with a sword, not peace, father against son, brother against sister." This means very obviously that there is a loyalty beyond the tribal, the family, the blood, the country, the loyalty of a man to his own soul's self, to his own true being. And since this loyalty is impossible to fix or stabilize, it sows constantly war. It is based on progression of being, movement, the very flux of life, on character, which is destiny. Yet without any contradiction there remains the possibility of a steadfast loyal friendship (not the homosexual, but very close to it—anterior to it, as it were). That is the unspoken loyalty of free spirits, of true anarchs who realize that growth is possible without mutual envy, rivalry, hatred. On this plane, the surface differences are only nourishment one for the other. It is a free give and take, but it requires a fundamental accord based on the same realization of the nature of the self. Such men sow discord only among the dull, feeble spirits stuck in the morass of unchanging symbol-worship. For them the presence of the "free spirit," the anarch, the outlaw—i.e. the creative type—is in itself a dissonant note. They want the way made smooth, understandable, whereas the anarch attempts to show them that it is only through constant change and conflict and pain that one can make a way, the real middle way!

Naturally Lawrence, who stood for such an idea, who made war on the forms and symbols of culture, could not find such a friend. Such men are too rare in the world. But they are possible and they do reappear from time to time. These precursors are the hope repeatedly voiced that a new type of man will appear. And once again that would spell the very death of Art, the coming of such a type. Then truly Art would have no *raison d'être*, no tyranny and no enslavement, walking perpetually in the mystery. There would be no need of manifestations, of the concretizing of abstract ideas of the soul. Each man would be the embodiment of the mystery. Life would assume its sacred character.

There is another thought, hinted at above, that one of the reasons for the failure to find friends and have right relations between man and man is that our present understanding is that what the friends seek in each other is the idealized self, the missing complement to one's own nature. This is, in a sense, based on the divided beings which most men are, and that is why it is idealistic and romantic and wistful (when at its purest, for example, as in the case of David and Jonathan, or of Tennyson and Hallam). In the artist, who is the personification of this dividedness, we see consequently how his friendship is always perfidious and treacherous, how it alternates and oscillates from the most lavish generosity, devotion and self-sacrifice to the other extreme of hate, denunciation, etc. (Nietzsche and Wagner, for instance). In these instances we are made to realize that what the artist really cherishes in his friend is the ideal image of himself in the narcissistic pattern of the split personality, the schizoid type. Such is Proust's behavior, clear because he is also an invert. In *Aaron's Rod* Lawrence goes, as we have seen, in true artist fashion, beyond the crude Murry-Lawrence affair, which he sensed early on was impossible to a probing of the very roots of the problem. He confronted the two halves of his own being, these two "friends" who remain eternally dissonant. In determining for himself, as best he then could, the insolubility of this problem (note that Proust ended here by declaring that we could never understand each other, and therefore never be friends in any real sense), Lawrence saw that his next step was to be a "leader" of men—that is, he would have to show them how to live, how to change their being, in order for friendship to be possible. And now Murry, once again inspired by Lawrence's vision (he considers *Aaron's Rod* the best of all, the most revelatory of the real Lawrence, naturally), Murry tries to act the disciple, the humble follower. But Lawrence knows that Murry will never understand his wisdom, and so he puts him off: "Let's wipe off all that Judas-Jesus slime!"

And finally, in another letter, the last letter to Murry, he says it magnificently:

If I am the only man in your life, it is not because I am I, but merely because I provided the speck of dust on which you formed your crystal of an imaginary man. We don't know one another—if you knew how little we know one another! And let's not pretend. By pretending a bit, we had some jolly times, in the past. But we all had to pretend a bit—and we could none of us keep it up. Believe me, we belong to different worlds, different ways of consciousness, you and I, and the best we can do is let one another alone, for ever and ever. We are a dissonance . . . .

So don't think of coming to Mallorca. It is no good our meeting—even when we are immortal spirits, we shall dwell in different Hades. Why not accept it.

He has reached his peak of wisdom. He has realized his true nature. He is *beyond* our conception of friendship. His friends—he is one in resurrection with them—are only the great spirits, past and future.

CHAPTER V

Destiny

I was the God and the creation at once;
creator, I looked at my creation;
created, I looked at myself, the creator:
it was a maniacal horror in the end.

L AWRENCE'S POEMS reveal his mysticism better than
anything else he wrote, and passages like this from
"New Heaven and Earth" demonstrate how solipsistic, how
Lawrence-centered, that mysticism was:

I was so weary of the world,
I was so sick of it,
everything was tainted with myself....

When Anaïs Nin discusses these passages she tells us something very significant about Lawrence as creative type: "Living
that everyday life, letting his mind associate and merge with
the world's mind and its activities, he realizes that he had
become an inseparable fragment of that world. So long as he
should identify himself with that world he was responsible for
it; all was in him, and he in all. He was its creator until he
should create something new."

Lawrence knew that Culture is always an affair of the masses, the collectivity. You might say it represents the divine
droppings of those birds of passage who by their flight give
tension and significance to the horizontal cyclical orbit which
is organic, biologic life. Culture then is always compounded of
the "dying ecstasies" of the creative type who contributes to
Culture only by his dying, not by his living. (That is why
Lawrence can characterize humanity as death-eaters, corpse
eaters, engaged in a sort of spiritual cannibalism.)

Life is the process of Becoming, the time-destiny movement
on the flat, as it were, a straight-line continuum or an orbit—it

amounts to the same thing. The creative type, though also a victim of this law of nature, proves by his living the impossibility, the illogicality of life. His living is the anti-Fate movement which transcends the dead biological movement of birth and becoming. By his divination of *Being* he breaks the time-continuum. The repetitious cyclical law still operates but, after his appearance, it operates on another place. He provides the axis of a new life.

And although he alters life itself in so doing, he also reveals his obedience to the life principle. He reveals this important fact as well that obedience to the life principle can be had or nourished only by flying away from it, by plunging into the abyss, with eyes closed, in the hope of the miracle.

The individual artist type is the creative type *par excellence.* He exists in a void, as it were, without support of collective ideology. His relation with and to the world is chiefly, supremely indeed, one of man to idea. He is a law unto himself. His function, or purpose, is to recreate an ideology for the world which is to come after him. He has no more connection with the existent ideology than he has with the folkways. It is his sworn and eternal opposition to mores *and* ideology which breathes life into the inchoate forms to come. He is the symbol of war itself: he clears the air of poisons, of miasma, of lying delusions. It is by his stubborn opposition to everything that exists that man is enabled to glimpse again the naked, visionary reality of the artist and thus destroy the cloying forms which prevent the healthy growth of the coming shoots of life. It is by his stubborn, fanatical opposition to the collective impulse that life is rescued from the biologic quagmire, the fungus of living death which a purely collective life signifies.

In order for new forms to arise, for a new Culture to have inception, the artist must now go mad, must become hallucinatory. He must become again a mantic personality. He can not and does not want to stay the death of the old forms, or even put new life into them. He does not strive to oppose destiny—the time spirit—because he is himself the incarnation of living movement.

It is here that the enigmatic role of Lawrence comes to resolution. Man of destiny? Anti-Fate? From the Spenglerian view, based on the study of the collective individual and the forms about which his world revolves, Lawrence is Anti-Fate.

But this is only the surface aspect. For the creative spirit, even when preaching death, expresses itself enthusiastically, with faith, with life hope. His pessimism is but a more profound, an invisible optimism. It is the obverse of the lying, current optimism which is based on fear—fear of death, fear of life—on a turning away from that reality which stares one in the face.

In another sense Lawrence *is* one with destiny, in that he speeds the end by his death-dealing powers. It is here that the mysterious dual aspect of the creator manifests itself strikingly. Like Siva the Destroyer—a bisexual god—he now reveals the feminine side of his nature by conserving the life instincts, while at the same time asserting the full force of his masculinity in the destruction of the existent forms.

This brings us back to the very roots of the problem—the conflicting bisexual character of this peculiar type of man who plays the role of Savior. We see in him a truly symbolic figure in whom all the manifestations of a world problem are rooted and expressed. The grand problems which had been analyzed away, scattered, diffused, made unintelligible, are reunited in him, the individual who symbolizes the whole world problem. As in one of those Peruvian skulls which one sees in the museum, the macrocosm is reduced again to tangible, comprehensible human proportions, to a size that will fit once again into the womb from which it sprang.

The artists of the future, of whom Lawrence is a forerunner, a primitive like Giotto, is a type who will work away at the joints of the new forms. They will appear and disappear in brief flashes of creativity. They will be stamped out quickly, because their creative value will pass unsuspected. They will be working underground, as it were, among the chthonian forces, in the unconscious strata of life, where the old archaic forms are buried, disintegrated, and forgotten. To those who remember only the old forms they will appear mad. No communication will be possible. And it is just here, on this dark strand of non-communication, that the hope for the future lies. Now is not the time to expect of the mass a faith which they are incapable of summoning. It is too soon. What is done underground, in quiet and mystery, will be seized only by the few rare spirits, the little flame of life preciously guarded and handed on from one creative spirit to another. A religious task. Hermeneutic, in the highest sense. Not for the profane eye, their task. It is in the dark underworld that the mysteries will be exhumed again. Here lie the secret forces of resurrection. Here among the dark gods of death who hold the power, the mystery, the revelation.

These "nascent" forms, with their first rude articulations, will be forged in the chaos and obscurity of the artist's own soul, in the very womb of the race. Here all that has been denied him as a livng being, the repressions out of which were created the cultural symbols of the past, will be exhumed again. His complete divorce from the common, outer, everyday, profane, vulgar reality of the mass is his salvation and the salvation of art.

Before these nascent forms can gain strength enough to assert their vitality, to go forward in their destined cycle of growth and decay, there will need to be a holocaust of individual deaths. It is these deaths, these individual deaths, which will provide the loam, the top-soil, for the ideological flowering of the future. A long process, a Dark Age. On the surface it will seem that art is dead. On the surface it will appear as though the biologic forces of the collectivity had truly triumphed, that life indeed were nothing but a paradise of work and reproduction. But that will be only the night in which life itself lies fallow, only life expressing itself through nature.

Gradually through the long night the soul will slowly gather itself together and the many will re-experience the miracle of oneness. That faith which will again arise in the mass will be the reflection of the faith which Lawrence stressed so vitally: faith in one's self! The individual's faith in himself when all outer faith is lacking. Like a spark there will come one day a fusion of these two faiths. That will be the moment when the mass recognizes and deifies again a great individual, one who is ready to gather up and take unto himself that inchoate faith with which the great world of men and women is overbrimming.

In the interim the artist must actually play the god. He must be God Almighty to himself. He must give *himself* and not just a work of art. He must put his whole self into his work so that he may, both figuratively and literally, be devoured. Each killing, each creative death, for the succeeding ages to come, will be like vital nourishment for the exhausted soil. It is the old drama of Dionysus and the mysteries, but it is played on a different level. In other words, the macrocosogony has reached its limit, the universe has been stretched to unreality. For in the act of withdrawing from the cosmos, of separating and personalizing ourselves, we have exhausted the meaning of macrocosm. It is empty. The opposite process now takes place. The cosmos must be shrunk, must be deflated, the bones removed, the skull boiled down. (It is not just this deflation of the macrocosm which has already occured and which produces in us the sensation of utter collapse?)

The world must be humanized again. We must draw it closer and closer to us, devour it again, so that we may live, as microcosm. We must "atone" for the sin of alienation. We must get rid of our feeling of guilt and become again *religious*. For we have put the god which is the cosmos outside the cosmos. And finally the god too has disappeared and there is left only our tiny, miserable, dissatisfied selves, the empty symbols of . . . of what? of nothingness. What Lawrence meant, therefore, when he used the expression "religious and godless" was the very real, vital consuming of the god-in-the-cosmos. Devouring God. Devouring that life which we have denied ourselves, which we have put outside ourselves, in a false heaven, a false hereafter. *Live now in the flesh! Follow out every desire!* Give play to the deepest instincts, to the deepest hunger for the living spirit. That is our hunger. For the flame of life. For life with meaning. To consume the cosmos is to give meaning to life—*by giving back life to God.* Only thus has "being" meaning. Stop the striving, the becoming. Take root and devour. Obey the deep, animal nature. Because the "spiritual" is exhausted. It has no meaning any longer. It was right for Christ to stress the spiritual side of life; but for us who have lived through the life of mind and spirit, there are left only the dark animal forces of life. We must put on flesh again: we are all mind and spirit now, ghosts of our real selves. How be crucified if there be no living body to nail up? How does one crucify a ghost?

* * *

Just as the individual, when he arrives at maturity, evinces his maturity by the acceptance of responsibility, so the artist, when he recognizes his real nature, *his destined role*, is obliged to accept the responsibility of leadership. He has invested himself with power and authority, and he must act accordingly. He can tolerate nothing but the dictates of his own conscience. Thus, in accepting his destiny, he accepts the responsibility of fathering his ideas. And just as the problems which each individual encounters are unique for him, and must be lived out, so the ideas which germinate in the artist are unique and must be lived out. He is obliged, therefore, to rule with tyrannical force. There is no ultimate distinction here between king, hero, saint, artist. The great human mass must be exploited in order to satisfy the sense of power rooted in the artistic instinct. The king works directly upon his human material; the saint works indirectly, through religious symbols. The artist works upon the human mass more subtly than any because he comprises in his nature all the primordial elements of which these archetypes are formed. At bottom he is the most tyrannical of all the creative types. He has absolutely no concern with humanity except to work his will upon it, to exploit it creatively. And this, indeed, is the explanation of the simultaneous or the alternating hatred and worship which he inspires. It is the sign of his deep alienation from humanity.

This is the crux of Lawrence's difficulties as man, as friend, as human being. To be and not to be! To help Magnus so as to rid himself of him. Magnus is an annoying test of rejected reality. He is like the stone was to the Berkeley idealists. One stubs up against the Magnuses when one wants to be a savior of mankind. So he aids him in an inhuman way, as much as killing him off. The Magnus type asks sympathy, brotherhood, understanding. But the savior, intent on providing for his own progeny, the coming of humanity, has precious little time for the Magnuses of this world. And he is not inhuman enough brutally to kill him off. Or not *human* enough! The human thing is to aid or refuse, not to aid and refuse at the same time. Lawrence gave Magnus a stone instead of bread. He killed Magnus, and that's the reason he wrote what he considered one of his finest bits of prose. With a guilty conscience! He sacrificed Magnus as the artist always sacrifices everyone, to his art. Magnus is the human sacrifice put in the cornerstone of the new temple of love which Lawrence was constructing.

The savior is the schizophrenic type *par excellence*. Unable to resolve his inner division, he arranges the world in its terms. Unable to save himself, he tries to save the world. There is in this type of man an unusual endowment of the feminine. In the artist, this feminine side works as a leaven, permits the masculine, creative side to renew its sources of fecundation. But in the religious type this feminine nature, consciously denied and suppressed, comes to be symbolic or representative of the outer reality from which the individual has divorced himself. Woman is deliberately made enigmatic, and hence shunned. The same pattern is at work regarding the conscious processes: the whole realm of reality, which man with his reason endeavors to explore, to lay out, to comprehend, is likewise denied, in order that ignorance may be glorified.

Identifying the old cultural world with the powers of day—with the Apollonian—he seeks to destroy it by setting up the counter-world of night, of the instincts, of the intuition. His language is always one of identification with the universe—the effort to posit himself as universe, as God. The more mysterious he becomes to himself, the more mysterious becomes the new life which he is trying to establish. The problem of fulfillment, of obedience to the inner urge, becomes the all important. In Lawrence's case we have the effort to arrive at fulfillment first through sex, a failure; then through friendship, also a failure. No matter what route he travels he comes back in the end to himself, to stark isolation. Since he is incapable of going mad, there is only one conclusion to which these failures can point: self authorization.

This is the true significance of the scene in *Aaron's Rod* in which Lilly massages Aaron's lower body with oil. The savior annoints himself, appoints himself to his role as Redeemer, since now there are no true friends, no disciples, no apostles to support him and sanction his authority. He feels not only supremely right, but supremely justified. As the self-appointed savior he will earn his fulfillment by regenerating the world. His alienation from man is now so complete that it is inevitable that he will discover himself, God. The whole drama now becomes one of using up his inner sustenance while at the same time glorifying it.

Now and then, weary of this futile, Promethean struggle, he expresses his longing to be human again, to participate in life's struggles. "I want to do something with living people, somewhere, somehow, while I live on the earth. I write, but I write alone. And I live alone. Without any connection whatever with the rest of men." It is in *Kangaroo* that Lawrence, through the mouth of Somers, voices these words. Here, already aware of his destiny, he allows himself to probe the problem of leadership. In "The Ladybird" it pops out again, in the words of Dionys(!): "as a *man* who is by nature an aristocrat, it is my sacred duty to hold the lives of other men in my hands . . . ." But here he represents himself as a special kind of artistocrat, the aristocrat of aristocrats, i.e., the spiritual aristocrat, Dionysus, Redeemer of Mankind. In *Kangaroo* it is a more human leadership, that of a man among men, that of a great political leader. He realizes speedily enough, however, that his concern is not with external forces, with social and political configurations. He has neither enough faith in himself, nor in men, to go through with the Caesar role. He realized that he belongs to another order of man, to the spiritual leaders of the world.

Just here, however, is where Lawrence departs from the fundamental type from which he stems. Instead of becoming a Christ, a Buddha, a Mahomet he elects to put himself forward as *artist*. It is here, moreover, where he has been so grossly misunderstood, that he shows a supreme wisdom. He is going to lead the world, but indirectly, as the potential artist type who reveals the mystery of life and thereby makes it possible for a new and strange element to appear. He knew, Lawrence, that it was the artist in man which had created all the religions, that it was the artist who created God. And he knew too that in a time of irreligion, of complete bankruptcy of the soul, it was useless to stress the religious element. He goes out instead to the dark, animal side of his being, to the obscene natural sources of life, to re-enthrone the Dionysiac element which has always represented for man the interpenetration of spirit and nature: "My great religion is a belief in the blood, the flesh, as being wiser than the intellect. We can go wrong in our minds. But what our blood feels and believes and says, is always true. The intellect is only a bit and a bridle. What do I care about knowledge. All I want is to answer to my blood."

Thus we have the enthronement of the dark god, Quetzalcoatl, the bird-serpent, a synthetic symbol of the conflicting human spirit that asserts its divinity by stressing its animal nature. He realized that there is an impasse which can never be resolved except by going beyond, and to go beyond is to fuse the two opposites. It is here, in a mystic symbol, that Lawrence reveals finally his supreme humanness—in the glorification of the conflict in which man is perpetually rooted. Since there is no ultimate solution for the divided being which man is, the thing to do is to deify the conflict itself. Thus the Holy Ghost, which represents the very quick of the creative impulse, becomes at the same time the seat of conscience, the guide and the law.

In this way Lawrence, by his very detachment from life, was able to create a world. By appointing himself a savior he is able to point the finger at his own corruption. To be sure, the savior is the most corrupt of men, since it is he who contains all the seeds of corruption; it is he who is sacrificed to corruption in order that others may live, may have new life; it is through the savior, through his assumption of the role of responsibility for mankind, that the world is able to free itself from the horrible burden of guilt, and of sin, which ever weighs it down. It is only when we have successfully killed the savior that we are emancipated from the drag of guilt, that we can move again as new figures, free to choose between good and evil, free again to worship, religiously to partake of life, to comprehend its final, sacred aspect.

As I hinted before, however, Lawrence had the wisdom not overtly to assume this role of savior. To repeat the role of Christ would have been to make himself less than Christ, a second to Christ. To Lawrence the two thousand years which intervened between himself and Christ had to be put down as a defeat of the spirit. It was not, as with other men, that he failed to understand Christ. He felt, as did Nietzsche, that he had surpassed Christ. For him, Lawrence, Christ had not died in vain; for the majority of men Christ had. Christ had come to set men free, but he left them more enchained than ever. Lawrence respected the power and the beauty of a tragic figure such as Christ, of a life that could cast the long shadow of two thousand years and still make itself felt; he regarded himself as a product of that culture which had been erected over the dead body and spirit of an ignorant Jew. "It has been 2000 years," he said, "the Spring and Summer of our era. What, then, will the winter be? . . . It is almost better to be dead, than to see this awful process finally strangling us to oblivion, like the leaves off the trees . . . .My life is ended here. I must go as a seed that falls onto new ground . . . .Really, I can't bear it; the past, the past, the falling, perishing, crumbling past, so great, so magnificent."

Like every true artist, he set himself up as a force to combat the dead cultural process. Like Nietzche, he seizes the hammer and ruthlessly smashes the old symbols, the icons, the dead letter of the law. He brings into evidence a new reality, the mysterious, creative reality of the artist which has its roots in conflict. He situates himself in the flux of life, in the psychological springs of action. He stresses the fecundating aspects of this eternal conflict in man, not the solution of it. Escapes there are, but solutions there are none. One may resolve the conflict—through action. The whole cultural process, in the eyes of the great artist, is the effort of the uncomprehending, uninspired masses to arrest the flux of life, to sit complacently or worshipfully before the empty symbols. The artist is he who creates and destroys at the same time. His purpose is to give to man's actions a significance which, in and of itself, his actions lack. Instead of solving life's problems he revives them, but he revives them in their fundamental nature. He hacks away the bric-a-brac of thought which clutters them, the misconceptions which have adhered to them. It is the struggle itself which finally stands revealed, and it is the struggle which is glorified.

All history is the record of man's signal failure to thwart his destiny, the record, in other words, of the few men of destiny who, through the recognition of their symbolic role, made history. All the lies and evasions by which man has nourished himself—*civilization,* in a word—are the fruits of the creative artist. It is the creative nature of man which has refused to let him lapse back into that unconscious unity with life which characterizes the animal world from which he made his escape. As man traces the stages of his physical evolution in his embyronic life, so, when ejected from the womb, he repeats, in the course of his development from childhood to old age, the spiritual evolution of the race. In the person of the artist the whole historical evolution of man is recapitulated. His work is one grand metaphor, revealing through image and symbol the whole cycle of cultural development through which man has passed from vital primitive to effete civilized being.

When we trace back the roots of the artist's evolution, we rediscover in his being the various incarnations, or aspects, of the hero which man has always represented himself to be—king, warrior, saint, magician, priest. The process is a long and devious one. It is all a conquest of fear. The question "why" leads to the question "whither" and then "how." Escape is the deepest wish. Escape from death, from the nameless terror. And the way to escape death is to escape life. This the artist has always manifested through his creations. By living into his art he adopts for his world an intermediary realm in which he is all-powerful, a world which he dominates and rules. This intermediary realm of art, this world in which he moves as hero, is made realizable only out of the deepest sense of frustration. It arises paradoxically out of lack of power, out of a sense of inability to thwart fate.

This, then, is the rainbow, the bridge which the artist throws over the yawning gulf of reality. The radiance of the rainbow, the promise it bespeaks, is the reflection of his belief in eternal life, his belief in perpetual spring, in continuous youth, virility, power. All his failures are but the reflection of his frail, human encounters with inexorable reality. The main-spring is the dynamic impact of a will that leads to destruction. Because with each realistic failure he falls back with greater intensity on his creative illusions. His whole art is the pathetic and heroic effort to deny his human defeat. He works out, in his art, a triumph which, since it is neither a triumph over life nor over death, is an unreal triumph. It is a triumph over an imaginary world which he himself has created. The drama lies entirely in the realm of idea. His war with reality is a reflection of the war within himself.

In carving out the artist he reduces his human figure to insignificant proportions. He tends to exhaust experience, not for living, but for his work. Finally the very change of reality he hoped to effect, the salvation he preached here and now, the personal, individual hope of resurrection becomes transmuted into the universal and spiritual reality of his art ideology. The drama which, as a type (Dionysian) he has elected to play has become real and eternalized. Against the world as god-man he fails. But his example and his work persist, and it is therein, as postponed destiny, that he triumphs.

* * *

In order to accomplish his purpose the artist is obliged to retire, to withdraw from life, utilizing just enough of experience to present the flavor of the real struggle. If he chooses to live he defeats his own nature. He must live vicariously. Thus he is enabled to play the monstrous role of living and dying innumerable times, according to the measure of his capacity for life.

Ludwig Lewisohn so very shallowly advises the American artist to stay at home and win his battles there. For him, Melville, James and company are neurotic weaklings who couldn't face reality, who couldn't stand the gaff. But it is the particular destiny, the very life pattern of these high sporadic types to get themselves ostracized and to take themselves elsewhere. This Oedipus/Ulysses myth is in our blood heritage. So Lawrence, realizing that it was his destiny to go running over the earth in his savage pilgrimage, at the same time detested the journey, was miserable, wanted to be with his own people, admitted his ineradicable Englishness. And his understanding of the pattern is magnificent: "Men are free when they are in a living homeland, not when they are straying and breaking away. Men are free when they are obeying some deep, inward voice of religious belief....Men are free when they belong to a living, organic, *believing* community, active in fulfilling some unfulfilled, perhaps unrealized purpose. Not when they are escaping to some wild west....Men are freest when they are most unconscious of freedom. The shout is a rattling of chains, always was. Men are not free when they are doing just what they like....Men are only free when they are doing what the deepest self likes."

There is, moreover, no help for it. *Fate*. This answers Murry on going into the desert, being a hermit, retiring from life, castrating oneself, being a saint. The point is precisely this: the savior type *is* obliged to retire from life, that is, from the ordeal of experience, in order to incubate, to take root in himself, to discover himself, to announce himself, to gird himself for the next step in the battle, martyrdom and crucifixion. He goes away to find his own faith in himself, but the going away is not the end. The end is to come back and challenge the world squarely! If he were to remain in the world and become its victim on its terms, he would surely be defeated.

No sense labeling this type as weaklings, neurotics, saints or saviors. (I myself am guilty of it!). Recognize them as a type, and rather envy them than decry them or pity them, for they are the privileged ones of the earth, totally involved in the greatest experience of all. They are not running away from life as cowards; they are retreating from the front to regroup their forces, and *en passant* they imbibe much wisdom, they widen their horizon, they put their ideas to the test, they touch other levels, alien depths of experience. Mark well too that they are productive! Productive neurotics, if you will, but all of them usually men of great output, great vitality, energy, will power, these Melvilles, Jameses, Gauguins, Lawrences. They are not paralyzed by the conflict. They emerged triumphant. They create. Rimbaud, Aragon—these are the types who are cowards and traitors, who have no resourcefulness left, no courage left, no will, no more creative ardor—surrendering ignominiously to life.

All longing for travel, adventure, exploration is based on a desire to experience life more fully. It is a protest, or admission therefore, against the flatness, exhaustion of the customary stale routine. But whereas the real life-adventurers go out to seek new life, to experience life to the fullest, the neurotic-savior type goes away into the desert—isolate, apart from man—to search out his soul, to give significance to that experience which he has already tasted, which is meager perhaps, and too much for him. He suffers from experience! He goes away really to strengthen himself for a new combat with life—in order to overcome it! Usually, in the wilderness, he punishes himself (for his Promethean guilt of alienation from mankind), he fasts and prays. All this to conquer any suspicious longings of the flesh for earthly experiences. He usually returns from the desert with his "message of salvation," prepared to save man and to be offered up as sacrifice, both. The Dionysian role. Lawrence could not and would not do this! Because his message was: "enjoy all experience to the fullest."

Lawrence went round the world seeing only what he wanted to see, that is, in the spirit of the prophet driven out of his own country, who merely confirms by his wanderings his own unique abnormal view of things. It is the classic attitude of the savior type. Because after his "contact with the world" (so-called) he will return, more set, more convinced of his own truths, more determined to overthrow the world and upset all its values. Lawrence must have known it was *not* his destiny to know the world. He was retreating upon his inner self, isolating himself more and more, to come out of the wilderness finally surrounded by a little group of disciples.

In another sense, his travels revealed that innate loneliness, that hard unyieldingness, that insularity, that superior attitude—moralistic, critical, intolerant, judging, rigid—which are so markedly the traits of the Nordics, the Anglo-Saxons, which make them such bad, nauseating tourists, so disliked everywhere, spreading a poison wherever they go. It is noteworthy that it was only when he was in Ceylon that Lawrence discovered his "Englishness." "English" in the teeth of the world. A hard, dire, consistency—, unchanging, unflinching, unyielding.

It is also characteristic of his *"voyage autour du monde"* that Lawrence interests himself profoundly not in the actual living peoples about him, but in their buried past, the ruins, customs, relics of their ancestors. And the two dead races which aroused in him the most passionate attraction were the Etruscans and the Indians (the Aztecs and Mayas chiefly). The Chinese he seems curiously uninterested in, although he wrote appreciatively to Eunice Tietjens about them and he mentions the "long green dragon" of the mandarins in *Apocalypse*. But it is evident that he did not like the Chinese reasonable, wise, philosophic attitude. He liked the Egyptians because they had a sharp sense of death and a great *symbolic* culture. About the Greeks he is indifferent apparently. But the Etruscans and the Indians—yes! Their violence, their livingness, their cruelty, their dark, passionate, mysterious and powerful qualities. Anti-mechanical, anti-scientific, anti-logical.

In spite of that, what a commentary he leaves upon men, beasts, plants, customs, peoples, continents, races, religions, morals. Quick judgments, yes. Erroneous impressions, yes. But always passionate, first-hand opinions, not derivative. Everything judged by his own standards, and what other standards are more important? Otherwise, one might as well sit at home by the fireside in an armchair and read a book, get things vicariously. The world's opinion of things is always formed vicariously. The world is wrong! At least Lawrence travelled in a different way from the tourist. He earned his disillusionment. "Perhaps it is my destiny to know the world," he said. Quite true. The artist is the wanderer-hero. The very theme of the Oedipus myth is this endeavor to escape one's destiny, this running away from the horror of one's conflict.

Lawrence the MAN, the wanderer-hero, the prototype of genius on his flight. I am tempted now to do in cinema-montage, in camera shots, in larger and larger type, in louder and louder sound his remarks disposing of people, of ideas, of religions, of civilizations, of whole epochs, of entire continents, screaming: "we're not living! no sign of life anywhere!" The MAN/GOD/GENIUS the CREATOR/DESTROYER, who whispers, tired of his journey, on his way "home," 'it's cunt thar't after."

For in his human moments the artist craves fulfillment through the woman—that is, as Lawrence says, *one* way of fulfillment. And in *Lady Chatterley's Lover* it is the very human Lawrence, the eternal male, who reappears, as Murry says, after a lapse of eighteen years. Mellors and Annable are the same fundamental being, the human male, which Lawrence never wholly was, could not be, in fact. But if, after eighteen years of journey and travail, of spiritual quest and soul struggle, the human Lawrence reemerged, with what wisdom and vision and sweetness did he do so! The antagonism is still there—male and female warring endlessly, in perfect consonance with the deep hostility which exists between the sexes. But Mellors is a far riper individual than Annable. The eighteen years have been replete with the most varied experiences. Lawrence now, in the person of Mellors, has stripped away from the eternal male the ideal grave-clothes of the impossible lover and husband. *John Thomas and Lady Jane!* That was another title (suggested to him by the morally outraged Juliet Huxley) he had wished to give this book. The penis and the vagina! Or he would have called it *Tenderness*, after the true tenderness that would take the stench out of the word *love* because it would restore to the man and the woman the primacy of their roles. A union based on love, which is war, and thereby providing a perpetual renewal of the spirit; a faith built upon the recognition of this innate antagonism, so that the man could go on to his beyond, to his business of creation in which the woman might participate, the clash of their separate worlds resolved in the harmony of creation. Such a fulfillment Lawrence envisaged and realized, through his art, as the possible destiny of the ordinary man and woman, the creatures of earth for whom the eternal conflict in sex has its importance also.

*   *   *

Lawrence, very much like Jesus—like Dostoevski also—had a very strong sense of the destined, fateful character of life. He lived in the immediate imminence of a new era. His was not the historical sense of a Goethe or a Napoleon. I don't know what word to use precisely to describe his attitude. "Cosmic" is perhaps the nearest, though in the mouths of those who today employ the term there is little of the meaning that Lawrence gave it.

In referring to the cults and superstitions which prevailed during the period of dissolution of the Antique world, he tells, in *Apocalypse*, how the rule of the heavens returned on man as never before, with a power of superstition stronger than any religious cult. "Horoscopy was the rage. Fate, fortune, destiny, character, everything depended on the stars....Their rule became at last a form of insanity, and both the Christians and the Neo-Platonists set their faces against it."

Lawrence was impressed, was overawed, as man has been from time immemorial, by the pageantry of the stars. His works are a veritable cosmological poem, if we choose to study them from this angle. "When I hear modern people complain of being lonely," he says, "then I know what has happened. They have lost the cosmos—It is nothing human and personal that we are short of. What we lack is cosmic life, the sun in us and the moon in us." He relates how "By the time of John of Patmos men, especially educated men, had already almost lost the cosmos. The sun, the moon, the planets, instead of being the communers, the comminglers, the lifegivers, the splendid ones, the awful ones, had already fallen into a sort of deadness; they were the arbitrary, almost mechanical engineers of fate and destiny. By the time of Jesus, men had turned the heavens into a mechanism of fate and destiny, a prison." "Only now," he adds, "are we passing over the border of Pisces [the astrological sign of our age], into a new sign and a new era."

It is curious to observe how a renewed sense of destiny and a renewed interest in matters cosmological have emerged out of the chaos of our modern, scientifically-minded world. When in 1781 Sir William Herschel revealed to the world the existence of the planet Uranus (which, according to the astrologists, is the dominant sign in our era of transition) there appeared on the horizon simultaneously that singular figure of destiny, Napoleon. With the close of the Napoleonic era the modern world was ushered in. Henceforth the word "destiny" acquires a new significance, a pregnant significance. A hundred years after Napoleon, after the organic, cyclical conception of life which ran contrary to the Darwinian—the Goethean view— destiny acquires its definitive cast for us in the monumental work of Spengler, entitled significantly *The Decline of the West*. Viewing the world-as-history, Spengler outlines a mor- phology of Cultures with the intention to enthrone the "idea of destiny" as against the prevalent "causality principle." Though he employs the methodology of science, Spengler dis- credits and rejects science itself. Spengler's is the logical wind-up of a process begun by Goethe, and extended by Nietzsche.

"We," says Spengler, "regard the *history of philosophy* as, in the last resort, philosophy's gravest theme . . . .In this work it will be our task to sketch out this unphilosophical philosophy—the last that West Europe will know. Skepticism is the expression of a pure Civilization; and it dissipates the world-picture of the Culture that has gone before. For us, its success will lie in resolving all the older problems into one, the genetic." "There are no eternal truths," he says. "Every philosophy is the expression of its own and only its own time . . .The difference is not between perishable and im- perishable doctrines but between doctrines which live their day and doctrines which never live at all . . .the essential is, what kind of man comes to expression in them . . . .Only its necessity to life decides the eminence of a doctrine.

Thus he can conclude: "my own philosophy is able to ex- press and reflect *only* the Western . . . soul, and that soul *only* in its present civilized phase by which its conception of the world, its practical range and its sphere of effect are specified."

Spengler's "genetic" philosophy, his world-as-history, however much it may be debated, or challenged, is not an isolated, unique view of the world, as we know. It is a view which has doubtless been expounded time and again, in the end periods. The attention given to this huge work, its "popular" success, even, is but the symptom of its timeliness. Havelock Ellis has pointed out that, unknown to Spengler, another morphology of history had been conceived and elaborated at about the same time. He refers to the *Revelations of Civilization* by Petrie, the Egyptologist, whose book was published just three years before the outbreak of the world war. Like Spengler, Petrie recognizes the "intermittent" character of civilization; he too defines the eight great civilizations, with an average length—for the civilizatory period—of about 1330 years. He too regards *our* civilization as having reached its climax about the year 1800. And he also envisages the possibility of our civilization lasting only another few centuries, to be finally dissolved by a fresh race, with a new cycle syncretically commencing out of the elements of the old.

In citing Spengler's pamphlet, *"Pessimissimus?"* Havelock Ellis remarks very justly that such a point of view is not at all to be regarded as "pessimistic," but as expressing "fulfill-ment"—a word strangely reminiscent of Lawrence, one of his key words, in fact. The curious thing to note however is, that though there is only a short interval between the appearance of Petrie's book and Spengler's—the period of the war—this period, brief as it may be, is sufficient to make the idea stick. Today Spengler's language is incorporated into our thought—just as the psychoanalytic jargon forms part of our mental stock-in-trade. It does not matter whether these views are "true" or "correct" they are now a definite, accepted part of the picture. They enter into and shape our picture of the world, appealing not to the "conscience" or the "intelligence" of man, but to some deeper, inscrutable layer of his being.

It is possible that the great Faustian Culture, which is now in the stage of arteriosclerosis, may enjoy the distinction of expiring more brilliantly, more catastrophically, than any Culture ever known. The dominant characteristic of this age, as the psychoanalysts have made painfully clear, is Fear—*fear of life*.

Fear is the cornerstone of this final edifice of neurosis which we have created as the seat of the last drama. And fear, as we know, is always fear of one's self. It is always inexplicable and illogical. But it is certain, just as the sense of destiny is certain. It is this fear of extinction which is driving us to extinction. The outer fatality is merely the crystallization of the inner feeling of despair, of failure, of emptiness.

The world that Copernicus opened up Einstein brings to a close on the fantastic figure of 35,000,000 solar systems, the axis of this incredible system having the immeasurable length of 470,000,000 times the distance from the earth to the sun. Coincident with the collapse of this bubble there emerges the cocky little skeptic, Lawrence, who, with something more like the imagination of a Kepler, throws the whole thing overboard. In place of the myth which science has elaborated, Lawrence struggles to reestablish a more creative, more poetic, more human myth, in which ideas are again related to living, and not merely to dead facts.

In *Art and Artist* Otto Rank has pointed out the close association between the idea of destiny and the idea of death. Man, he says, originally studied the heavens in order to read there his fate, and of course, to thwart it. But what he discovered, Rank emphasizes, was not his fate, but the science of astronomy. This picture of the multiverse has now reached its limits, as has the corollary picture of the atomic multiverse. What commenced in Chaldean times, or earlier, as body projection, with all the dream-sure certitude of organic evolution (as the lore of the zodiac indicates), comes to smash finally upon the old rock of reality. The conscious, logical processes, having arrived at the point of exhaustion, a new reality is hypothesized, with the seat of the soul, or the psyche, or the "brain," situated in the Unconscious. Man is still trying to read his fate, and to thwart it, but now he looks within, back through all the layers of dream and myth, through all the myraid strata of the geologic "I".

These two pseudo-sciences—astrology and psychoanalysis—represent the extreme poles of a constantly changing view of reality which forms man's picture of the world and must forever remain inscrutable. Between these poetic limits of apprehension, between these two poetic visions lie the changing cultural forms which appear and disappear on the surface of human history. One of these forms, or myths, has now reached the saturation point: the myth of science. The world senses vaguely, but definitely, that things are in a state of transition. The collapse of the world is the collapse of the myth.

The outward swing has reached its peak. With the turn of the tide we are swimming back to flood the psychologic gulf, the deep winter marshes in which are struck the empty symbols of the past. With the enthusiasm of pioneers and discoverers, we are bringing to light the flora and fauna of the world to come, a world that will be inhabited by the ghosts of ourselves. To reanimate these dead forms, to give them meaning and value, a religious feeling is imperative. No new "Culture" rears itself without the prime symbol—soul. What we have at present, even in its most hopeful aspect, is not in any way akin to a religious spirit. Our condition of mind is more like that of the disintegrative period of the Greco-Roman world, when sensing the death that was upon them, helpless, desperate, frantic, the peoples of that great civilization fell victim to the shallowest cults, creeds, doctrines, philosophies— anything that promised the stay of the inevitable. It was out of such a bacillic stew of ideas that the regenerative doctrine of Christianity was born. Then as now the key-words were hallucination, dream, mystery, resurrection. Rimbaud rode in on the crest of modernity frothing at the mouth: hallucination, dream, mystery. *Smash everything!* This, too, is a very real sense of destiny. It is our destiny.

Astrology, as has been frequently explained, is the attempt to read and to control one's fate. To him, however, who regards life as directed, irrevocable, fate-laden, says Spengler, there is no desire to control or thwart his fate. The man of destiny makes himself one with destiny. Such men have no need of the stars, nor of God. They feel themselves as much a part of the universe as the stars themselves, and they conduct themselves as gods. They are beyond human laws, human codes. Napoleon expressed it trenchantly in those memorable words uttered just before the Russian campaign: "I feel myself driven towards an end that I do not know. As soon as I shall have reached it, as soon as I shall become unnecessary, an atom will suffice to shatter me. Till then, not all the forces of mankind can do anything against me." These are the words of a man who *was* destiny, who *made* destiny, as we say. He was destiny incarnate. Contrast that inner certainty with the vague divagations of our leaders today, regardless of what field they choose as sphere of action. Contrast it, for instance, with the feeble mysticism of Jung, one of the latter-day champions of the Unconscious.

Beyond the phenomena of human activity lie incalculable forces. Both astrology and psychoanalysis have for their grand aim the revelation of the extent and magnitude of these forces. The motivating spirit of inquiry is based upon the recognition of life as conflict—whether the theater of conflict be projected outward to the stars, or driven inward to the unknown regions of the Unconscious, is relative and secondary. A sense of mystic participation with the universe, a religious awareness, is the all-important. Both views are founded in that older, sounder view of life which Lawrence proclaimed. "Early science," he says, "is a source of the purest and oldest religion."

> *The very ancient world was entirely religious and godless. While men still lived in close physical unison . . . an ancient tribal unison in which the individual was hardly separated out, then the tribe lived breast to breast, as it were, with the cosmos, in naked contact with the cosmos, the whole cosmos was alive and in contact with the flesh of man, there was no room for the intrusion of the god idea. It was not till the individual began to feel separated off, not till he fell into awareness of himself, and hence into apartness; not, mythologically, till he ate of the Tree of Knowledge instead of the Tree of Life, and knew himself apart and separate, that the conception of a God arose, to intervene between man and the cosmos. The very oldest ideas of man are purely religious, and there is no notion of any sort of god or gods. God and gods enter when man has "fallen" into a sense of separateness and loneliness . . . . Away behind all the creation myths lies the grand idea that the cosmos always was, that it could not have had any beginning, because it always was there and always would be there. It could not have a god to start it, because it was itself all god and all divine, the origin of everything.*

It should be clear from the foregoing that this is precisely the opposite of the scientific spirit, with its insane idea of conquest over Nature, over the mysterious forces of the universe. Where astrology, for instance, and analysis fall short, is precisely in their submission to the inquisitive, scientific spirit. The creative, the poetic, aspect which Science shares with all the arts is swamped by the pragmatic. The desire to subjugate the forces of Nature for practical purposes, instead of exploring them in a fictive, a metaphysical, a disinterested way, has brought about an empty *knowledge* of Nature, instead of a *wisdom* of life. Life and death lose their significance, their polarity. In place of the drama we have an empty continuum of work, the daily round, the monotony, the humdrum, the futility, the will-less, purposeless, directionless existence of humanity today. The craving for immortality, which has gone out of the modern soul, is due to man's having achieved immortality here and now. Death, instead of being something different, comes to resemble life itself. Life and death have fused into an inseparable mélange.

The greatest longing in the soul of modern man is the desire for death—to be able to die! To be able to have a clean birth and a clean death: a separate, individual life and death. His reawakened interest in the old sciences, the "pseudosciences," is an indication of his desire to partake of an individual destiny—*individual and cosmic.* Anything—even to go mad—seems to him preferable to this mass inertia, this mass inhibition, this mass paralysis, mass life, mass death. One can liken this pseudo-death, in which we feel ourselves to be enveloped, only to the pseudo-death of birth, that traumatic experience when the fetus, impelled by mysterious forces, is delivered from the nullity of the womb. A symbolic act wherein man, a biologic phenomenon, expresses himself historically, as individual.

From seed to flower and back to seed again. A drama of movement, change, struggle, growth, decay. Between the two magnetic poles, the fixed, constant poles of birth and death, flows the mysterious current, life. The measure of polarity between these two fixed poles is based on the religious index, that is, the sense of mystery. When the current is strong and unimpeded the individual becomes one with life, with destiny. The innermost desire then is not to escape the conflict, the drama, but to accept it—for better or for worse. Death is not more painful to endure than life. The individual does not consult the stars to secure a better "arrangement," to alter the invisible pattern, he consults his destiny to salute it! Regarded thus, the conjunctions of the planets, as they figure in his life-map, acquire what might be termed a "poetic justice." Life is acted out, not conceived in terms of reaction. The event is carried through—not postponed or aborted or traduced. Death comes as one of a series of events. It is neither a defeat, nor is it ignominious. Life indeed may be ignominious, shameful to the soul, as Lawrence has said, but death is never a shame. *Life may be a shame when it is lived in terms of death,* as we are living today. That is what he meant.

Looking at life in a historical-time-destiny sense we observe the fatal recurrence of type-men, type-situations, type-diseases, type-deeds, type-ideas, type-problems, which provide the melodic structure of our changing cultural forms and symbols, the architectonics of idea. No idea is ever thoroughly worked out, no ideal is ever thoroughly pursued, no destiny is ever thoroughly lived out. No magnum opus is ever complete. There is always an aura of unfinished business, a potential residue in which each new creative genius lodges himself. There are never any completed life-works, never any completed lives. And yet the fragmentary, the abortive can be sublime, grandiose—*sufficient*—if the integration is there, if one can decipher the rude hieroglyph of life which is art, if one can detect in the microcosmic effort the macrocosmic plan. For the rotary, cyclical time element which has fascinated men throughout all the ages, which is so ingrained, so innate, in our way of thinking, has its inception in the most primitive, fundamental aspects of life—earth, sun, moon, the four cardinal points, the seasons.

Life presents itself even to early man as a problem-situation represented by a closed circle. Life appears closed, hopeless, fatal. And so it remains— fundamentally. Out of each seeming impasse man is lifted by the time movement into another circle, another plane with different problems, which in turn present themselves as closed and insoluble. There never is any solution to a problem—except time. One simply moves on or up or out or down to another plane, into another zodiacal sign,

among other clusters, constellations, influences, agglomer-
ates, climates, soils. In each of these situations there is a cosmic set-up, a condition of weather (usually bad), charged with
this or that quality which acts upon the individual in a definite
way. And there is always a fixed, obsessional point, a magnetic
pole-star which is interpreted and named differently in different times.

Always there are the two phenomena: type and periodicity. It
is the story of the earth itself (at least, as we picture it to
ourselves), a planet containing the mysterious sign (life), which
in its orbital swing encounters fields of influence which are
supposedly the same but which vary as the earth and the whole
universe travelling with it constantly moves into new sidereal
space. Space-movement-time. And the time element deter-
mines the character-complex of every situation and the lives
bound up with it—the lives of individuals, of beasts, stars, suns
and constellations. The sidereal time picture is the constant,
just as light is the absolute in physics. We take the picture for
granted, examine it no more, because it is relatively fixed. It
may last ten thousand years, or ten billion years—or it may
dissolve tomorrow. Our conception of historical destiny is
merely the counterpart of our picture of scientific planetary
destinies. It is a "counter-concept." We plot, we describe order,
we can even prophesy with accuracy—all within a tight,
theoretical frame which may last a long time, as long as our
history—but where that stops is utter chaos, and the prognosti-
cation is, always, catastrophic fatality.

An artist, in the evolution of his works, which is simply the
historical record of his changing problems, reveals this cosmic
pattern, this obsession. He is not therefore and consequently a
magician, an astrologist, or a scientist, or a philosopher, or a
moralist, or even a psychologist. The prophetic and the musical
aspect of the poet's life and world spring from his fluid apprehension of the real nature of changing phenomena. He
stands outside all systems of thought—in the quick of a permanent cosmic order, or design. That is why he sings, music
being the essence of this unison with reality, this life that is
detached from image and idea. And that is why he is prophetic:
he has his finger on the cosmic pulse which beats eternal. That
is why he is anarchic, because all lesser forms of order must
perish to give way to the greater, unseen, unknowable order.
That is why he sings only about life, *how* things seem to him,
or *are*. He moves with the spheres, evanescent and changing,

yet changeless. He is always only one step removed from the charlatan, the criminal, the lunatic. The moment he loses his vision, his attunedness, he falls into one of these freak categories. His weakness is the desire to act out the more fascinating, the more facile, the more human roles of mountebank, murderer, redeemer. Ever at his heels, waiting for that human moment of weakness, is the mob. The mob is always there to crucify, to eat the corpse in order to possess the secret and the power.

* * *

In the same sense that Christ belonged to the future, so does Lawrence. ("Lawrence was the future; as much of it as we are likely to get in our time," said Murry.) According to a Spenglerian view of things, (had such a philosophy been voiced in Christ's time), our role would have been to submit to destiny, to do what we could do with our dying days. But those who were inspired by Christ refused to accept a living death. True, the old forms died—as a Spengler would have predicted. True too that Christ's doctrine was never realized by men. "I die that ye may be saved, that ye may taste of the life everlasting . . . ." And men weren't saved nor did they taste of everlasting life. No, the result of Christ's appearance was the establishment of a new way of life based on a vulgar compromise, a syncretic morale, syncretic philosophy, syncretic religion adapted to the existent mores. The collectivity is immune to ideas; it moves in and with the mores, always in the eternal dead present, the winter marshes where life is frozen, until a cataclysm occurs and the current folkways are displaced by those of a conquering people. The rise of the Gothic world out of the antique is the story of the gradual adaptation of Christ's mystery cult and doctrine by inferior but primitive races who had overthrown the Roman world. The success of Christianity, the religion, is an illusion, it is the rise and growth of a new culture *around* the cornerstone of the Christian forms and symbols. It was an accident that Christianity survived; it might as well have been another faith; it happened to be there when the barbarians came to power, and they preempted it.

The real message of Christ, the message of which his life was an example, has been understood and appreciated by only a rare few. Even Nietzsche, who detested "Christianity," had to admit that one could not aspire to a realization of his philosophy until he had first passed through the experience of

Christ's teachings. And Lawrence practically admits the same thing. He posits his philosophy as superior to Christ's, more timely, more true, or more valuable therefore. The doctrines of renunciation, he says, are for the aristocrats of the spirit—for individuals always: Plato, Jesus, Mahomet, Buddha, D. H. Lawrence.

Hence Spengler, in speaking of the coming "Second Religiousness," speaks of it as being a "syncretic" religion (with Gothic elements necessarily). It would be a mistake to suppose that we will go toward an Oriental religiousness, such as Buddhism, which is godless, wholly intellectual, wholly centered in the psychology of the self, a religion of old age. We have our Buddhism already in "Socialism"—in the Spenglerian sense of the word—the condition in which the individual is sunk in the collectivity, where life is wholly economic-ethical, the idealism of biology, the spirituality of statistics.

Lawrence on the other hand speaks in the true language of the creative spirit, of a restoration of a Cosmos "godless and religious," in the primitive meaning. It is in this sense that he envisages a genuine springtime. Let him bring forth hope who can! Such a view of a "new heaven and new earth," of a new personality, is deeply in accord with the Spenglerian idea of the death of our culture and all its forms. Socialism is not a hope, it is the condition of the fag-end, man delivered up to the machine!

In this sense Lawrence's role is justified: he represents most realistically the dying god who yields fertility when consumed. His life is of necessity sacrificed in a war on the old forms and traditions. His "truths" can be revealed only upon his death—by real, direct consummation. "What we want is a fulfillment, a consummation." Meaning by we, what he wanted. The life he was denied himself he gives to others. In order for him to reign as god absolute he must be consumed; otherwise he is a menace, an evil force, because a too real, too psychological god.

Lawrence then, in his Dionysian role, incarnates the Mystery. He deals death, as the magician did. His doctrine—fertility, vitality—is spread through contagion, by consummation of the host. Alienated from man through his possession of godlike powers (Prometheus who stole the fire from gods, the fire of civilizing influence) he expiates his guilt and sin through sacrificial death, to restore the old union with the cosmos. It is the divine self in him speaking, the self which has split through the great knowledge vouchsafed him. It is the sense of guilt which recognizes that he has made a part of himself like god and the other part human, all too human. When he rails against the *"too personal"* as he does repetitiously throughout his writings, let it be recognized that by "personal" he does not mean the ego, in the psychological sense in which Jung uses it, but the "persona" or mask. What he is searching for continually is the true self, that central source of power and action, which he has called the Holy Ghost, and which it may now be seen corresponds to that mysterious unknowable area of the self out of which the gods are born.

Restoration with the cosmos then comes to mean "restoration of man's divinity," of his godless, religious self, because there is nothing but god or this creative power. Consequently, too, he cannot accept the scientific hypothesis of an evolution of beings from a lower to a higher form of organism. He can posit only an "unfoldment"—life expressing itself through myriads of forms simultaneously, not with intent to become something different, something other, but to blossom forth in the glory of its own uniqueness, *to be more and more what it is.*

Consequently too he reechoes the ancient idea that there is no such thing as "creation," no "separateness," no God versus world idea. The cosmos always was, is, and will be. Only *we* have grown apart. And it is in this growing apart that we have developed the extreme notions of self, of the "personality" and of God, which is only the anthropomorphic production of the "self."

This little personal ego which is the all-in-all for us today corresponds again to Lowenfels' conception of "the one and the many," or the statistical *1* and the creative *one.* Lowenfels, in the "Elegy," speaks of "Lawrence (the poet), the creative One *and* the uncreative mass that creates him." Meaning, no doubt, the enigma of the appearance of a creative personality born of an unfruitful time. "Concrete reality versus visions, dreams." A confusion here. There are all kinds of reality, but it is never "concrete." It is Lawrence's reality against the "dead" reality of the mass. A creative reality, in other words, against an "as if" reality in which the collective herd moves as in a dream. Such a man is always living into the future, part of the future, because he is the very crest of movement. The concrete reality of the herd is the static present, the valley or trough of the wave. The dream, the vision of the artist is hence a thousand times more real than the so-called immediate, tangible reality. Far from being a "dreamer," in the the usual pejorative sense of the word, the artist is the one who is most wide awake, who knows what time it is, as Lowenfels says, only, to be sure, it is not "clock" time It is *real* time . . .destiny . . .direction.

It is not always true, as Aldington has it, that "People are . . . strangely unwilling to admit the genius of a living artist. They feel so meanly of themselves that they cannot believe that one of the gods is moving among *them*, that genius lives in *their* time. They are insulted by superiority and try to ignore it or crush it." It is true now, when the cult of genius, the religion of individuality, has about come to an end. The worship turns to hatred. The same feeling of separateness of course, but the ideal has been dethroned. Now people are insulted by superiority; the Lenins, Mussolinis, Hitlers, at too far a remove from them; that is their ideal and only so because it is realizable, attainable. They have brought genius down to their own petty level of comprehension: little familiar deities who can mean something to them!

In this connection, Luhan provides us with a marvellous revelation of the nature of Lawrence's genius: "If anyone asks you why he died, Jeffers, tell them that this struggle wore him out. And yet sometimes it is my fancy that he overcame himself. That, as he wrote me, he changed. And it is also my fancy that when he finally succeeded in making that change in himself, he had more work to do here in this world, and he was let off." And her analysis of Lawrence in a passage that immediately precedes this one is equally brilliant:

> *He was and he was not; he had it and he didn't have it! He was always double–split in two. He was forever two! He was born on the second of the month and he died on the second of the month. He was the Son–the second person of the Trinity–but (God help all women!) though we tried to overcome and possess him, yet secretly we always wanted him to be the Father! And, poor darling, his struggle lay between these two roles. Begotten a son, it was his destiny to raise himself to fatherhood. I imagine that was what he was here on earth for. He perpetually strove to adopt for his own the difficult and lonely role of Father, and as often he slid back to the shelter of the Beloved Son. Everything conspired against him.*

Here is the picture I am trying to paint of Lawrence: the tragic picture of that last man of genius, that last individual rebel, that lone spirit, insisting on having to say. That is why he is so ignored today. He waits for another age, and age again of men.

CHAPTER VI

The Sacred Body

THE WORLD, I fear, will remember Lawrence only through *Lady Chatterley's Lover*, and how is one to know Lawrence through this bitterly distorted, brilliantly defiant expression of his soul? He reveals himself partially in all of his works and *Lady Chatterley's Lover* is one of his most extreme self-expressions. The phallic mystic! Phallic obviously enough, but where is the mysticism? It is there well enough for those who know him and understand him, but it is implicit in the work rather than explicitly available. The prophet who has expressed himself tyrannically by parable and symbol throughout all his works, the flaming archangel who rises to frenzy and ecstasy through his vision of the sacred aspect of life, this man, like the prophets who stalked through the Old Testament covered with excrement, finally despairs of making himself understood: since there is no other way of making clear his message he does the crude and obvious thing, he performs a miracle for the crowd—he gives us a genital banquet. *Lady Chatterley's Lover* is no more the substance of Lawrence's gospel than are the loaves and fishes which Christ distributed among the multitude; it is only the evidence of unseen powers.

The book is obscene and there is no justification for it. Because it requires none. And the miracles of Jesus are obscene, because there is no justification for them either. Life is obscene and miraculous, and neither is there any justification for life. The crowd will accept neither life nor obscenity nor miracle; the sacred is taboo, nay, incomprehensible to the multitude.

Obscenity is pure and springs from effervescence, excess vitality, joy of life, concord, unanimity, alliance with nature, indifference to God of the healthy sort that takes God down a peg or two in order to reexamine him. Obscenity is a divine prerogative of man, and is always to be used carelessly, heedlessly, without scruple or qualms, without religious or aesthetic defense. When the body becomes sacred, obscenity comes into its own. Purity of speech is as much bosh as purity of action—there is no such thing. Obscenity is stomped down when the body is degraded, when the soul is made to usurp the body's proper function.

Obscenity figures large and heavily, magnificently and awesomely, in all primitive peoples; it is incorporated into the soul language, becomes part of the large, free, spontaneous gestures of life, the terrible aspect of life, allied to the fates, to nature, to the underground life of the race. The savage is not a sick man. The savage retains his sense of awe, wonder, mystery, his love of action, his right to behave like the animal he is; he does not fear words in this sense. His fear of words and things is grander, more terrible, more sound, part and parcel of the fear which art expresses, which creates all there is of culture forms and symbols.

If *Lady Chatterley's Lover* represents another of Lawrence's failures it does so only because of its impurity, its compromise. And by that I mean, only wherein it is obscene is it magnificent; in its obscenity lies its great purity, its miraculous, its sacred quality. The rest, that padding, that cotton-wool in which his visions are often wrapped, is the dead weight of the mass, the humus of decomposing bodies which he had not successfully sloughed off.

For the same reason in writing about *Lady Chatterley's Lover*, I would like to employ all of Lawrence's favorite obscenities and a few additional ones. I would like to tell the publisher that if he will not print them, he may leave a blank space for the offending words. But I will not edit the chapter, nor adulterate, nor castrate. I demand the right to provide an appendix to this chapter, revealing by c--- (a four letter word, standing for what every female has, or some such) the clue to its meaning, showing at the same time by this clumsy, ridiculous, roundabout language how infantile it is to keep up censorship, how one may obey the law (by not using the word itself) while yet revealing the full force and content: nay, more, that through consciously and deliberately evading the direct statement one only inspires and increases the lubricity, which is a *reductio ad absurdum* for the law. Also I feel that to have issued an expurgated volume of *Lady Chatterley's Lover* in America (through the connivance of Frieda) is a treachery of the highest order to Lawrence. No, Lawrence must enjoy the privilege of having his obscenity recognized and sanctioned—as is the case with the Bible and other Classics. Because, in accordance with the high wisdom of the learned judges who set up this law against obscenity, Lawrence himself said in his Foreword to *Fantasia of the Unconscious,* "I don't intend my books for the generality of readers."

It is a pity, however, that Lawrence ever wrote anything *about* obscenity, because in doing so he temporarily nullified everything he had created. Lawrence was a frightfully sensitive and a frightfully timid man. He sought to justify his violence, to explain it away, instead of leaving it as a fact, or a phenomenon. Violence is its own justification, a pure thing, one of the purest things in life. And obscenity is only one of the many forms of violence. It is the expression of the insufficiency of symbol, the explosion that occurs when the tension of antagonistic forces is no longer adequate to preserve the image. And of all the symbols which man has created to make his universe supportable—that is, understandable, meaningful—the sexual symbols are the least secure; for in the riddle of sex he comes closest to tasting the full savor of death. The great dread of ultimate annihilation, the evasion of death, the thwarting of destiny, this enduring, overpowering and all-pervasive phenomenon of fear on which all his culture is erected exposes its falsity when confronted with the sexual. Sex is the great Janus-faced symbol of life and death. It is never one or the other; it is always both. The great lie of life here comes to the surface; the contradiction refuses to be resolved.

It is nevertheless in *Lady Chatterley's Lover* that Lawrence comes the nearest to the whole man, the man who can live in the world and accept it as is. And alongside the usual bitter, denunciatory humor which he still retains, there is another kind of humor, broader, more tolerant, more understanding. Nearer to Rabelais and the great "medicos"—the earth man. Though his picture of the female (Bertha Coutts/Frieda) is even more devastating than that of Lady Cristabel (in *The White Peacock*) his obscenity is not expressed so much in his antagonistic reaction as in a ripe, earthy acceptance and enjoyment of the female, as *pure female.* His obscenity becomes positively delicious and quite unique, the more repulsive to the world, however, because it is so free of purpose, free of satire, mockery. It is nakedly, frankly *amoral.*

Here he reveals that one way of fulfillment (through sex) of which he wrote in *Fantasia*. (He is not now dealing with the other and more important way—that of fulfilling the soul's earnest purpose, etc.) Here the man and woman are stripped to their fundamental animal nature—wholly untutored, natural, amoral, without chivalry, romance, idealism. It is precisely a sample of that "tenderness" he is after. He wrote to Brett of it, calling it a "little warm flame," "a real kindliness and a wholeness." He is demonstrating that when the fake spiritual attitude (alternate glorification and degradation of the woman) is abandoned there then springs up a warm, true relation based on antagonism, on difference of role and function, but sympathetic and viable.

In examining *Lady Chatterley's Lover*, Murry finds it of no value whatsoever *because* Lawrence was merely trying to imagine a final triumph of his defeated masculinity. He rejects the creation because of its pathological basis. But if this tender book, as many believe, provides a very adequate description of what sexual fulfillment can mean then the livingness of this creation, the perfection of its achievement, is what is valuable and not the fact that life itself failed to provide the author with any such fulfillment.

The book is almost a posthumous chapter to the life of Christ, what Christ might have realized if he had had the chance to live his life as a man, if he had not castrated himself as Savior and Redeemer of mankind. Christ, if he had been allowed a cock and a pair of balls. If Christ could have walked around with John Thomas in his hand, what a lot of suffering we would have been saved. The very mention of this vital part of the anatomy in connection with Christ will send a shudder through many. It is the greatest blasphemy to call him a *man*! But later, in *The Man Who Died*, this is exactly what Lawrence does: he resurrects Christ (*himself*) and causes him to live it out on earth as a man with his woman. It is important to remember that first he had given us this perfect union in heaven above, in the "Morning Star" of *The Plumed Serpent*. Which is only another instance of the faithful and unconscious process in the artist who, in going through his evolution, recapitulates all the phases of the race.

In *Lady Chatterley's Lover*, it is as a fully-completed spiritual being who has conquered his animal nature by recognizing it that he glorifies John Thomas and Lady Jane. He refuses to deny his animal nature. This is why the Christ of *The Man Who Died* comes complete with cock and balls. Christ is now a whole man, not any longer an idealist, a castrated Redeemer. This new man is one who has earned his wholeness, his humanness, by making the complete cultural trajectory from earth through the heavens to earth again. After celestializing he humanizes. *The body fundament!* At last the Sacred Body in its full harmonious significance.

If, moreover, we revert now to our previous image of man as a mysterious phenomenon, as a sacred tree of life and death, and if, further, we also think of this tree as representing not only the individual man, but a whole people, a whole Culture, we may begin to perceive the intimate connection between the emergence of the Dionysian type of artist and the notion of the sacred body. When Spengler criticizes Nietzsche for being a "moral critic *and* moral gospeller"—pointing out that the two are incompatible, that the thinker must be beyond good (all good) and evil (all evil)—it seems to me that, though his criticism may be accurate and just, it nevertheless brings to light a more important truth: that the thinker is the victim of thought, that the thinker is he who makes a synthesis for the sake of a system. The thinker, he seems to say, must put Idea above everything else.

Now if Nietzsche was anything, he was an artist. "Art," he proclaimed lustily, "represents the highest task and the truly metaphysical activity of this life." The artist, in other words, nourishes life by relating ideas to living, by making his illusory, fictive world tangible and real. At the furthest reach of thought, when man has come to the apex of distendedness, of *pure thinking*, so to speak, there develops of necessity the Apollonian type of artist who is faced with the danger of being stuck fast forever in his dream of contemplation. There comes a point, if man is not to fall asleep in the mirror of his own creation, when ideas must be refunded into ignorance. Otherwise, as Nietzsche points out, there is the threat of paralysis of the will.

Pursuing further the image of man as tree of life and death, we may well conceive how the life instincts, goading man on to ever greater and greater expression through his world of form and symbol, his ideology, cause him at last to overlook the purely human relative fundamental aspects of his being—his animal nature, his very human body. Man rushes up the trunk of livingness to expand in a spiritual flowering. From an insignificant microcosm, only recently separated from the animal world, he eventually spreads himself over the heavens in the form of the great *anthropos*, the mythical man of the zodiac. The very process of differentiating himself from the animal world to which he still belongs causes him to lose sight more and more of his utter humanness. It is only at the last limits of creativeness, when his form world can assume no further architectural dimension, that he suddenly begins to realize his "limitations." It is then that fear assails him. It is then that he has a foretaste of death as it were.

Now the life instincts are converted into death instincts. That which before had seemed all libido, endless urge to creation, is now seen to contain another principle—the embrace of the death instinct. Only at the full summit of creative expansion does he become truly humanized. Now he feels the deep roots of his being, in the earth. Rooted. The supremacy and the glory and the magnificence of the body finally assert themselves in full vigor. Only now does the body assume its sacred character, its true role. The trinal division of body, mind and soul becomes a unity, a holy trinity. And with it the realizaton that one aspect of our nature cannot be exalted above another, except at the expense of one or the other.

When this fundamental, rooted, sacred character of the body is divined, what we call wisdom of life here attains it apogee. In the top-most branches of the tree of life thought withers. The grand spiritual efflorescence, by virtue of which man had raised himself to god-like proportions so that he lost touch with reality—because he himself *was* reality—this great spiritual flowering of Idea is now converted into an ignorance which expresses itself as the mystery of the *soma*. Thought retraverses the religious trunk by which it had been supported and, digging into the very roots of being, rediscovers the enigma, the mystery of the body, rediscovers the kinship between star, beast, ocean, man, flower, sky. Once again it is perceived that the trunk of the tree, the very column of life itself, is religious faith, the acceptance of one's tree-like nature, not a yearning for some other form of being. It is this acceptance of the laws of one's being, the law and the form of one's being, which preserves the vital instincts of life, even in death. In the rush upward the "individual" aspect of one's being was the imperative, the only obsession. But at the summit, when the limits have been felt and perceived, there unfolds the grand perspective and one recognizes the similitude of surrounding beings, the interrelationship of all forms and laws of being, the organic relatedness, the wholeness, the oneness of life.

And so the most creative type—the individual artist type—which had shot up highest and with the greatest variety of expression, so much so as to seem "divine"—this creative type of man must now, in order to preserve the very elements of creation in him, convert the doctrine of, or the obsession with individuality, into a common, collective ideology. This is the real meaning of the Master-Exemplar, of the great religious figures who have dominated human life from the beginning. Their isolation, in the heavens of thought, is what brings about their death. At their furthest peak of blossoming they have but emphasized their common humanity, their innate, rooted, inescapable humanness.

* * *

Speaking of man's need for a purpose beyond woman, Lawrence says in *Fantasia:* "if sex is the starting point and the goal as well: then sex becomes like the bottomless pit, insatiable. It demands at last the departure into death, the only available beyond....When sex is the starting point and the returning point both, then the only issue is death."

Now this theme of love and death, of going beyond the woman into futurity, is the theme of almost all modern tragedy. It is a mighty, mighty theme, the very nexus again of the whole problem of our world focussed like a navel on the very surface of the body today. The further we dig into this navel the more tender, the more revelatory, the more ramified and perplexing, the more dark and mysterious are the problems uncovered. In going into this navel, which is located outside the womb and above the sexual organ, which connects the child with the parent, which is the symbol of life once lived together in silence and darkness, a whole process that takes us back into the furthest past, in penetrating this closed wound we retrace ontogenetically the whole history of our problems, as sexual beings, problems antedating the historical and religious problems, the great ugly wound which in Freud is the clue to the whole problem (variously modified) and which displaces the problem of hunger (or individual survival) and puts it back again into the racial one of survival biologically, greatest of all problems. The whole religious problem, the question of soul and destiny, of God, etc., takes its stance and creates all the reverberations through the primordial one of survival: *sex*.

What Lawrence means to say by employing the dubious language of "going beyond her," of woman's necessity to have faith in man's predominant purpose, and so on, is this: that man, the catabolic agent, the insufficient, can only create a value, a reason for his existence by fulfilling his biologic function, fecundating woman, and fecundating woman, taken over on a larger scale, means the building of a masculine world—art, religion, architecture, *civilization*—in *order to sustain the illusion of his necessity*. Woman knows deep down that he is unnecessary; she merely tolerates him; she *created* him, actually, in order to live a larger life herself. Her role of bisexual creature, the all-sufficient, the fecundator and creator, was too limited, though highly satisfactory.

If we read into this scientific myth of the evolution of sex its deepest import we can superbly understand woman's role, her activity, her war and depredation, and we can stand it. That is, if we keep ever before us the image of Siva, the creator-destroyer (whole mythologies and pantheons of such deities have existed in the past, and exist now in our unconscious being), if we keep this image before us the eternal battle with woman sharpens our resistance, develops our strength, enlarges the scope of our cultural activities. Through her (and for her) we build our grandiose structures, our illusions, our myths, legends, philosophies, religions.

Lawrence, who so deeply understood this, was doing us an inestimable service then, in restoring the prime symbol of woman: the enemy! This of course, was understood in all ages, and perhaps more deeply and profoundly in the past, in the masculine periods. For example, the whole story centering upon the House of Atreus sounds the overtones of this then vastly important conflict, when the dying masculine world of Greece discovered in its bowels the snake that would destroy it—not just the specter of homosexuality, but the demon of incest worship which struck at the very core of survival, the most superb race yet turning in on itself, breeding inward and howling for fresh outside blood to nourish it. Incest, infantilism, narcissism, love of its own great self, that love projected in philosophy, in logic, in sculpture. This resulted in the closed, harmonious, static, present world of the Greeks, as opposed to the dynamic, spatial, conscious world of later days.

Lawrence's great passage on the magic of sex in *Fantasia*, to which I have referred above, has a deep meaning that I fear has been overlooked in appreciating his thought. Nor did Lawrence himself, so it appears to me, fully, deeply enough, understand all its implications. But he put his finger on it, he held it there steadily, and like a mesmerist (even with his limited intellect) he derived blindly, by the weight of his heavy blood and yearning, the import, the vast import of it. Moreover, not having the strength or the wisdom to go into things on a vast scale, historically, biologically, he developed impatiently (and also with intention to give his disciples a fresh impulse, though he knew it was an old reading) his peculiar language, his own dark terminology. He did this also in order to lessen the vicious influence (psychologic and historical) of those who occupied the intellectual stage, for they were artificial, false, superficial, scientific.

Parenthetically, we should consider the beginnings of Christianity and Keyserling's idea of Jesus the masculine symbol, of the world going down into night and lying for centuries in female torpor, depending on this one man, this one idea to fecundate it. It never did germinate properly but produced the monstrous abortion which we know as the modern, Christian world. If we remember that Jesus had nothing to do with woman, how he turned on his mother, how he lived celibate, how St. Paul with his crass but fiery understanding, created the contempt for woman which dominated the early church, how the business of love (which Jesus preached) had to wait for a flowering until the chivalrous period, when it was of course diverted, polluted, degraded, turned in on itself through long repressed bodily denial, then we can understand many contradictory things about the rise of Christianity.

The antique masculine principle had broken down, petered out; it was necessary for man (not woman) to restore his soul, to find again a nourishing faith. When everything had gone to smash in his world (his culture, his art, etc.) it required a mighty idea and a mighty antagonism (ambivalence) to build again. The doctrine of love which the outcasts, the poor and lowly, the disinherited took to their breasts supported them, fostered the cohesive action of faith, but underlying this doctrine of love was the heavier, sterner, more terrible doctrine (the essential masculine principle) of *war*, the salvation of man, the search for the kingdom of heaven within (which was the stress again on the instinctive, primal conscience, on the individual soul, on the blood).

It was the individual soul which had gone under with the collapse of the antique world; naturally men saw only the ruins, saw only the open wounds, interpreted the cruelties, the running sores which were on the body as the cause of the death; they failed to perceive that the running sores came from the internal malady. *They couldn't!* (Any more than we see things today—witness all our false doctrines, theories in every department of mind and thought.) And this love preached by Jesus and so eagerly seized on, was it not perceived how far beyond any ordinary love it was, that it was a cruel love that overlooked woman entirely.

Here we have what Lawrence hints at enigmatically, what he didn't express fully, the need for a love between man and man, a man's love (not at all a question of homosexuality), but a polarity between men which could embrace the ambivalent value of war, war that spells hatred, cruelty, death, and war that necessitates by its very utterance the idea of fierce, uncompromising love, the adherence to one's beliefs at any cost, the final triumph of love in death which is the meaning of crucifixion, and which man has embraced over and over again in his myths and legends. In this love and hate, this war, it is all a question of man's survival, man's world, man's soul. The war with woman is a side issue because man cannot and will not recognize that war in its true light; it is too ghastly and too shattering to his pride, to his male conscience and consciousness.

Man's wonderful world of moralities and religions, of codes of honor, of law and justice, or art, has been erected at woman's expense, in deep defiance of her, in a constant, painful effort to keep alive the illusion of his necessity in the scheme of things, which woman without saying a word, silently and by her mere presence, by her love even, negates. Because woman is amoral, woman is uncivilizing, woman is lethargy and night, woman is destruction in the profound sense that all creation is also destruction.

Man's battle to establish God, to posit the Absolute, what is this essentially but the avowal of his forlorn, desperate, hungry desire to prove woman wrong, to show that there is a permanency, a final limit, a court of last resort. The world of woman is built on flux, nature's flux, a living and dying, a birth and death, a metamorphosis. Man's great fear, is it not the primal fear of his defeat at woman's hands?

Now Lawrence, in restoring to woman her primary symbolic value, pays her the highest tribute and at the same time alienates her, and consequently this world of today, deeply feminine, distrusts or despises Lawrence's ideas. The world is dying in supine acquiescence, lulled to sleep in the scorpion's nest, and it prefers the most fantastic cures to the simple naked truth, the horrible truth with which Lawrence confronts it. Listen to his words: "The great goal of creative or constructive activity, or of heroic victory in fight, *must* always be the goal of the day-time self. But the very possibility of such a goal arises out of the vivid dynamism of the conscious blood. And the blood in an individual finds its great renewal in a perfected sex circuit."

Pregnant words. Deep words. Am I right in my interpretation of his language? This goal of the day-time self, is it not the masculine role (the great sun and fecundator, that which imagines itself the source and origin, the first cause, etc)? And is not its fight the desperate fight of masculine self-preservation? and does it not become most deeply aware of its aim in the sex struggle? does it not taste death and triumph in the sex union?

Ah, and man's coition, how ironic, mocking, comic it is in the last analysis—man lying on top of woman, dominating her, subjugating her, man the great fighting cock, the strong master of the world. He triumphs cruelly when he enters her and makes her obey, but it is the short triumph of a moment or two, just enough for nature to play her role, to wreak her havoc; and woman submits, submits so willingly (this alone ought to make him suspicious of her), submits so easily (and not just with him but with any one ... the great whore that she is) because she is accomplishing *her* destiny. In that brief gestation when she is tied to him like a disease (when they actually loathe each other, though men usually haven't the courage to admit it) she suffers her real ignominy (and man, the donkey, has tried to glorify that condition, not for her, but for himself, of course). The moment the child is born, however, she is through with man; as far as she is concerned now, as woman, he is finished, he can croak.

It follows that Lawrence is bitterly necessary to our world, especially to the Latin world which feels so secure in its attitude toward sex, toward woman. Springing from an Anglo-Saxon world where all the values had been reversed Lawrence arrived at the hard core of his philosophy; that accounts for both the enthusiasm by which he was there received and also for the antagonism; but notice the French attitude, one of pretended indifference, one of scorn and contempt, as if for an infant prodigy who had tried to shock them from their sweet lethargy. No, the French need to be aroused and incensed, as the more percipient among them really have been. For Lawrence strikes preeminently at the French stronghold, where the fight has been given up, where there is a grand indifference concerning woman, where woman becomes the toy, the amusement, the wife who joins in and titivates the husband, the husband listening respectfully, but not seriously, playing a hypocritical role of "friend." (Most often these are marriages of convenience because waiting in the wings are the patient mistresses who will provide the sexual orgies.) All is decay, inertia, languor, compromise, a happy compromise, true, and better for the nerves than the Anglo-Saxon duel which is fought out in the dark, neither side knowing what it is fighting for. Yes, the French need Lawrence because Lawrence knew the French. In the "Introduction to these Paintings" he first deplores the Anglo-Saxon attitude toward the body, and then he goes on: "And in France? In France it was more or less the same, but with a difference. The French, being more rational, decided that the body had its place, but that it should be rationalized. The Frenchman of today has the most reasonable and rationalized body possible. His conception of sex is basically hygienic. A certain amount of copulation is good for you. *Ca fait du bien au corps!* sums up the physical side of a Frenchman's idea of love, marriage, food, sport, and all the rest."

Meanwhile, the result of the Anglo-Saxons' complete reversal of values is that woman has emerged as man's "equal," man's "partner," man's "helpmate," and so on. How ridiculous this business of listening to woman! To be sure, we give her attention because we are indoctrinated with her ideas; our whole corpus of ideas is saturated with the feminine principle. She is crying for attention socially, politically, in all fields, including the arts, because she is actually eating up our world, appropriating it like the black widow spider, who after paralyzing its victim commences to suck its juices, raw and alive, or who in the midst of intercourse commences to eat. And that devout air of woman's today, her earnestness in pleading her cause, how like the praying mantis's hypocritical and deadly posture it is. But woman doesn't see it, nor man.

Now all this again is deeply revelatory. It has to do with the perversion of that maternal instinct in woman, the invisible thread that connects man with woman eternally, which when it is not properly expressed reveals the deeper, inimical, all-sufficient role of woman, becomes open scorn and contempt, usurpation of man's role in life, when man does not throw off the yoke of the swaddling clothes and the apron-string, the root-malady in the case of Joyce, Proust, and Lawrence. This pain, to which they never became adjusted, accounts for the direction, the tendency of their work (or the meaning expressed by their work), a disease which permitted them through the distortion of reality to understand better the nature of our sexual ills. (In the case of Alexander and of Napoleon, it could be argued, this malady enabled them to conquer the world!) In the history of all the mad Caesars and Czars, the Pharaohs and the Emperors, we have this background of mother domination, of incest, of patricide and matricide, of crippled men who conquer the world but are made *cocu* by their wives.

With the emergence of militant woman in the nineteenth century, moreover, came the dramas of Ibsen and Strindberg, the former showing us the social implications of the problem and the latter the biological. Strindberg stands out like a mad demon, the male driven wild by this condition, and creating out of his madness all his work. The value of Strindberg was to open our eyes once again to the deep import of the struggle in *Confessions of a Fool, The Father, The Inferno*; but Strindberg remained a misogynist whereas Lawrence (perhaps because of

his latent femininity) arrived at a higher or deeper understanding. His abuse goes out equally to man and to woman; he
stresses continually the need for each to accentuate their sex,
to insist upon polarity, so as to strengthen the sexual connection which can renew and revive all the other forces, the major
forces that are necessary for the development of the whole
being, to stay the waste of contemporary disintegration.

How difficult, hopeless almost, is the situation he reveals by
that terrible phrase: "if there *are* any such men nowadays"!
How, he asks, can woman desist from this hideous and obscene
love-will, this scorpion's nest that she has built, if men do not
believe in themselves? It is a vicious circle in which the one is
as much to blame as the other—and the real cause lies deeper
than this surface war between the sexes, as it is understood
today. The real cause issues from the evil seed of the Christian
ideal, which once had its value and nourished us, but which, as
must happen with all ideals, finally exhausted itself, The ideal
of love must go, he repeats over and over, like a cry of anguish.
This is not a plea for carnal, sensual love, sex in itself (which is
disastrous), however, but a plea to understand the limitations,
the paralyzing effects of *all* ideals—"the oblique, indirect
method of expression" to use Keyserling's words. It is the effort
to take the emphasis away from the abstract and external
(which produces merely oscillation and rotation) and restore it
to the center within, so that all our acts, all our expression, may
proceed from within outward, from the individual soul, the
final seat of authority. The Kingdom of Heaven is within us.

In this respect, the difference between Lawrence's and
Joyce's attitudes towards woman is instructive. Joyce, through
his filth and abomination, his throngs, mystery, flood of words,
is still bound to the woman in hatred. His is the primitive
Christian attitude which seized on the carnal, sexual role of
woman in order to exalt the spiritual, generative principle of
the male. Woman the whore, source of all evil, seducer of man's
natural innocence, etc. This gives to Joyce's descriptions of
woman (chiefly the Molly Bloom portrait) its great carnal attraction, its lubricity and obscenity, because it is based on a
fearful, overwhelming desire. His hatred of his own mother, of
her influence, and the Church's influence, is the admission of
defeat at woman's hands. Lawrence has really emancipated
himself. He puts himself above and beyond the sexual view of

religion. So, when finally freed of his incestuous bond, he restores a dark, cruel, mysterious and primitive male god (Quez-talcoatl, who is only one manifestation), and he can again enter into sexual relations with woman in the full vigor of unrestrained passion, animality, carnality. Because, not only through woman, but through all things that he pierces he will discover the eternal mystery of things. He does not seek solution to life *in* love, but *through* love.

Now the French, in appraising Lawrence as an obscene animal, or as an adolescent mind, or as a diseased Anglo-Saxon, reveal, as I have already pointed out, their own limitations. (Note how differently the Spanish treat him—they retain a more medieval view of woman; the French represent the Hellenistic view in decay.) In France, where there is the attempt to preserve the Greek view, woman has submitted to the tendency, the direction of tradition; at her best, the French woman resembles the Greek courtesan, friend and equal of the philospher, the only woman whom the Greek man respected. But actually, in the vast majority, she plays the trivial, insignificant role which woman assumed in the decadent periods of both Greece and Rome; she is not even regarded respectfully as a mother, as she was in the earlier days of Sparta and Tarquinian Rome. That is to say, she has failed to preserve her individual role, she has been conquered by that masculine world which the ancients represented.

In America, where there has never been a strong cultural trend, a tradition, a point of view, where everything has been in flux and disintegration, she has played just the opposite role, she has triumphed over man's world. Both attitudes are lopsided, and, as we see, have produced their ills. In Spain and Italy there remains yet the fierce antagonism between the sexes (witness the scorn of woman for man and vice versa in *Twilight in Italy*); but here the male attitude, and the female too, is blind and instinctive, no consciousness of the role to be played, of its significance. The essential antagonism needs to be brought out into the open, to be understood upstairs, as it were.

The Frenchman knows that the woman who thinks as we do has no blood relationship with us. He only permits the woman to imagine that she is his mental equal—he is too weary to fight her. But in Soviet Russia, where woman is the "comrade" and "equal" of men, where marriage as an institution has broken down (in Japan too, where divorce is so easy) we see the triumph of the love ideal, see man and woman joined together like oxen to illustrate the nobility of the philosophy of "work." The children are incidentals, given over to the State nursery, to hygienic rearing (a vast anonymous incubation), and parental love is reduced to a minimum, education becomes an affair of the State on a truly grand scale. This is all like an echo or image of the Aztec civilization, a paternal socialism with rigid hierarchies and castes, with production as the goal and the religion a bloody hecatomb of sacrifices. The sacrifices in Russia are just as bloody but not so patent—*everything* is being sacrificed to the end: Communism, the ideal!

Here, where the blood-relationship has been broken, where the woman thinks like the man, acts like the man, you have the quintessence of spiritual disintegration. Soviet Russia is irreligious (which would be excellent, were it merely a question of destroying an encumbrance like the Catholic church), but there is much more to it than this: it is the acceptance of all the scientific credos (with no appreciation of the myths behind them), the fulfillment of the materialism ushered in by erroneous view of scientific exploration (and since thoroughly exploded) in the nineteenth century. Russia is, in other words, what she has always been—the anachronism in history. It was just because she was inchoate, unformed, lacking in tradition, barbarous, vigorous, that she could take over a "wrong" idea; the revolution may have sprung from the people, from their sorrow and degradation, but the form, the trend of the revolution was established by an "intellectual" group: it is the outcome of the scientific, atheistic, materialistic doctrines of Darwin, Marx, Huxley, et al.

With Lawrence, who is also the product of that nineteenth-century milieu, however, we have a man who, like Nietzsche, though far less superior, places the whole emphasis on the Man, salvation through the self, through the creation of a higher, fanatical, Utopist idea which, nonetheless, is in accord with the wisdom of the best minds we know. Hence, the title of this chapter, "The Sacred Body", since it will not be the mind alone, nor religion, nor an ideal, nor an economic amelioration, nor education which will bring about salvation. What is called Lawrence's "sex mysticism" I want to show as an effort to give back to sexuality its cosmic character.

Lawrence unfortunately had not enough stamina to develop his ideas rigorously. But there is a "macrocosmic" character to his work which is all important. His effort to have done with *idealism*, with moralities, with democracy, brought him back to the body, the imperishable microcosm whose projection gives us the world. In the roll of iconoclast he performs the service required of us who are to precipitate the inevitable debacle. The revolt which he waged on every frontier of life is a thoroughly spiritual revolt, and the only one worth engaging in today. It throws into ignominious relief the petty bread-and-butter revolts going on now everywhere in the world. And this politico-economic revolt now appears dangerous, not because it is destructive of the old order, but because it may stay for a while the hand of destiny; it may usher in a brief, dying Renaissance (the pragmatic culmination of Christian thought) and thereby create false hopes.

For if there be such a pitiful *contre-temps* it will not be a humanistic revival, creative of rich personalities, as was the previous Renaissance, but a collective revival, its ideology based on the lowest common denominator, the average man, its goal Work, humanity being pensioned off in its old age, leisure arriving too late. That there can not be any worth-while human revolution until man reaches a consciousness of his own sacred individuality—and this, from all signs, is an improbability, since to emancipate himself he would have to renounce everything he considers necessary and valuable today—would seem obvious. But that Lawrence put his finger on the dilemma, that he diagnosed the disease, and pointed to the only, even if Utopian, remedy is also clear. His work, then, has great importance for us, wholly apart from its aesthetic value.

* * *

Lawrence, according to Luhan, "railed against dancing. He called it an indecent tail-wagging." But he could dance all right with the Indians, and it was dancing he spoke of in connection with starting a new colony which would find a central core of living. This attitude marks again his great distinction between "sexuality" which he hated, and a sensuality rooted in a primitive apprehension of one's relation with universe, with woman, with man. Sensuality is the animal instincts, which he wanted to bring out again; sexuality, the false cultural attitude which he wanted to overthrow, because it is a narrow interpretation of life.

And herein, too, is to be found the great difference between Lawrence's worship of the body and the modern emphasis upon action, sports—the "new humanism" as it is called:

> If there is one thing in the air at the present moment, above the melee of modernism, it is the note of evasion, of escape from the break-up of personality. One way out is the human body.... It might almost be said that what is taking place is a rediscovery of the body and the formulation of a new and mystic "humanism," with the body as a center. An escape is sought through sensuality, but not the sensuality that has been known of old—rather, the pure and rarified sensuality of the athlete, the man who triumphs with his body.... In all this may be seen a reflection of that necessity of action which the one who had just emerged from the period of the War felt: the necessity of acting in order that he might feel himself alive.... The end of it is, the physical man is to be resurrected, by way of giving a meaning to this mechanized universe in which we live. The body means action, and action is a refuge, possibly the most satisfying that there is, and it is precisely this refuge that the "new humanism" seeks.

Certainly the descerning student of Lawrence will realize that this "cult of Hercules" has little in common with Lawrence's emphasis upon the physical. The body as a refuge, yes; as an escape even, but for the soul's salvation. The clue to the universe for him was always the spontaneous living soul. Not merely integration of the personality, not just a Greek revival of body culture nor the establishment of a race of god-men, but a mystic union with the universe was his aim. And the body was but a means of renewing that contact, a symbol of a lost unity. The old, old theory of the macrocosm inspired him because it kept alive in him this sense of unity which he sought to reestablish.

His was not a "rare and purified sensuality" (whatever this expression may mean), but a thoroughly pagan glorification of the instincts; it was not the body he feared, but the mind, the court of death for the instincts. With this image ever before him of man's undying connection with the universe, he fashioned his own cosmogony, his own psychology, his own physiology. It is a mystic body through and through, and it carries with it its own morality, none of which is acceptable, or comprehensible even, to this age. Ridden and obsessed as we are by all the old ideologies—religious, social, ethical—saturated and perverted by the scientific jargon which we no longer have the courage, or the will, to criticize (let alone reject).

"All Lawrence's philosophy was deeply affected by the idea of the mystical body," writes Frederick Carter:

> *once he had dipped into the subject of the body and its relation to the true man, and the belief that in it his full powers slept or were obscured and must be brought to activity, thereafter it often, perhaps always, motivated his imagery and defined his method of approach in psychology. He caught there a glimpse of that profoundly simple ancient idea of man the microcosm and the pattern of the universe.... It was this idea of the mastery existent in Man, this vision of each man as the microcosm holding the pattern of the universe within himself, that held the deepest fascination for him. A man with all the wonders of the stars burning within him, born from the stars and native of the whole wide world from middle core to outmost deep, this was the figure and symbol that he hailed.*

It is this mystic element in Lawrence's writing—Carter is quite right—which cannot be stressed enough. It is the element which gives his work its strange appeal, its urgency. In a way which only the mystic can fully appreciate, Lawrence strove to use the inner and outer view of the world into one valid, vital psychologic reality. In that book which has baffled so many of his readers—*The Plumed Serpent*—we see with what passionate, creative strength Lawrence reinvested the old myth of the dragon.

In *Apocalypse,* where he has written at length of the myth of the dragon, where he has stated again for the last time his mystic view of the universe, he concludes: "What we want is to destroy our false, inorganic connections, especially those related to money, and re-establish the living organic connections, with the cosmos, the sun and earth, with mankind, and nation and family. Start with the sun and the rest will slowly, slowly happen." There is nothing vastly unfamiliar here to those acquainted with Lawrence's way of thinking; a certain triviality, almost, in his reference to the importance of *money*. But the important line, the really cryptic line, is the last: start with the sun and the rest will slowly, slowly happen. From the very outset, as evangel of the new order, he had stressed the sun: it is the Alpha and Omega for him.

Now this imperative need in him to restore the generative principle which the sun symbolized for the older masculine Cultures arose from his awareness and fear of the emasculate nature of our civilization. The disintegration which he perceived everywhere he felt most keenly in the world of sex. He saw everything going grey, opaque—typical Lawrencean adjectives. He saw a danger of the flame perishing, the fire dying down and all the color of life running out. He did not want to accept the current myth of the sun as the source of life, of our temporal, planetary life, because he could not face the thought of a possible end to life. His own fierce desire for life is so strong that he anthropomorphizes the universe; he not only will not concede that there are any dead planets, but he will not even concede that the source of our earthly life is the sun.

The idea which science has rendered familiar to us, that life on earth, all forms of life, will some day be extinguished as the fires of the sun die down, this idea was anathema to Lawrence. And so he reverses the process. It is we, the living, he insists, who give life to the sun and the stars. The origin of life— whence come we, whither go we?—he admitted that he knew nothing about. He dismissed them, even as Lao-tze dismissed the idea of God, and the soul, and immortality. There is no solution to these problems, he says over and over again. He knew only this thing called Life, whose heart is mystery—life ever-renewed, a perpetual flame, a source unquenchable. And if the intellect deny this, he would say, then there is something wrong with the intellect, then the intellect must give way to the blood. It is the mind of man, he insists, which has created all the snares and pitfalls. It is the mind of man which would deny the life instincts.

The whole process in Lawrence, as I have said above, is one of microcosmizing the universe. Man must again consume the cosmos. There must arise the process of extraversion. Having ingested the cosmos, man must spew it out again. From being overwhelmed he must overwhelm. The mere blob of dust, the sporadic, enigmatic phenomenon, *man*, a mere incident in a chain of inexplicable cause and effect, must rise superior to its understanding. The mind which is capable of reducing life to such terms must be disowned. The mind which has reduced life to such insignificant proportions has also, in the past, exalted life to fabulous proportions. Life rises and sinks in the thermometer of the mind.

Lawrence fixes himself permanently in this mercurial fluid of the mind. It is a vacuum, but he does not seem to be aware of it. He registers new degrees, or imagines he does, but they were fixed in advance. The whole corpus of thought is fixed in the body—there is no escape. The mind may utter the most fantastic thoughts, but the body is anchored, and all the forms of thought are fixed therein. Deep surprises there may be, but there is always a reconciliation. And so, when Lawrence gives free rein to his mind, or his spirit, or his soul, or whatever he chooses to call it, he is brought back; he may cover the whole trajectory of man's longing, which is what an artist usually does in his work, but ultimately he is brought back. He is brought back to the mystic fundament of the body, and through it he experiences the dissolution of all things.

During the Renaissance it seemed, indeed, as if the body had come into its own again—but this resurgence was only to nourish and sustain the soul. The vast re-making of language, coincident with the Renaissance, was brought about by the great creative individuals of that period to fit the changing soul concept. In the case of Rabelais the gusto and violence of that language may be said to have swept like a plague through the soul of his people; there is not only the joy of life in it, but the joy of death. The imminence of death was still there, and its triumph was celebrated. Even in death Rabelais' language gave joy, courage, wisdom—whereas in our modern ghost of Rabelais, James Joyce, there is not even hope. The sense of life, we say, ran high, but this sense of life was based on a feeling for death.

In Shakespeare it is already deteriorated, as Lawrence has well pointed out. That canker in the soul of man, of Western man, that poison of doubt which assails him more and more from Shakespeare on, had its roots in the very soul of Western man—in the Hamlet-Faust antagonism. The great dynamic aspect of the Faustian soul has its counterpart in the myth of

Hamlet. The great Will carries within it the germ of its own destruction: *doubt*. Certainly this poison makes its appearance in every civilization, as it progresses onward toward its death, but the peculiar Western skepticism reveals a particularly insidious and fatal quality. It makes its appearance in the tempestuous soul of a Shakespeare in the very bloom and vigor of the Renaissance, at the very moment when the Western soul is asserting its conquest over Destiny. The great, yearning Faustian spirit which had opened up new worlds, which had made itself drunk with new horizons, and in Rabelais which celebrates that drunkenness, this same spirit emerges in the space of a few generations with the most terrible incarnation of its malady: *Hamlet.*

Proust has exposed this canker in our souls magnificently by his treatment of the "Albertine" theme, by his whole *exposé* of the soul of the invert wherein doubt and jealousy together assume stupendously significant proportions. Lawrence has touched upon it in his references to Cézanne in "Introduction to these Paintings" when, in speaking of the inability of the English to produce any but a very few genuine painters, he comes to the conclusion that the fault lies in the English attitude towards life. They are paralyzed by fear, he says. *Fear of what?* "It is an old fear, which seemed to dig in to the English soul at the time of the Renaissance. Nothing could be more lovely and fearless than Chaucer. But already Shakespeare is morbid with fear, fear of consequences. That is the strange phenomenon of the English Renaissance: this mystic terror of the consequences, the consequences of action . . . . " He goes on to speak of the difference between the Oedipus myth and the Hamlet legend. "Orestes is dogged by destiny and driven mad by the Eumenides. But Hamlet is overpowered by horrible revulsion from his physical connexion with his mother, which makes him recoil in similar revulsion from Ophelia and almost from his father, even as a ghost. He is horrified at the merest suggestion of physical connexion, as if it were an unspeakable taint."

The cause of all this Lawrence traces to syphilis: "The appearance of syphilis in our midst gave a fearful blow to our sexual life. The real natural innocence of Chaucer was impossible after that." He adds that some one ought to make a thorough study of the effects of "pox" on the minds and emotions of the various nations of Europe at about the time of our Elizabethans. Gradually we are led back to his perennial theme—that we are afraid of the instincts, afraid of the intuition within us: "Now we know one another only as ideal or social or political entities, fleshless, bloodless, and cold, like Bernard Shaw's creatures. Intuitively we are dead to one another, we have all gone cold." We have a dread of everything but ideas, he says, ideas which *can't* contain bacteria!

I quote this characteristic piece of Lawrencean dogma because, however susceptible it may be to ridicule, there is in it nevertheless, as indeed there is in his wildest flights, a provocative germ of truth. The studies which he desired to see made were already made, and in abundance, before he had ever set down his thoughts. Not only had the "pox" been studied, but all the flora and fauna of disease which from the fourteenth to the seventeenth century ravaged Europe. Indeed, no vital understanding of the Renaissance is possible without a deep study of the phenomena of death and disease out of which it emerged. But Lawrence grasped a vital point when he read into the legend of Hamlet this blow at the procreative body. For when sex is the prime symbol, every blow from without is a blow to the procreative body. And so, when Lawrence approaches the Hamlet theme, it is to appropriate it into the corpus of his thought, to weld it as he has welded every other theme, to the nexus of his cosmological scheme. Hamlet struck a blow at the universe, not at man alone. Hamlet *is* syphilis, the syphilis of the mind. Hamlet, the disease, strikes at the blood, at that blood-consciousness which Lawrence has raised to such importance. One can well understand that for Lawrence syphilis was not just another disease, or even a phenomenal disease: it was a mortal disease which could make its appearance only when the body had been utterly denied and despised.

We might well ask ourselves if those great plagues which ravaged Europe from the fourteenth to the seventeenth century were not the outward, visible manifestation of that warfare which had already begun to devastate the soul of Western man. The man of the Middle Ages was still an integrated being; but by the time of the Renaissance the great trinity of body, mind and soul is shattered. The Reformation is the finished expression of that great dissolution of the holy trinity. From the Reformation on there is the ever-increasing divorce between soul and mind, the exaltation of the latter above the former, with its culmination today in the complete bankruptcy of the mind and the paralysis of the instincts—all of which had its inception in the Middle Ages.

After the Crusades came the Black Death. Upon the discovery of America, syphilis. Coincident with these blights the significance of life fades, the body withers, the soul decays. The exuberance of Lawrence's language is the joy of the body recovering its soul—or of its attempt to recover the soul, for Lawrence knew that such recovery was impossible. He was born with this white syphilis in his veins; his work is permeated with it. And when he rises to a fury and passion, when he fulminates in a bacteriological stew of dream and frenzy, it is to work off this toxin, to shoot the virus into every living organism, every pseudo-living organism, in order that he might free us of the white death. As in the old days, when the Black Death flourished and the wildest cures were rampant, he recommends sometimes that one stand on an empty stomach in the early morning over a latrine and inhale the stench. You are not dying fast enough! he yells. He saw the world full of death—but a cellular, biologic death. He wanted a death on all fronts, a vital, spiritual death! He saw that we were dying piecemeal, a tripartite death: first the body, then the spirit, and now the mind. *Only die altogether!* he begs us. Die out utterly, so that a new race of man may be born!

To return once again to Murry who says that sacrifice is the *be-all* of existence, the very condition of existence. "Man dies in his personality, to be raised again in impersonality." This sounds almost like the genuine thing, but Murry does not go far enough. If instead of sacrifice of the personality we put "surrender of the self," we understand Lawrence's Dionysian role, the total surrender. That is, a fulfillment. What man wants is the fulfillment of his deepest desires, Lawrence says over and over. Not sacrifice, such as Jesus made. It is true that the whole drama is played out on the theme of sacrifice, but it depends on the interpretation one puts on it, the manner and way of sacrifice, its significance.

Lawrence realized that by sacrificing his life he had sacrificed the most precious thing he possessed. It was the fullest expression of his total being. His doctrine, that *we must sacrifice existence to being* (not to "living," please note) presents us with a hopeless tangle we never escape. Murry does not distinguish between the sacrifice Lawrence made through his art and the man's own vision of Life. He takes him literally, as he takes Jesus literally. He doesn't get out of the conflict himself. He merely takes sides: Jesus against Lawrence. He misses both. For at bottom they are the same fundamental type. Lawrence worships the human, worships life; Jesus worships the divine. Both are inhuman, or superhuman. Both horribly conscious of their humanness—which is their frailty, their dividedness. Jesus denies the flesh, Lawrence accepts it, glorifies it. Lawrence is the logical culmination, the apotheosis of 2,000 years of Christian idealism, now gone over into its opposite. Now when we have stopped striving to become like Jesus, when we have recognized the evil of that striving, we discover that we are really that which we were striving to be.

To acknowledge the sovereign independence of the spirit, as Murry writes, is to put this world under a shadow. This is a living death, in a perpetual dream and hope, a futile war between the antagonistic elements of one's being. It is the spiritual domination which Lawrence fought against, because, as he said, we have had enough of it; Christianity has served its purpose; man has been spiritualized; he is withering at the top of the tree. He must be reminded that he is a tree, not just leaves and branches. Lawrence voices the despair of the ages, in which it is felt that man has been crucified by the spirit. Unless we can give the *coup de grâce* to this hegemony of mind and spirit, unless we can decapitate this head which is out of all proportion to the rest of the body, we shall never resume our human role, we shall never live again in the flesh, as complete human beings.

Consequently Lawrence was right, when in his Introduction to *Fantasia,* he said that Freud did accomplish one good thing: he made us aware of our animal nature, of the body which we have repressed. For it is here that we have a chance to connect again with the universe, through the dark gods within. And the analyst is to be praised who has this for his aim: to reveal to the patient the true nature of the self, of personality—the analyst who gives his patient a real center of gravity, a vital and concrete axis upon which to rotate *with* the world in place of the tiny egoistic axis upon which he has been spinning around in a dead nullity of being. The other kind of analyst, the one who offers absolution and salvation, the one who caters to the petty ego is disgusting and a fake.

But especially Lawrence was right, when in answer to Huxley's scientific proofs regarding evolution, he put his hand on his solar plexus and said: "I don't feel it *here.*" What a primitive and deeply revelatory gesture. Like putting his hand on his soul!

Throughout his life Lawrence emphasized the instinctual life, blood-consciousness, the solar plexus. He was a man of spirit himself, a super-Christ, as he regarded himself. He understood the overwhelming need of modern man to recapture the attitude of the ancients towards the body. In *Apocalypse,* as well as in his essay on Cézanne, he reveals the process of degeneration which set in with Christianity. He fulminates against the Judaic view of the world, against the idea of personal immortality, against the Socratic view of self-knowledge, against the sceptical attitude of science, against knowledge itself, against education. He has the early Greek feeling for the body, the early Greek conception of Eros. He is interested in the astrologic view of the ancients because it offers a cosmic view of life, a macrocosmic pattern of the universe. Only in this way can life acquire purpose and significance.

In a sense, Lawrence, in the short span of a lifetime, recapitulated the long struggle for human freedom which the Greeks, in their hey-day, apotheosized. He realized that man's struggle was to live as god, and that only when he had attained this goal, could he become truly human.

What I have referred to as the Chaplinesque character of his life is due only to the fact that for a "new" or "nascent" personality there is no sphere of action in this world of as-is, the world of mores. A fanatical man looks either crazy or ridiculous. The dignity and eloquence of Lawrence's gestures thus lie in his works. It seems anomalous and grotesque that a coal-miner's son should be intoning Christian hymns in Cornwall and dancing in suede and bells with the Navajo. Yet, foolish as this latter activity seems, it is as gesture that it counts. He himself told us that there was no real going back, but that one could dip backward retrospectively, as it were, in a greater curve of livingness.

This of course marks the gulf between Lawrence's and the contemporary attitude of whites toward the Indian, one of oscillating hatred and admiration, of guilt that sequesters and isolates the Indian while at the same time it grants him lands, etc. This is what leads to the state of affairs in which many Indians, under white "domination," are paradoxically better cared for than our own white brethren! For the Indian Lawrence had not false admiration, no guilt, no sentimentality. He went to them, not to Luhan, to learn from them about life, through the living experience of them, not through ethnology!

He thought, like Jesus, of establishing a "new world" (like the Transcendentalist Brook Farm, perhaps) here on earth—in Florida, Mexico, the West, the Andes, Australia, Canada even. Again he is the artist wanting to make concrete his ideas. As savior and redeemer he plays a dual role. His vision makes him realize his godhood and the necessity of self-sacrifice; his humanity makes him want to renounce his role and live in the here and now. Would he ever have conquered the Romantic in himself, like Goethe? Perhaps there is no answer; his life was cut short. We have no idea what he would have evolved into had he lived longer.

CHAPTER VII

Philosophy

IT SEEMS as if an appreciation of Lawrence must always be half-antagonistic. Perhaps the reason for this is that conflict is what he himself best expressed. His first essay was called "The Crown"; but in spite of *The Plumed Serpent*, his subject is not really the crown, the prize, but the antagonists who are fighting for it, the lion and the unicorn, a continual metaphor of his own struggle, first to be and then to know himself. A momentous attempt to learn, by living, *to be* and to learn, by living, *to know*, is what his autobiography discloses.

The dual or antagonistic elements in him furnish the clue to his use of symbols. Look for the repetitious words, they give the clue to his conflicting self, by expressing the opposite of what he is, what he is striving to be. For example:

"The dark gods"	*a man of light, of the spirit, an intellectual.*
"The Absolute"	*a man divided, seeking unity; one who saw the relativity of things, the tolerance of indifference, as Spengler says of the "civilized" man, and was hurt by it.*
"Beyond woman"	*one who is chained to her cruelly, through his bi-sexual Redeemer nature, by Oedipus complex.*
"Corruption and death"	*one who is free of evil, of distintegrative qualities, one who is flow and movement, not fixed in winter marshes of living death but vitally alive, a flowering of being!*
"Dark potency"	*one whose potency is upper, spiritual and only too obvious.*

"Non-human, non-   *because he is too human and too*
personal stress"   *personal an individual.*

His choice of dark god, Quetzalcoatl, Bird-Serpent, is significant. Even in his choice of god he retains the duality—he resolves his problem by uniting the discordant elements. And this hybrid god in both its aspects is the symbol for the soul. He arrives at his highest symbol by reverting to the animal world. He wants to define the god through the substantial image, with its emphasis on instincts and feeling. Consider the serpent, evolved from the original soul-worm that left the corpse, it stands for the wisdom of the earth, a creature chained to the earth, obliged to crawl always on the surface with its belly, deriving its wisdom from belly contact, through sense of touch which Lawrence says we most keenly lack. For he deplores the impoverishment of our sense of touch.

This wisdom of the serpent, earth derived, is the *only* wisdom—it is the sign of the perpetual limitations that confront the soaring, inquisitive mind of man. It preserves the body feeling, the sense of origin. It also bespeaks the sensuous nature of man, the apprehension and appreciation of life through the sacred body. Renewal through the earth, through life instincts, through shedding the old skin, through constant metamorphosis, through the wisdom of experience, through contact with tangibles, realities. The whole allegorical significance of the serpent, the sense of sin, of evil, is splendid and revelatory.

The bird represents the highest metamorphosis of the soul-idea among all the symbols of spirituality found among animal worshippers. The bird, like the worm, rises from the dead body, and in point of evolution the bird evolves from the serpent. Here, parenthetically, we should note that the transition from earth to heavens, as done in primitive man's macrocosmizing, is an abrupt jump from earth to stars—the long, devious route back to earth through man again. The bird is the instrument to bridge to the beyond, the great spiritual quest of man.

Thus the two predominant traits of Lawrence's nature: close, close to earth, wisdom from body, contact, relationship, cruel wisdom or truth from reality. The serpent we fear most—most malign, deadly. Treachery. False teacher. Destroyer of innocence. And then the bird who satisfied his craving for immortality, for things beyond the reach, its delicacy, its ethereality, its lordliness. Thus, by an Absolute that combines the dual elements of his being, he resolves the schism in his nature. All Absolutes, upon analysis, turn out to be Relative, to be the union of irreconcilable things. It is his very dualism, his disunity, that leads him to posit the opposite: Unity.

In playing the role of Unifier, however, (which is a violation of his real nature, of man's real nature—an assumption of that which he is not, but forever aspires to be) he pays the penalty, he suffers the pangs of guilt, he is haunted by the other side of himself which he has denied at the expense of glorifying the one. His sense of guilt leads to the expression of his crime by the apprehension of his double—the alter ego he has denied—for the sake of a metaphysical victory. This is why when man is most religious the god he has created is opposed most vigorously by a Satanic force. And Satan is always more real, convincing, because he springs from the sense of guilt. The problem of evil is therefore most baffling and cruel, enigmatic, for the great saintly characters. The stronger the god element, the stronger likewise the human element (as with Dostoevski!), and this is so because the god-like quality of the man is reflected in his Narcissism.

Lawrence hovers around this question, unsuspectingly, or unconsciously, when he answers the Luhan woman on the Self: "When you are final master of yourself, you are nothing . . . ." He knows that the love of self brings about the disintegration of the ego. He comes so perilously near to this insanity, this schizophrenia, that it is only by a herculean effort that he arrives at a solution—in his dark god, Quetzalcoatl. By surrendering his trust and faith to the lordship and dominance of a god he absolves himself of the responsibility and trust which he had by implication asked his fellow-man to believe in, when he appointed himself artist, that is, God. Throughout his work, his sense of guilt is terrific, and there is the obsessive, persecution mania which leads so often, in these cases, to paranoia: "We can retreat upon the proud, isolate self"—and rot there!

The greater the sense of mystery the greater the obscurity in the artist's work. Dostoevski and Lawrence are fairly equal here—only with Dostoevski it is a struggle on the religious plane, all a question of soul; with Lawrence arriving later, representative of soulless civilized man, it is a struggle, or problem of the human-animal nature. Dostoevski glorifies the spirit and Lawrence the animal nature—both are wrestling with God—because one can arrive at the divine by digging down through the dark unconscious layers or one can arrive by expanding the consciousness to its most evanescent. In both there is the same intensity of conflict, the Dionysian conflict, the same self-sacrifice through work, the question of man's salvation and freedom from sin and evil through redemption, of resurrection into another better world, of wholeness, final union with the universe.

The trance state of the mystic and the hallucinated state of the schizophrenic are almost similar. Both are conditions of madness. With the mystic it is momentary and rejuvenating; with the diseased man it is permanent and killing, which it would be with the mystic if prolonged. Indeed Dostoevski has explained often enough that the moment of ecstasy is insupportable, that it is sufficient to last a man all his life, that it brings an overwhelming joy and clarity! And Proust also has explained it marvellously when describing the various revelations that were made him.

Enough to mark mysticism out as a taint, as a variant of madness, as a nervous disorder which can move on to complete insanity or to the highest religious efflorescence. The important point is that it is a species of insanity, that the mystic or the epileptic or the neurotic or the schizophrenic, when seized, is completely broken apart: the split has divided him so completely that his ego disintegrates and he becomes one with the universe.

When the mystic's body and soul are intact his ecstatic, religious nature acts as a mildly permanent and salutary power. The conflicting forces in him are in a fine balance, and the tension between these opposing halves of his nature affords him the sense and enjoyment of mystery. The truly religious spirit exists in man only when he is whole and his soul is young—that is when he is well polarized. All life then has a sacred character. With age, whether individual or cultural or racial, the religious feeling dies down—it is revived desperately as a refuge and escape, toward the very end of life, when all other solutions fail. It has not been the animating force of his life. The wisdom of age constitutes the ability to accept reality, which is the knowledge of certain death—substantial, personal, individual extinction. It no longer seeks to disguise the fundamental cruelty and terror of life because it is too weary for further struggle. It is not the acceptance of destiny so much, as the *succumbing* to it.

In youth (Spengler says "only youth has a future . . . *Destiny is always young*"), destiny is accepted *for* its terror. The terror inspires. This is the reason for Nietzsche's reminding us that the "tragic sense" arose only in the youthful Greeks, that it was a *neurosis of health*, that it was not pessimism but a joyous acceptance of life! In old age the symbols which inspired youth are explained away. Old age sees behind the illusions—too weary to deny any more the ultimate truths. It has learned, with sorrow, that the fundamental problems of life are insoluble. It learns to accommodate itself to the pain and the discord. This accommodation is the approach, naturally, of death.

Conversely, the ability to erect ever new, ever more numerous symbols is the sign of vitality. A people, a race, a culture, an individual, die only when the ability to create illusions is exhausted. The interest in history is the interest in our own dying. History reveals to us the progress of life from one set of illusory symbols to another. It reveals the drama, that is the life-struggle, centered upon each nourishing dream and illusion. It vitiates and negates them all by explanation, by genetic accounts, by theories of evolution, by problems of relativity, points of view, perspective. It stands outside and apart from the pure stream of movement, which is life, and scrutinizes these things coldly and aloofly, skeptically, unbelievingly, also *regretfully*. For old age the last sustaining myth, or symbol, is science—knowledge. Science is the faith of the mind displacing the faith of the soul. It explains the death of all things. It offers as consolation wisdom, which is the sorrowful man's burden. Joy is wiped out. Enthusiasm also. All the instincts are perverted, and only at the very end is it realized that the deep wish in man, which has enabled him to live with his science, is a wish for annihilation, for death. And this is so obvious, so patent, in our day, as science moves on to destroy all hopes, all illusions, all myths, all religious fervor, all sacredness, in its theoretical domain, and in the practical, applied sphere of activity, inventing the engines of ultimate physical extinction.

From faith to knowledge is from life to death. That is History.

Just as the double haunts the guilty conscience of the artist, so the unconscious, the unknowable, the mysterious, the reservoir of instinctive, animal life, haunts the modern superconscious being. It is his Satan, and it is incarnated in the machine to which he has become the docile slave. It is his evil genius, his alter ego, his *doppelgänger*, his destroyer. Where the religious man suffered from sin, the atheist suffers from insanity. That is why the exorcism, the demonology, of modern scientific psychology resembles so strongly that medieval nonsense. The drama of good and evil which was once played out in the soul is now played out in the mind. The unconscious, which is the seat of the devil, wreaks its vengeance on the conscious mind. The Absolutism of the Mind is defeated by the negative powers of the suppressed soul which are struggling to come to the surface. There is no conflict any longer between animal nature and the divine because there is no recognition of a soul which would nourish this sharp dualism. The mind is supreme, absolute, and it is splitting—and the history of the rise of all the insanities of modern times is the history of this increasing schism. The glorified Self is falling apart. It is haunted by the Unconscious.

Lawrence's search for God is this attempt to arrive at the source of life, the fountain itself, and it matters little whether God be a plumed serpent or an Idea; or rather, for Lawrence it had to be the dark, animal thing, since the vessel of life had been drained of all spirituality. When in *The Rainbow* he came to pay his tribute to the spiritual forces in man, by the very imagery that he employs he admits the great dynamic principle which religion symbolizes, even though it be the tyrannical power of the spirit which the cathedral embodies. He sees in the cathedral that absolutism which carries humanity along like a great tide; he sees also the even as humanity is being borne along by the tide, engulfed and overwhelmed, it is conscious of its fate and resisting: "These sly little [gargoyle] faces peeped out of the grand tide of the cathedral like something that knew better. They knew quite well, these little imps that retorted on man's own illusion, that the cathedral was not absolute . . . .Apart from the life and spring of the great impulse towards the altar, these little faces had separate wills, separate motions, separate knowledge, which rippled back in defiance of this tide . . . ."

This is the woman Anna's view of the cathedral, the woman anchored in the reality of the flesh, anchored to earth, who regards the clinching and mating of stone arches in the dusky beyond of man's spiritual world as a deadening thing, a life-destroyer. Through the woman Lawrence presents the powers of earth, the wisdom of the serpent, the destroyer of divine innocence and youth. Woman it is who by her deep rootedness in nature resists that idealistic urge toward the destruction of the flesh which the questioning spirit of man, as presented in the cathedral, forever symbolizes. In the sly, impish faces that peer out of the grand tide of the cathedral she sees the separate will, the separate knowledge, the human, individual defiance, of the tyranny of the abstract and the absolute. She devines that the hidden secret of that great communal sacrifice which allowed the cathedrals to be reared lies in the significant work of the humble, human craftsman, he who is not the great architect or artist obeying an impulse beyond him, but a tiny microcosm imposing on the grand facade this decorative touch of personal, individual will, and that he expresses his religious-ness by a form of obscenity, in creating these gargoyles, these self-likenesses.

The God who is personified in this grand cathedral with its flaming windows and its rushing arches, that God is something in us that is borne along on a human tide and it is we, the grotesque, the despised, the ignoble who must also be immor-talized in the body of the cathedral. We have erected it and we adorn it, and we can destroy it too when it suits us. It is not absolute. We have fashioned it in durable stone as a testimony to the permanency of the spirit in us, but we are not going to be engulfed in the tide; we will peep out eternally, with sly, incorrigible, human faces, to mock the eternal spirit of man, to remind him of that which he wishes to ignore, albeit that it is his glory.

Something of this Lawrence hints at when in his poem on the Tuscan cypresses he recalls the living memory of the Etruscans and says,

> They are dead, with all their vices,
> and all that is left
> Is the shadowy monomania of some cypresses
> And tombs.

The shadowy monomania! As if he wished to impress it deep upon us, this eternal quest of the Absolute which has strewn life with monuments, with mournful trees, with regrets, with tombs. And he expresses this in its most extreme form when, as if to present this spirit, which he himself so deeply represented, he transfers to the carrion beasts, the vulture and the hyena, his hatred for the Absolute: "The carrion birds, aristocrats, sit up high and remote, on the sterile rocks of the old absolute, the obscene heads gripped hard and small, like knots of stone clenched upon themselves for ever." This is among the most revelatory passages of all Lawrence's writing, a self-portrait as convincing and terrifying as were the obscene figures in the cathedral to the woman. "The vulture can neither see nor hear the living world, it is one supreme glance, the glance in search of carrion, its own absolute quenching, beyond which is nothing." Who can deny that this is Lawrence himself, the male who in sexual embrace terrifies the woman with that impenetrable, stony absolute forever clenched upon itself. The stony self, beyond the ego, inhuman, uncompromising, devouring and tenacious, annihilating woman, sex, friendship, loyalty. The stony eye, petrified in that one supreme glance—the glance in search of carrion. Always smelling corruption, perched on that rock of the absolute, aristocrat of birds, high up and remote, drawn back on its own nullity, because beyond it there is nothing. Like the hyena again, which can scarcely see and hear the living world. Deaf and blind to the human tide, to the roar and crimson flood of life; fixed eternally on the sterile rock of the self, the divine spirit of man in search of its own curruption.

Finally, however, he attempts to unite the antagonistic elements (bird-female; serpent-male). He embraces woman's biologic cruelty of inexorable race-will, mere species perpetuation; her wholly self-satisfied and deep abiding earth wisdom; her belly and womb contact with life. Astrologically, Lawrence is dominated by fire and air: hence his instinctive selection of the *Phoenix*, the one bird of all that rises from the fire, the ashes of life, into the free air. His complementary nature, which was lacking, which he sought again instinctively in the too-too-solid flesh of a Frieda, was water and earth; he needed woman's fluidity, because he himself was in danger of being fixed in that upper stratum of "ideas"; and he needed her deep earth fixity, whereby he could unite in brotherhood with man and woman, as he could so well with bird and beast and flower. His emphasis on the non-human in order to get at the quintessential human nature, what is that but the roundabout way of the fire-and-air man who has to arrive at things through the spirit, through the mask of ideology. It was the core of things he sought—not the phenomena. This is pure epistemological striving. So through the bird he satisfies the questing, restlessness, flight, unseizability, the corrective again to his own intellectual aloofness and detachment.

* * *

Lawrence's whole life was a struggle and his philosophy of life is based upon a sense of struggle. This is the Dionysian view of truth apprehended not through the intellect, but through passionate experience. Instead of the absolutes imposed by abstract thinkers he offers a relative absolute based upon this realization of eternal conflict. Wisdom, he sees, consists in accepting this state of eternal conflict: the resolution of two opposites in the flux of living. "The Crown," written when he was thirty, moves toward the quintessence of his philosophy in his struggle to convey the idea of the Holy Ghost versus an absolute God, his idea being to make God real and psychological, or as I have said before, to make the world religious and godless.

Lawrence wrote "The Crown" when the war had been on for twelve months. He wrote the essay for a little magazine called "The Signature," at Murry's instigation. In his Note to "The Crown," Lawrence tells us of his initial feelings: *"To me the venture meant nothing real: a little escapade. I can't believe in 'doing things' like that. In a great issue like the war, there was nothing to be 'done,' in Murry's sense. Probably not for many, many years will men start to 'do' something. And even then, only after they have changed gradually, and deeply."* He goes on: *"I knew then, and I know now, it is no use trying to do anything—I speak only for myself—publicly. It is no use. trying merely to modify present forms. The whole great form of our era will have to go. And nothing will really send it down but the new shoots of life springing up and slowly bursting the foundations. And one can do nothing but fight tooth and nail to defend the new shoots of life from being crushed out, and let them grow. We can't make life. We can but fight for the life that grows in us."*

Does anybody remember having heard of "The Crown" during the war, or even after it? It seems to have been completely ignored, even more than was *Fantasia*. And yet, in my opinion, this long essay, written at Lawrence's mystical best, is the most important thing that came out of the war. This alone should have proclaimed him the man of genius that he was. All the rest may go someday, but this will remain. For this is the very core of Lawrence, the quick of him, translated into a language that transcends the ultimate meaning. He never surpassed this utterance, nor equalled it indeed. It was written when he was fired with faith and hope, when he believed that it was still possible to recreate man. Coincident with *The Rainbow*, it contains the whole of his philosophy, his radiant vision of life. All the themes he is later to elaborate in his novels, all the symbols he is later to exploit and give ever new meanings to are contained therein. The enigma is stated explicitly, accepted as a challenge, and expressed as a poetical fact. It is packed with God, with the deepest reading of life that our age has witnessed— and it fell by the wayside, was ignored, was misinterpreted by the very man whose promise of friendship gave him the courage to write it.

"The Crown" is difficult, almost obscure—because we have lost the power to think and feel as this man of God felt and thought when the quick of him was touched. The horror of the war was so real to him, such an affront to his poetic vision of life, that he had either to go mad or find a wholly new interpretation of life, one that would include the war and transcend it. Here lies the terrific sincerity of Lawrence, his *integrity*, if you wish, for incurable idealist that he was, he would not close his eyes to the stern realities of existence. The war lacerated his spirit a thousand times more than it did the bodies of any who fell in the trenches. For the great majority of men went to their deaths as they had gone through their lives—blindly, insensitively.

Lawrence faces the issue squarely. He sees man imprisoned in the form of his culture, a foetus in the womb of night struggling to be born. And we accept that life within the darkness as the *only* life. We relapse back whence we came, never having seen the light. That is the condition of our life (very briefly stated) today. The horrible reality of the war, then, becomes to Lawrence merely a symbol of a still greater reality: the struggle to be born! This it is, I say, that sets Lawrence high above the other men of our time who tried to reveal to us, through their suffering, the meaning of the war. There are wars that are sterile, he says, that yield nothing. Triumph is sterile! We want a consummation, a fulfillment.

Lowenfels criticizes my views by asking me to ask myself "for whom the world is dying." It is useless to ask the question, it seems to me. Men are not divided into economic and spiritual beings . . . unfortunately. And yet I see that when hope rises anew it is always an oscillation—one time we place it in a spiritual regeneration, another time in a social or economic re-alignment. And one acts upon the other. When an old order dies the mass seems to assert itself, but that is only a fallow period until a *new* order is established. There is always a hierarchy, of men and of systems, and of values. And this threatened economic revolution, whereby Lowenfels would have me put my finger to the pulse of things and consequently interpret Lawrence as the symptom of the death of an old order, does not appear to me as a new adjustment of outside forces. It represents merely the actualization of a revolution that has already occurred.

That is what Spengler means, I take it, when he says that already in the nintheenth century Socialism ceased to be a problem. The idea is merely being acted out. We have now the reduction to a statistical average, each man the equal of his neighbor—not any more as an individual, but as a cog in the grand machine. And the desire to avoid warfare is perhaps the recognition of an organic unity—no part of the body can war upon the other because it would destroy the functioning of the machine. The body is reduced to an integer, to a screw or a bolt or a nut—each equally important functionally. But this machine requires its master! The machine cannot function alone. That is the ideal of the present revolutionists—to have the machine function of its own volition. Because it is happy just being a machine!

Just as it is impossible to imagine man conquering the devil in him (that is his "other" nature) so I conceive it also impossi-

ble for him to subjugate the machine—for the machine is his
own supreme creation and he has made himself in its image.
Man today is nothing but a personified machine (his
mechanized conquest of space and Nature is matched by his
metaphysical conquest of space in the scientific extension of
his senses which his instruments represent, and through which
he ideates a mechanical universe). He has, like Faust, sold
himself to the devil (which is how the machine was always
justly regarded hitherto). He is hopelessly enslaved and dominated by it, in thought and action.

It was impossible for Lawrence, as it is now impossible for
me, to imagine that having invented all these instruments of
destruction (he has never employed his scientific instruments,
or his machines except to *conquer* something, to wrest power
from Nature, which Spengler interprets as the signal illustra-
tion of Faustian will)—impossible to imagine that he will not
employ these devils eventually upon himself. Man has invented machines as his own unique method of finishing his
destiny. Once he regarded the machine as anything but a curious phenomenon, or discovery, he was lost. He did not have the
courage or the wisdom to leave them alone (which is tan-
tamount to saying he was not another type of man). He sought
to employ them for his own end, to conquer Nature, an idea
rooted in the belief that knowledge is power and salvation. The
same fallacy reveals itself in the science of psychology—this
"know thyself" which began with Socrates and which comes to
an end now with the rediscovery of *mystery*, the great reservoir
of the Unconscious where the libido (God) reigns.

In parentheses, we should note that there is little or no talk of
creating new worlds—only of destroying old ones. Even the
earth itself is threatened with destruction—in theory, which is
merely the projected anticipation of an end. The current theory
of entropy, of our extinction through the earth's death, is
merely the myth we have invented in response to a death
feeling in our souls. We have envisaged our own end, and the
whole world dies with us. We have tasted destiny and, though
we deny it everywhere in conscious thought, it emerges in
scarcely any disguise in our most firmly held theories of life.
True, we also theorize about life as everlasting, as going on
elsewhere, on other planets, but this is mere evasiveness; it is
the concession we make to our instincts. It is this which

perhaps also caused us to create the idea of a *multiverse.* We can never shut the door, never wholly believe in our own rationalistic conceptions. And before us the Hindus had conceived also of staggering worlds, of grand impossibilities of conception. They too were intensely scientific. Just as we get most of our religion from them so also we get most of our fundamental scientific cast, our flexible, functional mathematics. With us the Will is always imperative, always expressing the deep life feeling. We establish an immortality through the symbols of physical sciences, the Hindus through a surrender to the great All.

But relative to my previous remarks on the discovery of the Unconscious, the irony is that these men of wisdom do not perceive the travesty of exploring this seat of the soul by empirical methods. There is, however, the hint that in discovering therein the vast power of myth and dream they will fall victim again to the spell of substantial and fundamental beliefs. Something like this must have been in Jung's mind when he said that Sun worship was the only rational religion. It is not rational, to be sure, for no belief is rational. For us everything has to be either rational or irrational. We rationalize now about the irrational. We have no power of irrationality any longer.

Further, the emphasis on the Unconscious reveals the fact that man, in his finished state, recognizes with his conscious mind that he has attained the limits, and that to rediscover the sources of his inspiration, that magic of primitive life, that mantic quality of language, he must return to the dark, obscure, soul regions. But as he is no longer able to interpret things spiritually he elaborates a scientific lingo to explain the secret. The exploration of the personality, its unconscious depths, is but an imitation of those other external explorations—paleontology, archaeology, geology, etc. The "I" is conceived of in geological terms, the fossil layers of the being!

We can learn from Lawrence that instead of the grand irrational fear which has eternally characterized man's life-history we have now a *fear of life* by which was created that *empire of neurosis* to which we become more and more subject. All art now appears as compensatory, substitutive, escapist, to use the psychologic parlance of the day. (It is no longer possible to think of life except through this ideology of disease!) The study of the neurotic (and as I have pointed out above, the artist is the supreme example of neuroticism) leads to the discovery of the preponderance of the incest motif, or the desire for death and rebirth—significant language! In this age of skepticism there can appear no aspect of the eternal religiousness in man's nature except negatively, in this backward flow toward the womb, the fount, the matrix of life.

Coincident with fear of life is the growing terror of reality (part and parcel of the same thing), for this reality is death, a destiny to which man is trying to shut his eyes. With the slackening of the life impulse man also loses his fear of death, that is, his urge for immortality; with the removal of this instinct, or at least with its effective weakening, the artist has no *raison d'être*. He comes, by a long and devious route, to the discovery of self: a cross-roads at which he may either create a new religion or develop a new personality.

It is at this point, the most crucial point in our history, when pausing, reflecting, criticizing, appraising, we are obliged to interpret everything genetically, that the significant character of our souls must decide. There is a unanimous opinion in every field agreeing with Lawrence that we have arrived at the end, at the bankruptcy of the soul, and yet vague, mystical hopes, lies, illusions, romantic deceptions remain. The force of Will, the dynamic character of our culture, tends to nourish the life illusions, the eternalizing of *our* contribution, the perpetuation of *our* type. But it is obvious that—soulless, rootless, mythless—we can neither create a new religion nor develop a new personality. The great personalities lie behind us, before the Climacteric of the Culture. The study of the self leads nowhere, except to a feeling of futility, because psychologism is the admission that we are dead, killed by the intellect's triumph over the soul.

Again it is Lawrence who tells us that the dead cannot resuscitate themselves, that they can only be resurrected. What was great in us will be revived—later! It is only thus that we retain the illusion of imperishability. The study of the Western soul (by its foremost experts) yields the unanimous verdict that there is no further development possible. The complete discreditation of that idealism which has characterized our whole history shows that the only possible hope lies in the cultivation of *wisdom*, the metaphysical attitude that lies above striving and willing, above faith and deeds. But the very constitution of our mentality precludes this, our language even, the creator of our ideologies, our deities, our mores, is against us. From the standpoint of wisdom the Chinese proved themselves more wise than we, but the history of man shows one thing—the inability of man to profit by wisdom, to act according to wisdom. That is reserved to the few always and everywhere—it cannot be taught. With wisdom comes the tragic sense of life, which the Greeks in their golden age possessed. But there is no evidence to support the view that our destiny lies in the direction of increasing wisdom. All the trappings of our life reveal the opposite, reveal the meanness, the vulgarity, the crassness, the callousness, the spiritless quality of our livingness.

There is, however, always a possibility of Renaissance instead of Dark Age, but this depends entirely on the quality of "individual" artists to come. A Renaissance must of necessity be based on a misunderstanding, on a backward-looking spirit. No, a Dark Age is preferable—a long night in which life lies fallow and the few rare spirits work with knowing mystery for the resurrection of a new body, a new spirit, a new culture.

To the few sensitive spirits left it is apparent that the Dark Age is already here. That transvaluation of all values which set in at the tips of the tree, in the very quick of our spiritual bloom, becomes daily more and more understandable. It becomes the dominant, obsessive idea of the artists who are left. Lawrence carried on in this tradition, Nietzsche the artist-philosopher, Lawrence the philosopher-artist. The ability to formulate thought, to marshal it in any grand philosophic style, weakens. Nietzsche rescued thought from the philosophers of his time by the sheer force of his artistic endowments. Lawrence rescues art from the psychologists through his religious endowment. We have in both the prophetic type. Men who prepare the ground for a new religious feeling—not for a new scheme of philosophy. It is at the top that the tree withers first—to all outward appearance. Thought decays. But the death, of course, is at the roots. The decay of thought is only the symptom of that death which is hidden in the trunk where the sap is drying up. But first the superstructure dies away.

The artists who now appear—those at least who have the right to be called "creative"—are the ones who refuse to let life degenerate into a completely fungoid state wherein the only activity worthy of the name is ant-industry. Instead of the horizontal metaphysics that stretches like a bridge from peak to peak we get a new vertical philosophy of life based on a profound awareness of the fundamental antagonism between life and death. It is this organic, cyclical, cosmic view of things which stands out in strong contrast to the existent threat of a perpetual state of China. It is a view of life based on a reading of death. It is non-cultural, non-aesthetic, non-purposive. It is based on conflict, not harmony. It is destructive, thoroughly destructive. Annihilating.

Death, which during youth and maturity had seemed a long way off, hidden behind the mask of cultural forms in which we moved with joy and freedom, death now becomes the magnet that draws us fascinated toward the abyss. Death resumes its role of fructifier. We now make the distinction between "creative" death and other forms of death. Life arranges itself in terms of death. *Death philosophy.* Once again we hear the language of the Mysteries, the language pregnant with fertility orientation. Because the obsessive fear is sterility, exhaustion, and the fear expresses itself not: "shall we be able to live?" *but:* "shall we ever be able to die?" For we realize now that if we do not die neither shall any new thing be born. We have the grave problem of whether the living (so-called) will be able to consume the dead gods. The danger lies in the fact that the gods may walk the earth unnoticed and die a futile death because unconsumed. The problem for the coming Orphic artist is how, by what means, to restore a magic sense, a magic relation between himself and the herd. For him the whole problem of existence narrows down to one of restoring a vital connection or relationship between man and man, between man and woman, between man and the universe. To restore, as Lawrence exhorts us in *Fantasia,* a sense of *Cosmos.*

Lawrence's chthonic language and his brilliant and obsessive use of symbols are impressive and presage a type of artist to come, a type that will work away in the dark, forging the matrix of the new forms which are destined to emerge. Lawrence appeared when there was still a measure of communication between the artist and his audience. But his world is rapidly disappearing and with that world a whole race of artists for whom there will be no use. The era of the collectivity—the fungoid era—is upon us and in this dark age the struggle for bread will override all other struggles. Whereas Lawrence's dark language is painfully clear, the language of the few remaining artists will become more and more cryptic, noncommunicative. As external remedies fail, as the belief in social panaceas wanes, the dark symbolic language of the artist will gather force again until it sweeps the masses like a contagion.

The revival then of this magic contagion between artist and collectivity is of paramount importance because it is precisely the sense of awe and mystery—religious feeling—which has atrophied. And since the tree, in its dying, manifests its death first in the most remote, extended branches, the only language possessing vital, contaminating power is this virile, symbolic language of the roots where the primal, *real* death is taking place.

Herein lies one of the most remarkable differences between a "modern" such as Joyce, and Lawrence: the language that each has created. The impulses are diametrically opposed: Joyce wants to avoid significance, and consequently language for him is a barrier to be erected against the world; while Lawrence places almost exclusive emphasis upon significance as a way to tear down barriers. Seeking to escape the nightmare of history, as I pointed out earlier, unable to cope with the world, Joyce seeks to dissolve it. Inspired by the same profound disgust, equally unable to cope with that world, Lawrence destroys it to build it anew, to create another, more integrated world. Joyce reverts to the world of nature in Molly Bloom, his only solution to the struggle a surrender to the biological forces. Lawrence dies a creative death, a death in which the universe is annihilated with him, in order to be reborn.

Language is a prime symbol: in its dual function of communication and expression it is the most potent and the most delicate symbol of the soul. In the confusion that ushers in the final chaos, language is the last thing to be altered. When language is perverted the final dissolution has set in—there are no more barriers to be broken down. The "revolution of the word" marks the utter collapse of our world; it is the counterpart to the disintegration of the ego, to the fusion of the sexes, to the automatism of our machine-made life. The great Hamlet-Faust legend, which made its appearance after the death of the "individual" man, comes to logical fruition in

Proust and Joyce. In our efforts to emancipate ourselves from the shackles of religion we have become more miserable, more saddened, more enslaved. The very factors in our civilization, using the word in its broad sense, which promised good, contained in themselves as we now see, the seeds of disaster. The very urge which gave to our civilization its tone and character, its strength, falls like an arrow blunted and bent, to the earth again.

We see now how, in the organic evolution of a great Culture, there arose the peculiar and appropriate myths that formed the underlying key pattern of the vast superstructure of art, religion, morals, customs. We have seen how the language of a people undergoes alterations in the soul's adaptation to these changes and developments. Looking at our own Hamlet-Faustian soul which sprang from the matrix of the Antique world, we can recognize today the great trajectory we have described; and as the arrow speeds to earth, its velocity ever increasing, our consciousness and our fear of the end is heightened beyond words. While the common man strove desperately to remain a vestige of hope, the artist centuries back was already signing the end, blindly,intuitively, at first, but with more and more awareness, more and more poignancy as time ran down. Until today it is no longer a cry of pain or anguish, but a long, drawn-out, agonizing scream. Today it is no longer possible to heed the danger signals: on its iron rails, our engine has past the last semaphores.

Wisdom, which at the Climacteric of a Culture was the sole prerogative of the artist, wisdom is today relegated to the sage. And for us today the sage is represented in the person of the analyst. Because wisdom is always the adaptation of the individual to the world about, to whatever ideology reigns, to whatever mores prevail, wisdom now represents stagnation. We must be rescued from the men of wisdom.

Lawrence is sometimes regarded as the novelist of psychoanalysis. Though he sometimes used its terminology, however, the point of his books will be missed if they are interpreted pathologically from the point of view of a science which replaces the Fates and Furies of classical tragedy with "infantile experience" and makes it, with its power of deciding events before they have happened, as fatal to dramatic interest as any prematurely introduced *deus ex machina.* In Lawrence's novels, an essential capacity of his characters is the ability to wield power over their own fates, or perhaps the ability to abandon themselves to their fates.

It is marvellous, moreover, how intimately Lawrence's ideas coincide with the highest flights of Jung and Spengler. He arrived at his ideas independently and coincidentally with them, "The Crown" (germ of all) written in 1915, precisely the period in which Spengler and Jung are busily developing their ideas of history and the psyche. And Lawrence remains above them, an antecedent to them both, as the artist always does, proving my constant assertion that the true artist does not owe anything to the psychoanalysts, nor the scientist. It is they who are indebted to the artist. They pillage him, erecting dead schemes out of his living vision of things.

For Lawrence wrote *Sons and Lovers* and *The Rainbow* without accurate knowledge of the psychological jargon. To my mind again it proves that what is fatally wrong about "psychology" is the systematizing, the huge and ridiculous terminology, the hocus-pocus—bad as any other scientific system, and an end in itself—whereas always the really creative individual possesses a "psychology" of his own, the natural, instinctive, intuitive psychology.

This is part of what defines Lawrence as the *magic* type that endeavors to operate on man by contagion. His wisdom was attained through personal struggle, and hence he sets up no codes, no laws, no theories for emulation. For each one his own discovery, through "passionate experience." *The kingdom of heaven is within you.* This is the wisdom perpetually repeated in various ways by the highest types of man throughout history; it is an unfolding of the personality. His Holy Ghost, enigmatic concept, is merely his way of referring to the mysterious source of the self, the creative instinct, the individual guide and conscience, which the psychologists have tried to explain in terms of the "position of the self" in relation to the Ego and the Id.

* * *

The spontaneous, living, individual soul, this is the clue, and the only clue. All the rest is derived. This is how Lawrence regarded the world. This is Lawrence's challenge to the myth of science; this is the living, vital faith he offers as an alternative to the lifeless faith of science concerned with death, with fact and phenomena, with names, with sense-connections, all devoid of meaning. This is why Lawrence can so justly pay tribute to the world of the Indian, of primitive men in all times and all places, whose worlds, if tiny by comparison with ours, are nevertheless unified, solid, meaningful. Lawrence doesn't care if his cosmogony seems childish: he wants a world in which man can *live*, a world that will restore to men their faith, give impulse and direction to their living. And so Lawrence becomes, as it were, the Apostle of Day, as Proust and Joyce seem to me the slaves of Night.

What is the reason, I ask myself, for the great difficulty in grasping this clue to Lawrence's personality? The obscurity is powerful, so powerful that it requires all my powers even to grapple with it. Perhaps the answer is that Lawrence has purposely created the obscurity, and consequently all these efforts to clarify him mean a going back and a wrestling anew with the same problems that confronted him. He brings one back to the source.

He is forever bringing one back to the source, to the very heart of the cosmos, through a mystic labyrinth by means of symbol and metaphor. Phoenix, Crown, Rainbow, Plumed Serpent, all these symbols center upon the same obsessive idea: the resolution of two opposites in the form of a symbolic mystery. Despite his progression from one plane of conflict to another, from one problem of life to another, the symbolic character of his work remains constant and unchanged. He is a man of one idea: *that life has a symbolic significance.* Which is to say that life and art are one.

In his choice of the Rainbow, for example, one sees how he attempted to glorify the eternal hope in man, the illusion on which his justification as artist rests. In all his symbols, the Phoenix and the Crown particularly, for they were his earliest and most potent symbols, we observe that he was but giving concrete form to his real nature, his artist being. For the artist in man is the undying symbol of the union between his warring selves. He has to give life a meaning because of the obvious fact that it has no meaning. Something has to be created, as a healing intervention between life and death, because the conclusion that life points to is death and to that conclusive fact man instinctively and persistently shuts his eyes. The sense of mystery, which is at the bottom of all art, is the amalgam of all the nameless terrors which the cruel reality of death inspires. Death then has to be defeated—or disguised, or transmogrified. But in the attempt to defeat death man has been inevitably obliged to defeat life, for the two are inextricably related. Life moves on to death, and to deny one is to deny the other. The stern sense of destiny which every creative individual reveals lies in this awareness of the goal, this *acceptance* of the goal, this moving on towards a fatality, one with the inscrutable forces that animate him and drive him on.

It is this interaction between art and life, the paradox of the artist, which Murry cannot understand and which makes his praise of Lawrence so ultimately vicious. An outstanding intellectual himself, Murry regards *Fantasia* as Lawrence's "greatest" work—"radiant with life-wisdom." Now I agree that Lawrence's ideas are more exciting in the abstract than when they are presented through his fiction; there is something lacking, something incomplete, something sterile and artificial about his characters and novels; they do not sum up his ideas, or rather they do sum them up, but only arithmetically, as it were; Lawrence is greater than his characters, greater than his books. But it is not really this that encourages Murry to make *Fantasia* the pinnacle of achievement from which to evaluate all of the man's works.

Murry himself has said much that approaches the profundity of Lawrence, but without the ecstasy, without the vision. He is important, Murry, in any consideration of Lawrence because he represents precisely that cold type of intellectual man that Lawrence wanted destroyed, and yet ironically (perhaps not so ironically either) it is this eternal enemy of Lawrence who gives us the deepest interpretation of him to date. "Even when we are immortal spirits," we have seen Lawrence write from his death-bed, "we shall dwell in different Hades." And so these sickening female friends who worshipped at Lawrence's shrine find a singular delight in exploring the rift between Murry and Lawrence. Murry is the Judas who "under pretence of intellectual sincerity" endeavors to annihilate his Savior. To them "intellectual sincerity" is in itself a suspicious phrase. And of course they are right, these vultures, since the only substitute Murry has for his lace of genius is his "intellectual sincerity." It is Murry who has the practical wisdom which Lawrence lacked. Murry seems to have apprehended this now and again. Particularly does he reveal it when he writes: "But he was not a great artist. He was a prophet, a psychologist, a philosopher, what you will—but more than any other single thing, the great life-adventurer of modern times." Now what Murry means, but does not say, is that Lawrence *was* a great artist and *not* a prophet, psychologist, or philosopher, because here, in the realm of abstraction, Murry can easily grapple with him and show his superiority, which is indeed the whole aim of his book—incontestably so. The thing that Murry is envious of is Lawrence's genius, all that which made him alien to Murry and incomprehensible also. And when he calls him the great life-adventurer of modern times, sincere though his utterance may be, we know that behind it lurks malice and envy, because once again Murry proves only too conclusively that the great pilgrimage was but another symptom of the man's infirmities.

And yet, for the cold intellectual who lacks the capacity to go forth and partake of life's experiences, even this ignominious flight around the world which Murry punctuates with shafts of ridicule represents an unadmitted achievement—at least, it is a sop that he can throw out less grudgingly to Lawrence's admirers. For as the importance of Lawrence increases, the importance of the Murrys must diminish. Murry understands this full well, and it is because he understands it so well that he made the truly splendid effort to attach himself permanently to a share of Lawrence's glory. To admit, therefore, that there is envy and rancor and malice as well as love and admiration and devotion in Murry's attitude is not to detract at all from the merit of his book. It is an illuminating book, one that raises even deeper problems than Lawrence acknowledged to himself. Questions, I must say, which do not appear in other works on Lawrence. And one of the cardinal problems which Murry takes up is the question of the "artist" in Lawrence.

Wholly aside now from the admitted human prejudices of Murry, the friend and rival, he does state in the chapter on *Fantasia*, and elsewhere in this book, what might be regarded as the central problem in all of our discussions of "art" today. It is a view which has a singular and unique interest for us, one which would have been inadmissible in the past. At bottom, says Murry, Lawrence was not concerned with art. What others

regarded as a shortcoming—not being enough of the artist—
Murry considers as a proof of his eminence. Lawrence really did
tower by a head and shoulders above his contemporaries, says
Murry, by this very recognition that the necessary conditions
of great art are lacking in our age. Here it is necessary, I think,
to quote Murry at length:

> *The artist needs to serve an authority which he acknowl-*
> *edges to be greater than himself, whether it be God or King*
> *or both together; he does not question the powers that be.*
> *Then, and then alone, is he free to be an artist, with all his*
> *heart and all his mind and all his soul. These conditions do*
> *not exist today, and they will not exist for a long time to*
> *come. The artist to-day finds no spiritual authority which he*
> *instinctively acknowledges. If he acknowledges any it is the*
> *authority of Art itself, which is mere wordy nonsense. Art is*
> *not an authority, it is the means by which authority may be*
> *revealed and expressed. So that the artist who is conscious*
> *enough to be capable of great art is inevitably involved in the*
> *endeavour to discover or to create the authority without*
> *which his activity as aritst is either trivial or anarchic.*
>
> *Lawrence intuitively grasped the situation; he understood*
> *it better than any other artist of his time. He gave up,*
> *deliberately, the pretence of being an artist. The novel be-*
> *came for him simply a means by which he could make*
> *explicit his own "thought-adventures," the poem a means*
> *for uttering his immediate experience.* His aim was to dis-
> cover authority, *not to create art . . . . To charge him with a*
> *lack of form, or of any other of the qualities which are*
> *supposed to be necessary to art, is to be guilty of irrelevance.*
> *Art was not Lawrence's aim. It might have been, if the world*
> *had been different. To say or to imply that it ought to have*
> *been his aim, is to reveal oneself ignorant of the fundamental*
> *necessities which Lawrence knew.*
>
> *Much better "art" has been produced by Lawrence's con-*
> *temporaries; books better shaped, novels more objectively*
> *conceived, poems more concentrated. Beside Lawrence's*
> *work they seem frigid and futile. It is simply that they are*
> *not commensurate with our deep needs to-day. Our modern*
> *art is all obviously, irremediably minor. And it must neces-*
> *sarily be minor, so long as its aim is to be art. There is, and*
> *always will be, a place for minor art; but to produce it is not*
> *the function of a major soul. Lawrence was a major soul.*

Once this fundamental viewpoint of Murry's is grasped we can understand the seeming inconsistencies of his devastating attacks upon Lawrence. Murry conveniently divides his "object of spiritual knowledge" into three parts: the man, the artist, the leader. With the pathetic hunger and longing which characterize the men of our age he singles out, as the most important element in the trinity, the leader, that is, the prophet and Redeemer. It is the hope of salvation which Lawrence promised that attracted Murry to the man. Even when he had been disappointed in the *man* he found again his Savior when he read *Fantasia*. The artist whom he had sought in the beginning he was ready to sacrifice for the sake of a greater gift, though once he has received the supreme revelation, in the great Gospel of *Fantasia*, he can rediscover the artist, as he does in the case of *Aaron's Rod* and *The Plumed Serpent*. But the thing which his "intellectual integrity" cannot support is the failure of the leader of mankind, the prophet, the Savior, the Redeemer. Once he has perceived the bankruptcy of his deity he has no other recourse save to crucify him with words. This same "intellectual integrity" will not permit him to go back on his extravagant words of praise; the simplest thing, therefore, is to drive the very words of the Gospel, the sacred words of the Redeemer, like spears into the hollow sides of the scapegoat. That Murry betrayed him is of small consequence; it was Lawrence's destiny to be crucified. He had appointed and ordained himself for the end he met. He even chose the man who was to betray him.

There is in this drama a striking and ludicrous resemblance to the other dramas which it typifies, the Christian drama particularly. Just as the ignorant disciples of Christ literally and vulgarly believed him when he promised a heaven and a resurrection, so Murry seems once to have believed the Lawrence's promises would be literally fulfilled. He completely loses sight of the fact that it is only a great artist who can make these insane prophecies seem realizable. In the case of Jesus he knows that it is not a problem of art—of an "art" at any rate which can be put in quotes—which is only to say that Jesus was a superior kind of artist, one who defied brackets and parentheses and quotation marks. Jesus was a mystic, a visionary, and his medium was the living word. Lawrence was also a mystic and a visionary but the time is less ripe, the word consequently less living. In this sense Murry is right when he tells us that "the conditions of great art are lacking in our age." The faith in himself which the great artist has always had (this is the only authority which the artist has ever served!) is gone. The faith in himself, by virtue of which he could not but be a prophet and redeemer, this faith is what gave him his authority, and by virtue of this same authority he created art, religion, science, what you will. It is the artist who created God and all other illusions which nourish us. And today the faith and the authority, both, are gone. That is the tragedy of Lawrence's life—THAT HE SOUGHT WHAT IS IMPOSSIBLE FOR US ANY LONGER: A FAITH AND AN AUTHORITY. It is because he was a genius, and especially because he was a visionary genius, that his fate touches us so deeply. Literary artist or spiritual artist—what difference does it make? He was an *artist,* and a minor artist with a minor soul. He was one of the few artists of our time who possessed a soul at all. The passionate experience of life which he talked about we can gauge by his "thought-experiences" as recorded in the novels; but great life-adventurer he was not.

And so, when we come to the chapter on "Death" in Murry's book, we get the sequel to the overture on *Fantasia.* In *The Plumed Serpent,* which Murry calls Lawrence's greatest work of "art," we find, according to Murry, that the quick of Lawrence is in dissolution: "The 'I,' the fundamental self, has fallen apart . . . .Lawrence, who discarded 'art' for prophecy, has reached a point where he must discard prophecy for 'art.' And this is acknowledged, consciously or unconsciously, in *The Plumed Serpent* . . . .But the triumph of the 'artist' is the defeat of the prophet." A remarkable passage, this, in which Murry summons all his powers to grasp the real nature of the man whom he adored and to explain the conflict that produced him. Here Murry sees Lawrence as a man who "from the beginning . . . has been engaged, body and mind and soul, in the effort at self-creation. In obedience to that all-dominating impulse, he has abandoned 'art' long ago, and made his books intimate and personal documents of his progress towards self-creation." For the man who is essentially a prophet, says Murry, the return to "art" is manifestly the beginning of a decline. And the effort towards self-creation Murry now finds impossible "because the self *cannot* be created." He regards Lawrence's return to art as a *pis-aller—"because* it is a *pis-aller."*

And here we come to the very crux of the problem: Ramon and his Morning Star, in *The Plumed Serpent*. "Lawrence's last effort at complete expression of himself in his fullness." . . . "There is only one thing that a man really wants to do, all his life [says Ramon]; and that is, to find his way to his God, his Morning Star, and be alone there." So far, so good—Murry agrees. But the sentence that follows discourages him: "Then, afterwards, in the Morning Star, salute his fellow-men, and enjoy the woman who has come the long way with him." This, for Murry, reveals " The old courage, and the old weakness. To be alone, and not to be alone. The old, impossible demand; the old self-deception. For if the Morning Star is verily what it seems to be, the sign and point of the surrender of the personal being to the unnameable and unknowable God, companionship in that place is unthinkable and impossible. No man or woman communes there save with the unknowable God himself. Ramon, no more than the actual Lawrence, can accept his loneliness. He sees the path but cannot take it." For Murry, now interested solely in the prophet and redeemer, would have his savior perform the classic gesture and depart alone into the wilderness. "Why not go," he says, "as the great men of the spirit have gone before?" He has just quoted the passage in which Lawrence expresses Ramon's helplessness: "This was how Ramon felt at the moment: I am attempting the impossible. I had better either go and take my pleasure of life while it lasts, hopeless of the pleasure that is beyond all pleasures. Or else I had better go into the desert and take my walk all alone, to the Star where at last I have my wholeness, holiness . . . For surely my soul is craving for her consummation, and I am weary of the thing men call life. Living, I want to depart to where *I am*."

Here, in what is perhaps the most poignant and crucial passage of all Lawrence's writing, is contained the very root of the conflict, hence the importance of regarding it at some length. It is not yet the end of the Morning Star; for what follows, as Murry very justly points out, marks the chasm between a Lawrence and a Jesus. Here the world will be forever split: in the gulf between the human and the "divine." Lawrence remains the *man*, the tortured, divided human soul who wants all his life to find his way to his God, his Morning Star, and to be alone there. "The moment comes," says Murry, "when the heroic human soul striving after self-creation *must* be alone. Friendship, marriage—these things vanish in the twinkling of an eye. There is no 'I' to be bound by them; and they dissolve away. Then a man must choose. The choice is as Ramon puts it: to abandon the quest for self-creation, or to face the terror of an ultimate isolation. And Ramon, no more than Lawrence, has the power to choose; like Lawrence, he shrinks away from both, and cries for the impossible."

I must confess that it is precisely this yearning for the "impossible" that makes Lawrence interesting to me. It is the proof of his genius. It is this "impossible" which he seeks that alone makes him worth while—not a solace and a comfort, to be sure, but an urge, a goad. He tried to remain human, though the demon in him drove him on to madness. Again and again he came face to face with the mysteries, he saw the utter futility and frustration of life, he experienced the union and dissolution of the mystic who for a moment becomes one with the universe; he tried to give us what he had experienced, which is impossible, since each man must experience it for himself and most of us never do. He knew that the eternal harmony, the attainment of the One and Absolute, could be experienced only through the annihilation of the self.

When one comes face to face with this enigma one must realize also that there is no solution, except death, that this is the wheel upon which one is broken. The return to art is the only solution life offers, for art again is the imaginative resolution of the inner conflict, the deep lying mask of illusion through which we can at once face the cruel enigma and bear with it. To attempt to separate the artist from the prophet, or the seer, or the visionary, or the madman, or the hallucinated, or from God, is an act of violation. The artist is he who carries in his soul the cruel mysteries, who gives expression to them, not in order to divest them of terror and insolubility, but to sustain the heroic image of himself through and by which he has empowered himself to play the God. For if it is true, as Lawrence says, that all his life the one thing he wanted to do was to find his way to his God, his Morning Star, let it be understood also that by God he means himself. The authority he wishes to serve is the authority which he has vested in himself, and like that God which man has projected out of his own image, he finds it difficult to believe in himself, to say simply *I am* and let that suffice. If it was weak and human of Lawrence to have wanted a woman in the Morning Star and a man, a friend, it was also very weak and human of God to have created a world of men and women instead of existing alone in his own absolute void.

That Lawrence profoundly understood these things seems indisputable to me. "The fact remains," he wrote, speaking of Gurdjieff, "that when you cut off a man and isolate him in his own pure and wonderful individuality, you haven't got the man at all, you've only got the dreary fag-end of him . . . .In absolute isolation, I doubt if any individual amounts to much; or if any soul is worth saving, or even having . . . .So that everything, even individuality itself, depends on relationship . . . .Strip us of our human contacts and of our contact with the living earth and the sun, and we are almost bladders of emptiness. Our individuality means nothing . . . ." But he can say also: "But never mind, the tragic is the most holding, the most vital thing in life and as I say, the lesson is to learn to live alone."

The contradictions and anomalies fall away when, facing the issue squarely, he tells us that the whole business of life, at the great critical periods of mankind, is that men should accept and be one with their tragedy." By this he meant to present to us the grandeur and sublimity of creative suicide, the choice which coincides with destiny, the acceptance of one's fate as an historic event, illuminative, meaningful, and not an *incident*, an identification of the personality with the trend of destiny, converting the fatality itself into an act of creation—the highest form of self-creation.

"I profoundly believe," said Lawrence, "that a single individual may prove to be of more worth than the whole generation of men in which he has lived": a truth so patent that it seems hardly to have been worth stating, and in truth it would not except that in this day the belief in individuality is almost extinct. That is more truly why Lawrence represents the future: he identified himself with this age by putting before us the creative symbol of his own struggle with that dead mass which is dragging life down, and with it art, religion, individuality. By his immolation he represented to us creatively the triumph of the mass. He painted his own crucifixion as a symbol of the futility of raising that inert mass to life. By this creative suicide his death becomes, to use his own words, "a climax in the progression towards new being."

Murry would like to dramatize Lawrence's defeat by attributing his death to his own self-betrayal: "no man ever is betrayed except he betrays himself." "Jesus," he says, "was betrayed by Judas, to his victory. Lawrence is betrayed, by Man, by Woman, by the Many, to his own defeat." Defeat? Victory? These depend upon one's point of view. *What* victory for Jesus? I see it as a marvellous fiasco! There *was* only one Christian and he died on the cross. I say that Jesus went to his defeat, that Napoleon went to his defeat, and Buddha, and Mahomet and all the other heroic souls who, in their defeat left such a triumphantly bitter taste of their individuality in our mouths that we are possessed by them all our lives, that even when we deny them, revile them, slay them anew, ridicule them, blaspheme them, we nevertheless and even in so doing render our homage unto them. The victory and the defeat are identical, simultaneous and inseparable. Victory or defeat, it is quite immaterial— the important thing for the man, for the artist is the struggle.

CHAPTER VIII

Form and Symbol

L AWRENCE IS hardly dead and already a vast literature is
growing up around him. Even before he died it was admitted that his importance was not so much for us as for the
future. To quote Murry again: "Lawrence was the future; as
much of it as we are likely to get in our time." Indeed, he says a
great deal more than this, which I feel it important to set down
here because it is so revelatory of the influence Lawrence
exerted over men, even those who have most frequently misunderstood and reviled him.

There seems, indeed, to be an avowed agreement, among all
the biographers and critics of Lawrence thus far, that he
preached a gospel which may not be ignored: "But there is this
to say," writes Murry. "In the order to which Lawrence belongs, nothing is lost. He is a symbolic man, one of the world's
great exemplars of what a man may be; one of the chief of those
rare spirits who bring men to a consciousness of their own
strange destinies." This gospel of "consciousness" Lawrence
wrote explicitly, in different manners, first in "The Crown,"
then in *Fantasia,* and again in *Apocalypse.* The novels are an
elaboration of these truths which he had experienced again and
again, and which he set forth in multifarious ways. It is upon
the gospel which he recorded in the essays—as the other, lesser
works fade away, and as the man we knew, with all his faults
and shortcomings, dissolves into a legendary figure—that the
works of future commentators will center, creating no doubt a
morass of controversy in which the authentic Lawrence will be
obliterated. Dire as the times may be, we have not yet scraped
the bottom, not yet reached that point of absolute despair and
disintegration which would enable us to raise a potential
savior, such as Lawrence, to the legendary stature of a Christ.
But we have witnessed, in our life-time, what can be done by a
servile mass with such flimsy material as Mary Baker Eddy and
Lenin.

Moreover, Murry has high praise for the potential of Lawrence's gospel: "if Lawrence's message is ever accepted, there will be no more Lawrences." But it is a foregone conclusion that Lawrence will *not* be accepted, any more than was Jesus, or Mahomet, or Buddha. For Murry tells us that *Fantasia* is, to all intents and purposes, an utterly neglected work: "If people are momentarily moved by it," he says, "straightway they forget it. They go on in the same old way as though it had never been written; they adhere, in their inertia and ignorance, to the same old system which is decaying about them. They are not changed at all." And then, like a true disciple, he adds these sorrowful words: "But I hope and I believe that a generation will arise to whom it will be a direct quickening of the soul. From it the warm life will pour into their veins. They will read, and they will act. What will prevent them from acting, if once they understand?"

The radiantly simple wisdom of *Fantasia*, which any not too intelligent man must understand and accept, remains nevertheless quite unaccepted. Murry has completely overlooked the fact that it is the very simplicity of this doctrine which makes it so difficult for men and women to accept. For it is this utterly simple message, and one other, which the great seers of every epoch have enunciated. And it is this monstrously simple view of life which men and women, from time immemorial, have rejected. To be one with the universe, to *accept*, is so divinely simple that one must needs be a god—and man cannot have God and *be* God at the same time. For when we eliminate God by becoming God there is no longer any struggle: the very basis of existence is removed. We may not have wisdom and the drama at the same time.

As if to clarify the enigma for himself, Murry adds that the men and women to whom Lawrence addressed himself could not be saved in their own lives, any more than Lawrence himself could be: but life, he says, can be saved: "by that knowledge we can save our children from the woes that have befallen us. We can stand aside and let them *be*: not negatively let them be, but positively let them *be*."

Now, if what Murry says were true, of what use, we may well ask, would it be "to save *life*"? Of what use to save life if we ourselves cannot be saved, in our own lives, in our own lifetime? Of what use the "radiant life-wisdom" of *Fantasia* if not for *us*? Of what use life-wisdom if we cannot have life in its fullness? Are we to consider ourselves nothing more than the sacred guardians of a mysterious thing called "life"? Are we not to live, except for a future that we shall never know, for a posterity which despite the self-imposed tortures of deluded saints and would-be gods, has always known how to take care of itself?

This great concern about *life*: whenever we hit upon this theme we may be certain that we are dealing with men who have felt the absence of it in themselves, men who in the endeavor to compensate for their own deficiency, impose their struggles, their yearnings, upon us. It is the men who are empty of life who are always talking to us about life! It is these ghosts from beyond the grave, these specters corrupted by wisdom and infected by death, who cast a gray, pallid breath upon the world. The life they would offer us, the life everlasting, is but the reflection of that death which has already gripped them, a death which has impelled them to convert the substance of life into vague, meaningless symbols. Not any dream of a prophet has ever yet come true—but their dreams have nourished other dreamers, and the poison of their dreams it is, that hangs over the world like a miasma, and stifles the living.

Lawrence understood, only too profoundly, that it is always the failure who presumes to show us the way. Unable to save himself, he would save the world. That is the irony which forms the invisible scaffold of these heroic lives. Commencing with a denial of the validity of reality, they end by triumphing over reality. That is their way of taking revenge upon life, which has cheated them. The drama, the poem, the edifice which they raise around themselves makes us blind: we forget their own naked, pitiful admissions, the premise of defeat on which is erected the gorgeous logic of their lives. We are hypnotized by the struggle; we identify ourselves with them, with *their* struggles, *their* conflicts, *their* triumph. Those who come after, who resemble them and are cursed like them, repeat the same monstrously simple doctrine. But even they, they who speak the same language, are obliged to close their eyes to the wisdom of their precursors. They, even as we, make themselves blind, for in their inmost being they know that it is not the doctrine to which men become attached, but the symbol— the spectacle of conflict, the heroism of that conflict. And so they blind themselves to wisdom in order that they may sing. They become as fools in order that they may experience for themselves this wisdom which is prized but never heeded, which indeed it is impossible to heed.

The man of genius—it is almost too platitudinous to repeat—is the apotheosis of conflict, and man, as the very incarnation of dissonance, bows down of necessity before genius. Since it is the illusion of triumph which sustains us, it is in the art of genius that we take refuge, not in the lie that created it. Over and over again the man of genius—be he saint, hero, prophet, poet—announces to us agonizingly that he is a divided, humiliated, tortured, defeated being; his life and his work are but the monotonous repetition of this theme. But so keen is our denial of ultimate defeat that we give no heed to the cries of truth; we are instead beguiled and enchanted, deluded and ravished, by the music wrung out of the agony which consumes us all and deafens us to truth or wisdom or salvation. For who that is *alive*, who that bears within him, by simple virtue of being, all the pain and chaos of which the universe is composed, would want to silence this music, resolve this eternal dissonance?

Peace, harmony, salvation: the gospel of death. If any man railed against this trinity, hated this trinity, fought this trinity, it was Lawrence. Frail, consumptive being that he was, consumed by the living flame that was in him, he realized better than most men how all too quickly the discordant elements are composed, how the fever of life tends to bank down, how murderously quick comes the tranquil, soothing negation of death. Here, in death, he realized, is where eternity begins, and that great impassable void of peace, love, truth. Here in the beyond which is perpetually postponed may begin perhaps the reign of that trinity which we shall never know—the frozen images of the Absolute which man creates and destroys and creates and destroys again and again.

What was it, do you suppose, that led Lawrence to write about Cézanne in the Introduction to his own book of paintings?: "The most interesting figure in modern art," he says, "and the only really interesting figure is Cézanne: and that, not so much because of his achievement as because of his struggle....He is not a big figure. Yet his struggle is truly heroic." What Cézanne had been trying to do, he explains,

was to express what he suddenly, convulsedly knew: the existence of matter. Here, with an almost distressing eagerness,
Lawrence seizes upon that modicum of success which
Cézanne was actually able to realize. Cézanne did succeed in
giving us the apple, he says, and he comes back to it again and
again, passionately, vindictively, as though the whole universe
were contained in that apple. "Cézanne's great effort," he says
(he might have added—*his triumph!*), "was to shove the apple
away from him, and let it live of itself."

Now, however slight may be the value of such a viewpoint in
the minds of the "art" critics, it seems to me, nevertheless, that
in thus approaching Cézanne's work Lawrence penetrated to
the very heart of the problem. For Cézanne's eternal plaint
was that he could not realize the truths which he had perceived. He was a recluse, failure, an embittered man. "Poor
Cézanne," says Lawrence, "there he is in his self-portraits
....peeping out like a mouse and saying: 'I *am* a man of
flesh, am I not?' For he was not quite, as none of us are. The man
of flesh has been slowly destroyed through centuries, to give
place to the man of spirit, the mental man, the ego, the self-
conscious I. And in his artistic soul Cézanne knew it, and
wanted to rise in the flesh. He couldn't do it, and it embittered
him. Yet, with his apple, he did shove the stone from the door of
the tomb."

And Lawrence! how he too wanted to rise in the flesh! But he
could accomplish it no more than Cézanne, no more than any
of us today. It was not salvation in a vague hereafter that
concerned him, nor even a Renaissance, but a resurrection here
and now, *in the flesh.*

When one reads his penetrating pages on Cézanne one
realizes only too clearly that the failure of Cézanne, which he
grasped profoundly, is the failure of D. H. Lawrence himself. It
is a terribly human failure, the sort which only men of today,
like ourselves, can appreciate and elevate to grandeur. It is the
failure of the artist who is born too late, the artist who can
triumph only by giving expression to his failure. What Cézanne
struggled to realize does not lie revealed in his paintings; the
struggle is there, but the realization died with Cézanne, as it
did with Lawrence. The discrepancy between the man and his
art may be interesting for the coroners of art, the post-mortem
may even establish clues, but the man, the flame that was in

him, the revelations that inspired him, are lost. They are lost because they were impossible of birth. This Lawrence who often emerges in the poems, and never more vividly, never more successfully, then in "The Crown," this Lawrence, I say, was never given a chance to be born. This Lawrence was rejected, scorned, crushed out.

Lawrence has acquired considerable importance as a crusader, as a phallic mystic, as a champion of the sacred body. But this is not the important Lawrence, this is the Lawrence created by outer conflict. The real Lawrence is the man who grasped death in his momentary visions. It is Lawrence the Apostle of Death who has value for us—the prophet, the mystic, *not* the rebel. And the prophet in Lawrence is confused, he utters contradictions, and finally he goes the way of all prophets. For what the world accepts is what the wold understands, and no more. Never do we accept the ultimate Lawrence, never the dreamer, the fanatic, the Utopist.

*   *   *

"Men live and see," Lawrence says in the Foreword to *Fantasia*, "according to some gradually developing and gradually withering vision. This vision exists also as a dynamic idea or metaphysic—exists first as such. Then it is unfolded into life and art. Our vision, our belief, our metaphysic is wearing woefully thin, and the art is wearing absolutely threadbare. We have no future: neither for our hopes nor for our aims nor for our art. It has all gone gray and opaque. We've got to rip the old veil of a vision across .... Rip the veil of the old vision across, and walk through the rent."

Lawrence tells us that *Fantasia*, which is regarded as his book of "life-wisdom," came after the novels and poems. In a sense this was a concession to the dull public which always demands of the artist signs and landmarks in order to get its bearings. The novels and poems were so unrelated to the current ideology that, in order to create an audience for them, it was necessary to furnish some clue, some philosphic elaboration of the ideas which he had expressed poetically. This necessity is only another example of the present day estrangement between artist and public: it is another proof of what has been called the bankruptcy of the cult of genius. Today the artist not only has to create his works, but he has also to create a public;

in the deepest sense he has to create a new type of man, a type which will understand and appreciate his ideology. While this has always been more or less true of the relation between artist and public, today it is cryingly so.

Today the idea that art is dead—art as we know it—has taken hold of men's imagination. It is evident that there is no longer a polarity, an antagonism between the individual and the mass. Every little scribe considers himself a potential artist who is prevented from becoming one in fact only because of external forces—the social-economic complex. But one thing is certain: the rise of the collectivity spells the death of the individual artist.

This, however, is only a way of speaking. When we speak of the death of our world, or the death of the ruling class, or the death of art, what we have in mind is simply the dissolution of all the old forms. Once again things must return to the button-moulder, to a primordial chaos, in order to be reintegrated, to emerge with new vitality. Art never dies, nor does the creative personality ever disappear. The creative instinct cannot be eradicated because it is the very essence and core of life. The death of art would mean the death of the artist, which is equivalent to saying the elimination of life itself. To say that art is dead is simply another way of looking at things, another poetic utterance. But unless that feeling, that view of life, is sincere and activating, unless we really believe that art is dead and behave accordingly, no new art can possibly emerge. The vision comes first. The vision becomes animating idea later. Therefore the vision is important.

If it be true that the vitality has gone out of the forms of life, of art particularly, it does not mean an exhaustion of the creative forces, the creative instinct itself. That is absurd and impossible. The question is, to put it narrowly—who has life, and where?

The possibility for revival, for resurrection, lies with a very few—those who have the hope and the will. The Lawrence who said, "We have no future: neither for our hopes nor our aims nor our art," this same Lawrence also said: "Nothing will ever quench humanity and the human potentiality to evolve something magnificent out of a renewed chaos." But what we must do, he emphasized, is to rip the old veil of a vision across, rip the veil of the old vision across, and walk through the rent.

Art reveals itself through form, through the concrete representation of abstract idea. This is as true of primitive art, of body ornamentation, for example, as it is true of modern art. The substance of art, which is really the spirit, the intangible, the mysterious, the inchoate, must, in order to be apprehended, take form. The form contains the meaning and the substance alike. If now we consider that the artist's creation, which is his sole significant contribution to life, is the spirit of life in him, transmitted and apprehended through the art-form which he has chosen, then it must be apparent that, for those in whom the life force is vested today, a complete break with the past is absolutely essential.

Lawrence is, in my opinion, the forerunner of the new creative type destined to emerge out of the ensuing nightmare and to be defeated again and again in the bread-and-butter warfare which faces us. We are at a point where the death of the old forms contains in itself nothing of a revitalizing character. Usually, when we think of death, we think of a pullulating cadaver from which the new shoots of life emerge. But now the very soil in which the corpse rots is exhausted; the soil has been thoroughly worked out. We have on our hands a desert. Nothing can grow, except in tiny, isolated spots, in the oases where the subterranean rivers of life have bubbled up to yield a sparse growth. The problem is how to irrigate this soil, how to refertilize it, so that the desert may bloom again. For this it is necessary that there be *creative deaths!* We have not the power to create life, said Lawrence. We can but guard what life there is in us, nourish it, make it bloom forth. The waters of life are there eternally, sometimes driven below and difficult to tap, but they are there all the time. It is for us individually, each in his own way, to bring the waters to the surface again, to work the bloom and magic which our destiny prescribes.

It is a struggle, in other words, between the one and the many. To surrender to the play of external forces, to the mob spirit, is ignominious. Here indeed it is better to die in the struggle—a hero-death rather than a hunger-death. Lawrence died a creative death. Rimbaud and Aragon, on the other hand, committed creative suicide. There is an important difference. The one offered himself up whole, with faith—not in order to protect himself against life, but to give something through his dying. He died for something. the others died to escape something. Lawrence, by emphasizing the negative reality of life, which is death, could embrace life. This is where extremes meet. He who has life does not fear death. And he who grasps death has no fear of life. Today we have no choice. We are in death, the living death which the apocalyptic souls embraced in order to bequeath to us their vision of life. Part of Lawrence was already in possession of the new life, but there was no place on earth for him to live it.

The drama which Lawrence staged is the old drama of the individual versus the collectivity. The tragic view of the universe, this attitude towards life which makes the creative individual drunk, arises precisely out of his distorted vision of things, out of his wrong way of looking at things. It is the Dionysian view, created out of the terror and awe which Nature inspires. The immolation of self through art which every great artist experiences, which he accepts joyously, though not without pain and conflict, is symbolized for us in the lives of the dramatic scapegoats who throughout the course of history have offered themselves up for crucifixion. Such, for example, despite sharp antithesis, are Jesus and Nietzsche, homologous types, precursors of the last Dionysian figure, Lawrence. The poem Lawrence lived was antipodal to the vision which inspired him—as was the case with his predecessors, Jesus and Nietzsche. The conflict with the mob distorts the vision; the conflict with dead forms distorts the inner poem.

The human significance of his creation only his peers can estimate and appreciate. Only a greater man than Lawrence will continue the line of tradition which each new genius transmits by breaking with the past. His struggle with the world was not to convert others like unto himself, but to convert the inert mass into a living spirit myriad in its manifestations, each a law unto himself, each striving to express himself to the fullest. The kingdom of heaven is within—this he knew, as Jesus knew it, and he gave voice to this knowledge again and again. But this is too real a truth, too devastating for the mob to accept.

What the mob wants is the symbol around which it can build its faith; it does not seek to grasp the meaning, the substance hidden in the form. It wants an ambivalence and always will set up an oppositional mechanism of God-versus-man. I has no alternative. And it is here that the true failure, the noble failure, of the artist is revealed. Possessing the clue to life, he imagines of necessity that the flame can be handed down to others, that the one can become the many. Here is the very heart of the Dionysian character, the mystery of the antagonism between the hero and the world, the mystery of the fertility of the dying god. It is the struggle of the oasis with the desert, the struggle of the living spirit against the death forces of nature.

In reality there is never anything but the individual, the artist through whom life manifests itself.The mass is biology—organic life, not *creative* life. The soul of a people resides in the artist, and all ideas and ideals, all faiths, beliefs, cults, religions, are the product of the individual soul of the artist. The whole history of art is the struggle of the individual to give expression to his soul beliefs. And the history of man is the history of art. The forms which the artist's expression assumes are the dead things which the dead mass accepts in its search for life. This is the false, deathly cultural reality in which the mass tries to live. It is the tomb which the artist erects over his dead body. For the artist and his vision die in the form. Civilization marches on with the dead host.

Civilization, in the highest sense, always represents death, the death of the creators. For the artist, though he is obliged to express himself through form and symbol, the artist nevertheless is always *against* form; he is always an iconoclast because he requires chaos out of which to establish order and harmony—*his* order, *his* harmony. The truly creative individuals, be they poets, heroes, prophets, saints, have always been idol-smashers, always been fanatical, uncompromising, anarchic, abnormal, pathologic, *degenerate* if you like, so long as by "degenerate" is meant something other than is understood by those who have usual recourse to the term.

It was the recognition of his own bitter failure as a man—not a failure in the ordinary sense, but failure from the artist's standpoint—that prompted Lawrence, so I believe, to set forth his understanding of Cézanne. In this remarkable and poignant exposition of Cézanne's failings Lawrence states most eloquently and penetratingly the problem of his own life and work. It is the problem of creating a new world wherein art itself will no longer be necessary, wherein men will not need to live vicariously through the artist, but each man, as he says, would create that world of art which is the living man, each man would achieve that piece of supreme art, his own life. For now, as he truly remarked, we cannot be. *"We are Hamlet without the Prince of Denmark."*

And there we are. Nobody in the world today, apparently, is able to go on where Lawrence left off. He offered us a vision of things, a very personal vision—the only kind there is. The revolution required to accept that vision of life is a revolution which has never yet come off. But it is just this pursuit of the miraculous, just this illusion, which sustains the artist: he rips the veil and walks through the rent, imagining that the world is behind him. But no one follows. It is this veil of illusion which gives the artist his *raison d'être;* in sundering the veil he gives us his art. But when he has torn the veil it is only to discover new veils. That is his mission: to tear asunder the veils in order to reveal new veils. To uncover more and more mystery, to create more and more longing, to spread more terror, more discord, more dissonance. Chaos! He thrives on chaos! Not to make life more bearable, but to make it more grand; not to make life more livable, but to make it more potent, more death-dealing: to communicate the great nameless terror which is in his soul, the wild, primitive fear which Nature herself inspires and which gives the lie to the feeble illusions on which all civilization is nourished.

In his ecstatic rapport with the very heart of things the artist grows dumb; the vision which is permitted him he finds impossible to communicate, because every form which he adopts for his purpose is an obstacle to his expression. The vision is incommunicable—that is why he comes down from the high place uttering gibberish. The end is gibberish—it must always be thus. The flame and the vision are the soul's utterance, and that which is called art is a compromise, a lie. Art is the tomb in which the soul's image is buried.

Out of this sterility in which we are lodged it seems well-nigh impossible that anything violently different, anything that would truly upset the course of things, may develop. Yet in man resides the power to alter the trend of destiny—for in a man reside all the miracles of which his destiny speaks. History is nothing but the ruins left in the wake of the creative invaders of life. Lawrence, while accepting the rise and fall of the historical chart, Lawrence, I say, while accepting this picture of destiny, emphasizes at the same time that which the "thinker" is loath to admit. It is not in the thinkers that the life-force resides. The artist precedes the thinker, always. And if, in his dual role of creator-destroyer, the artist prophesies doom, it is also in that same role that he proclaims the power of the miraculous. Not we have the "freedom to do . . .the necessary or nothing," as Spengler puts it, but: "nothing will ever quench humanity and the human potentiality to evolve something magnificent out of a renewed chaos." Always the possibility of the miraculous. *Nothing but the miraculous!*

Indeed, it is because the artist sees so clearly, sees further than the "thinker," that he places his hope in death. To attain a new mode of life it is necessary that the old mode die. And man must want this end, recognize this need, if he is to have a rebirth. Always it remains with man, individual man, in whom are contained the seeds of past and future, of birth, of creation, of destruction.

The inherent logic of things is with the thinker. The artist is antilogic. The mystics have appeared in every age and season, and always they have spoken the same message. In the mystic is the dream-logic out of which springs the world of the thinker and artist. At any and every moment of man's history, according to this anterior logic, there is the dual process of growth and decay going on. Always the individual and the seasonal. And in every age there must be manifest to those who are creative the vast opportunities, the potentialities, which are never lived out, neither by the individual, nor by the race, nor by the cultural stream in which the two are borne along. There is not just one historical destiny—there are innumerable destinies lying open before us always. The thinker, wedded to facts and events, is always a backward-looker. What we look back upon and sum up and describe as inevitable, as *destined*, was never the hard, inexorable *fact*, which the philosopher of history makes so clear. There was always the choice, the necessitous choice, the historian will say. But the creative individual sees infinite choices, not just one. In accepting his destined role he makes himself a part of history, he helps to sway that choice, that decision. Events cannot take place without him, or *despite* him, like a machine obeying a blind will. Certainly he is conditioned by that force which is forever rolling up behind him and which finally engulfs him, sweeping over his dead body and spirit. But he affects the course of that powerful stream; he alters it, in the same way that other great spirits, other *individuals*, through their vision, their integrity, and their will, have likewise contributed to it, likewise affected it. He joins himself to the great stream of which he is a part, and that stream becomes history.

It is exactly because he was an artist, a Dionysian artist, exactly because he was a man of destiny, that Lawrence remains a tragic and a fecundating symbol. It is because he was a mystic that he crucified himself; that he chose art as his cross does not make him less an artist, nor less a prophet. Like all mystics he had his speculative side and his religious side. He could contemplate Nature and be appalled by the truths he perceived; he could preach the way of salvation and be faithless to his own vision. He could formulate a wisdom of life, as in *Fantasia*, and mock it by the way he lived. In his art he strove to reconcile all the antagonisms which his momentary visions had sundered. Like Nietzsche he could say—"I am convinced that art represents the highest task and the truly metaphysical activity of this life." Like Proust. Like Dostoevski. Like all the great souls who, confronted by the mysteries and refusing to be paralyzed by the blinding illumination, have had recourse to art as "a saving and healing enchantress." In the one being he united the dark animal gods of the chthonian world and the sexless, substanceless spirit of the beyond. Through his art he explored the whole gamut of these two worlds which are eternally divorced and which, by the effort of will, the imagination seeks to reunite.

From the highest, most delicate and evasive flights he could descend to the most obscene depths. That he had not the stature of some of his forerunners is another matter. One observes his limitations more perhaps in his descents than in his flights. Compared to Rabelais, Swift, Cervantes, his obscenity is mild. And this is possibly a charge to be brought against him—against the age even more. For what underlies the tremendous obscenity of the great spirits, what marks their more than ordinary violence, frenzy, hatred, disgust, is their more-than-human understanding. The vile, blasphemous outpourings are there as a Dionysian recognition of intangible, invisible things, of sublime truths seized in moments of ecstasy. It is only when one descends to the lowest depths of the human, to the sub-human, that one approaches the divine. For what is this divinity of which man speaks if not the projection of his most abysmal self into the beyond and the unknowable. It is this span between microcosm and macrocosm which the artist flings across the void again and again; it is this impossible task, since it is always fictive, that makes the artist at once a savior of man and a destroyer. He is a hero and a liar both. He incarnates in his own being the pain of individuation, and he pays the penalty for it with his life. But he is glorified at the same time. He assumes the role which no one else can play. He is sacrificed so that we others may live. Through his madness, his genius, if you like, the opposition between the two worlds is temporarily annulled. Through his saving and healing art, the magic, sacral quality of life is restored. In smashing the old symbols he opens again the veins of instinctive wisdom, beats out the uncharted realms of the blood. It is he who releases the orgiastic frenzy which is at the core of all religions.

It was the artist in Nietzsche which led him to prophesy the coming of a tragic age; it was the artist in Lawrence which led him to embrace the tragic when the tragic spirit was most hopelessly absent from the world. The destiny which Lawrence accepted was to incarnate this lost tragic spirit, to reenact for us a drama which is no longer possible. He spent himself in an effort to restore a feeling, a view of the world, which in this age it seems impossible to summon. As poet and mystic he sought to give body to his faith by the establishment of new symbols. Even when, at times, he appeared to have abandoned art, it was only that he might nourish himself in the dream of contemplation. His human triumphs and defeats, the traumas, the schisms, the experiences by which the analytical mind would endeavor to interpret his art, constitute nothing more than the plastic material which, of necessity, he was obliged to use as a medium of expression. The complex web of conflict in which his nature was rooted forms the invisible pattern of his life and art. But, as Elie Faure well says, "the important thing is to set the passions free. *The drama is everything, the cause of the drama nothing.*"

To say that Lawrence was occupied all his life with task of self-creation is simply to say that he was an artist. To say that art is a *"pis-aller"* is also true. There is no contradiction here. For the problem of the artist is the problem of the personality. It is in the creation of the personality that the religious, the moral, the sexual, the ethical problems receive their form, their color, their substance. *The problem of the self antedates all other problems.* For the artist there is no demarcation between salvation and creation. In the elimination of evil, the purification from sin, the discovery of God, the union with the cosmos, the break with history, in all these varying, deeply identical modes of purging himself of sin-guilt-neurosis, the artist creates his world, which is *our* world, the world of psychologic reality—the only world that has validity. His very existence is at once the admission of conflict and the ironic denial, or triumph, over it. That is why there is neither victory nor defeat—or both, rather—in his achievements. His art is neither born of his experiences, nor can it be interpreted by them. His experiences are the result of his nature, of that fundamental conflict of the personality which his art creates and which in turn is created by his art. He is in a state of constant becoming, a dream and a frenzy; he is the span between microcosm and macrocosm, the little soul-worm growing out of the dead body, the phoenix rising from the ashes, the *Anthropos* drawn and quartered in the heavens. He is a tiny, baffling enigma emerging from corruption and, like a magnetic needle, pointing steadily to a new corruption.

The problem of God is not a religious problem, it is the artist's problem. The problem of evil is not the saint's problem, it too is the artist's problem. The solution of all problems lies with the artist, because in him are contained all the enigmas; and if there be no solution to our problems it is because he, the artist, desires no solution.

The balm of his art, then, is a poison. He offers no solutions, no remedies, no panaceas. Not to the intellect does he appeal, nor to the heart; his wisdom is incomprehensible, his sympathies monstrous. It is not even the fear of death which leads him to immortalize himself. It is not fear at all, but *acceptance* which drives him onward to annihilation. He has looked into himself and discovered the insanity of existence. God, love, crime—this is the trinity that leads him towards the brink. For in his mother's love he has tasted death; in crime he has experienced salvation; in himself he has known God.

As artist he refuses to let life coagulate into law, morality, custom, religion. As artist he does not believe in art either, since he must first destroy art in order to discover it for himself. He must destroy everything and confuse everything in order that he may create, and he must create because there is no other solution to the conflict which has shaped him. Such is the artist, and by these terms such is D.H. Lawrence.

"He was a man of one idea—that all civilization was the painted fungus of rottenness. He hated any sign of culture." This is how Lawrence describes Annable in his very first novel, *The White Peacock*. Annable is the first of a line of his doubles which Lawrence gives us throughout his novels. You might say that the Annable type represents the fundamental, potential Lawrence, the ideal-hero image of himself which was aborted in conflict with the world. As a man Lawrence was divided, but as poet he was single. As poet and mystic he saw with the inner eye which pierced the visible death about him. He saw into the eternal livingness of things. "If only we would shut our eyes," he wrote; "if only we were all struck blind, and things vanished from our sight, we should marvel that we had fought and lived for shallow, visionary, peripheral nothingnesses. We should find reality in the darkness."

At the heart of him, the one goading impulse, is Mystery. You will find behind every reiterated utterance of his, scored and underscored, that word *mystery*. In the poems it flames up and defies all approach; in the novels it gets smothered under the excrescence of fact and incident; in the essays it flowers again and turns to ash which the mind blows hither and thither, as if frantically seeking for a form which is anterior to language, for a form which would be a blend of music and idea.

At its best, when he is swept along by his paroxysm of hate, there is in Lawrence's language so rich, so dark, at once so lucid and enigmatic, a direct and overwhelming appeal to the blood and soul of man, as if he had surmounted all the barriers which language imposes, a direct appeal to the blood. There are poison and fire in his words, and a terrible naked beauty, as if like the dragon of life itself he found himself caught in the very whirlpool of flux and writhed and lashed there eternally. With its heavy load of fire and blood, of curses and threats, with its parables, liturgies, symbols and dreams, its drugged passion and gem-like brilliance, his language seems to be wrung out of the groans and despair, the frustration and perpetual hope of man, wrung out of deep, burning purpose; *sincere*, so sincere that his language scorches, leaves holes in the canvas, creates meaning for itself as it goes along, creates meaning out of the holes even, rips the veil between meaning and expression, flames into highest symbol, flames and dies on a page, in a line, in a word; a perpetual birth and death, a perpetual renewal from the inner source, a moaning and cursing, a dancing and soaring, a sheer fountain of icy clarity leaping from chaos and back again to chaos; a saturation of man and universe so complete, so devastating, that we have in us the illusion of his undying existence.

This is the real Lawrence, the corpse whose elements are strewn in the dust and the stars. This is the meaning of annihilation, of primordial chaos out of which order and harmony are established. This is the Dionysian Lawrence who escapes literature, who mocks at the man and his philosophy. This is the riddle of the universe whose solution crucified him.

The *soul* of the man—that is his gospel! And there, if we could follow him, lies our salvation. He is like one of those frightening figures which he described in his journeys through the Tyrol—a withered, emaciated, grotesque thing nailed to a cross. A horrible symbol of man, but an inspiring one. The scapegoat of modernity!

He did not promise a hereafter, a spiritual salvation when we are dead and gone. He talked about consummation now, *here and now*, in the living moment. He worshipped power, aristocracy, blood, race, distinction, personality, conflict, darkness and ignorance too. He ran against the whole trend of historical destiny. He took up his position in MAN, not in history, not in religion, or culture, or law, or custom. He looked death squarely in the face. Death in all its phases. Death on all fronts. Not through evasion or subterfuge, not through conversion or sublimation, not through spiritual palaver and hocus-pocus, but through *acceptance* did he find life. Inside him was an idea, a purpose, a flame. He was a man of one idea, a man dominated, ridden, consumed by idea. You cannot take the poetry and discard the idea. He saw to it that that would be impossible. And that is why the warfare goes on, and will continue to go on ceaselessly and forever, over his dead body. His ideas are embedded in the poem he left behind, the poem which he lived: "Ye must be born again. Out of the fight with the octopus of life, the dragon of degenerate or incomplete existence, one must win this soft bloom of being, that is damaged by a touch."

That mad, rasping, frantic, fanatical note in his voice—is it despair, or hope? Or both? Both, no doubt. I see him as a sort of intellectual savage restoring to man that nomadic quality which he has lost, sending him down the open road to God knows where. A road without end—but he sends him down it filled with ecstasy. Mad! Mad! Thoroughly impossible. Fanatically idealist. A super-idealist. And yet, the only way, the only thing. Death. Bitter, ultimate death. So that out of the corruption there may spring forth a new life, a blazing, magnificent life such as man has never known, never even dreamed of.

I see him working on the human body, neglecting art for the pursuit of a chimaera, yet putting back into art the only thing which will restore it and keep it alive: a passional content. I see him coming in the end to Revelation and reading there the undying will-to-power in man, its sanctification, its final triumph.

I like to think that this heroic, quaking little soul whose voice was almost muffled out by the dead drag of our world had the courage to realize that art is not dead at all, but dead only as man is dead. The moment a real, live man appears, a *soul*, art is restored. In Lawrence there is this intimation.

* * *

Lawrence was full of contradictions because life itself is full of contradictions. I want to impose no higher order upon the man, his works, his thought, than life itself imposes. I do not want to stand outside life, judging it, but in it, submitting to it, reverencing it.

I speak of contradictions: and immediately I feel impelled to contradict this. For example, I wish to make it clear that a man like Lawrence was right, right in everything he said, in everything he did, even when what he said or did was obviously wrong, obviously stupid, obviously prejudiced or unjust. (He is at his very best, to illustrate what I mean, in such writing as his studies of Poe and of Melville.) Lawrence was opposed to the world as is. The world is wrong, always was wrong, always will be wrong. In this sense Lawrence was right, is still right, and always will be right. Every sensitive being aware of his own power, his own right, senses this opposition. The world, however, is there and will not be denied. The world says NO. The world is eternally wagging its head NO.

The most important figure for the entire Western world has been for two thousand years the man who was the quintessence of contradictoriness: Jesus Christ. He was a contradiction to himself and to the world. And yet those who were opposed to him, or to the world, or to themselves, have understood. Even though denied, he is understood by all, everywhere. Is it because he was a contradiction? Let us not answer this immediately. Let us leave this question in suspense . . . .

Here, touching on this point, we stand very close to something which vitally concerns us all. We are approaching the enigma from behind, as it were. Let us think a moment. There was Christ, the one splendid, shining figure who has dominated our whole history. There was also another man—St. Francis of Assisi. He was second to Christ in every sense. He made a tremendous impression upon our world, perhaps because, like those Bodhisattvas who renounced Nirvana in order to aid humanity, he too elected to remain close to us. There were these two resplendent figures, then. Will there be a third? Can there be?

If there was any man in the course of modern times who most nearly attained this summit it was. D.H. Lawrence. But the tragedy of Lawrence's life, the tragedy of our time, is this: had he been this third great figure we would never know it. The man was never fully born—because he was never squarely opposed. He is a bust perpetually bogged in a quagmire. Eventually the bust will disappear altogether. Lawrence will go down with the time which he so magnificently represented. He knew it, too. That is why the hope and the despair which he voiced are so finely equilibrated. *Consummatum est,* he cried out towards the last. Not on his death-bed, but on the cross, while alive and in full possession of his faculties. Just as Christ knew in advance what was in store for him, accepting his role, so too Lawrence knew and accepted. Each went to a different fate. Christ had already performed his work when he was led to the cross. Lawrence nailed himself to the cross because he knew that the task could not be performed, neither his own task nor the world's. Jesus was snuffed. Lawrence was obliged to burn himself out. That is the difference.

Lawrence was not the first such modern type. There were others before him, all through our period, who had been doing themselves in. Each suicide was a challenge. Rimbaud, Nietzsche—these tragedies almost brought about a spark. Lawrence goes out and nothing happens. He sells better, that is about all.

I said a moment ago that the contradictoriness of Christ brought us very close to something vital, a fear which has us in the bowels. Lawrence made us again aware of it, though his message was almost instantly dismissed. What is the essence of this enigma? To be in the world and not of it. To deepen the conception of the role of man. How is this done? By denying the world and proclaiming the inner reality? By conquering the world and destroying the inner reality? Either way there is defeat. Either way there is triumph, if you like. They are the same, defeat and victory—it is only a question of changing one's point of view.

There is the world of outer reality, or action, and the world of inner reality, or thought. The fulcrum is art. After long use, after endless see-saws, the fulcrum wears itself away. Then, as though divinely appointed, there spring up lone, tragic figures, men who offer their own bare backs as fulcrum for the world. They perish under the overwhelming burden. Others spring up, more and more of them, until out of many heroic sacrifices there is built up a fulcrum of living flesh which can balance the weight of the world again. This fulcrum is art, which at first was raw flesh, which was action, which was faith, which was the sense of destiny.

Today the world of action is exhausted, and also the world of thought. There is neither an historical sense nor an inner, metaphysical reality. No one man today can get down and offer his bare back as support. The world has spread itself out so thin that the mightiest back would not be broad enough to support it. Today it is dawning on men that if they would find salvation they must lift themselves up by their own boot-straps. They must discover for themselves a new sense of equilibrium. Each one for himself must recover the sense of destiny. In the past a figure like Christ could create an imaginary world powerful enough in its reality to make him the lever of the world. Today there are millions of sacrificial victims but not enough power in the lot of them to raise a grain of sand. The world, and men individually, is out of whack.

We are on the wrong track, all of us. One group, the larger one, insists on changing the external pattern—the social, political, economic configuration. Another group, very small but increasing in power, insists on discovering a new reality. There is no hope either way. The inner and outer are one. If now they are divorced it is because a new way of life is about to be ushered in. There is only one realm in which inner and outer may still be fused and that is the realm of art. Most art will reflect the death which is taking place, for only the most forward spirits can give an intimation of the life which is to come. Just as primitive peoples carry on in our midst their life of fifty or a hundred thousand years ago, so the artists.

We are facing an absolutely new condition of life. An entirely new cosmos must be created, and it must be created out of our separate, isolate, living parts. It is we, the indestructible morsels of living flesh, who make up the cosmos. The cosmos is not made up in the mind, by philosophers and metaphysicians, nor is it held in existence by God. An economic revolution will certainly not create it. It is something we carry within us and which we build up about us: we are part of it and it is we who must bring it into being. We must realize who and what we are. We must carry through to the finish, both in creation and destruction. What we do most of the time is either to deny or to wish. Ever since the beginning of our history, our Western history, we have been *willing* the world to be something other than it is. We have been transmogrifying ourselves in order to acclimatize ourselves to a mirage. This will has come to exhaustion in supreme doubt. We are paralyzed; we whirl about like drunken dervishes on the pivot of self. Nothing will liberate us but a new knowledge; not the Socratic "wisdom," but realization, which is knowledge become active.

For, as Lawrence predicted, we are entering the era of the Holy Ghost. We are about to give up the ghost of our dead self and enter a new domain. God is dead. The Son is dead. And we are dead only as these have gone out of us. It is not death really, but a *Scheintot*. Of Proust it was said by someone that "he was the most alive of all the dead." In that sense we are still alive. But the axis has broken, the poles no longer function. It is neither night nor day. Neither is it a twilight. We are drifting with the flux.

When I talk of drift and drifting I know very well that I am using only an image. Myself I do not believe that we are going to drift forever. Some may, perhaps a great part of the world of men and women. But not all. So long as there are men and women the world itself can never become a Sargasso Sea. What creates this fearsome image is the awareness in each of us that, despite ourselves, we *are* drifting, we have become one with the ceaseless flux. There is a force outside us which, because of death, seems greater than us, and that is Nature. We, as living beings, are part of Nature. But we are also part of something else, something which includes Nature. It is as this unrealized part of the universe that we have set ourselves up in opposition .o the whole. And it is not our will but our destiny which has permitted such an opposition to come into existence. That force which is beyond us, greater than us, obeys its own laws. If we are wise we try to move within those laws, adapt ourselves to them. That is the real element of livingness, as Lawrence might say. When we refuse to move with the movement of that greater force we break the law of life, we drift, and in the drift Nature sloughs us off.

Where the great spiritual leaders have succumbed was in the conflict between these two forces, epitomized and symbolized by their own lives. Each spiritual gain has been signalized by a defeat at the hands of Nature. Each spiritual gain meant the upsetting of the equilibrium between these opposing forces. The distance between one great figure and another is only another way of estimating the time required to obtain a new and satisfactory equilibrium. The task of each new figure has been to destroy the old equilibrium. Nothing more. Nothing less.

Today it is vaguely felt that we are in a period of transition. To what? To a new equilibrium? On what fulcrum? On what are we to find a point of rest? Lawrence saw that the fulcrum itself was worn out. He felt the tide carrying him along. He knew that a new order was establishing itself. Against this new cosmic order he set up no opposition. On the contrary, he welcomed it. But as an individual he protested. He was not fully born. Part of him was stuck in the womb of the old. Half out, alive, fully conscious, super-conscious in fact, he voiced the agony of that other half of him which was dying stillborn. It could not die quickly enough for him, even though in that partial death his own individual death was involved. He saw that the greater part of the world was dying without having been born. Death in the womb. It was that which drove him frantic.

It is no idle figure I use when I say that only the upper half of him emerged: the head and heart. A blinding consciousness he had, and a tender bleeding heart. But a potent figure of man he was not. He had only the sustaining heart—and the voice, which he used to the fullest. But he had a vision of what was to come, and in the measure that he was able to he identified himself with the future. "Only now," he said, "are we passing over into a new era." He spoke about it over and over, cryptically, symbolically: *the era of the Holy Ghost.* I notice that he expressed the idea when writing to someone about the Renaissance. He had just finished reading Rolland's essay on Michelangelo. "The world is going mad," says Lawrence, "as the Italian and Spanish Renaissance went mad. But where is our Reformation, where is our new light?" And then he added: "One must live quite apart, forgetting, having another world, a world as yet uncreated."

Lawrence's use of the word "forgetting" is worthy of attention. Whereas Proust was able successfully to live apart, *remembering,* creating his own very real, fictive world, Lawrence was never able to live apart, nor to forget. Proust, by a complete break with the outer world of reality, was able to live on as if dead, to live only in the remembrance of things past. Even then his was not an absolute break. A thin, almost invisible cord connected him with the world. Often it was an inanimate object which, through his exaggerated sensory faculties, brought him with a shock to a reality which he had buried deep within himself. His was not a remembering in the usual sense; it was a magic revival of the past through means of the body. The body re-experienced the joys or the sorrows of the buried past. From a trance-like state Proust thus roused himself to a semblance of life, the powerful reality and immediacy of which was greater than in the original experience. His great work is nothing but a series of these traumatic shocks, or rather the expression of their repercussions. For him, therefore, art took on the metaphysical aspect of rediscovering what was already written in the heart. It was a return to the labyrinth, a desire to bury himself deeper and deeper in the self. And this self was for him composed of a thousand different entities all attached by experience to a mysterious seed-like Self which he refused to know.

Proust's was a path, a direction, exactly the opposite of Lawrence's. It was an effort, one might almost say, to retrace his life and, by collecting all the images of himself which he had ever glimpsed in the mirror, to recompose a final seed-like image of which he had no knowledge. The use of sensation here is entirely different from Lawrence's use of it: because their conception of "body" was entirely different. Proust, having totally divorced himself from his body, except as a sensory instrument for reviving the past, gave to the human individuality thereby an entirely irreligious quality. His religion was ART—i.e., the process. For Proust the personality was fixed: it could come unglued, so to speak, be peeled off layer by layer, but the concept that lay behind this process was of something solid, already determined, imperishable, and altogether unique.

With this conception of a personal ego Lawrence had no patience. What he saw was an endless drama of the self, a whirlpool in which the individual was finally engulfed. Lawrence was interested in the development of man as a unique spiritual blossom. He deplored the fact that man, as MAN, had not yet come into his own kingdom. While emphasizing the unique quality of the individual he placed no value on uniqueness in itself. What he stressed was the flowering of the personality. He was impressed by the fact that man is in a state of infancy, psychologically speaking. Neither the dynamic attitude of the West, anchored in the will, in idealism, nor the attitude of the East, anchored in a fatalistic quietism, seemed satisfactory to him as practical philosophies. They were both inadequate. "Man as yet is only half-born," he said. "No sign of bud anywhere."

His first significant work, "The Crown," is concerned primarily with an attempt to make clear the meaning of the Holy Ghost. It is his way of referring to the mysterious source of the self, the creative instinct, the individual guide and conscience. In the realization of its meaning he visualized the resolution of the god problem, an end to the vicious dichotomy of demon-angel, god-devil, an end to the alternate belittlement and aggrandizement of the personality. What he searched for continually is the true self, that central source of power and action which is called the Holy Ghost, the mysterious, unknowable area of the self out of which the gods, as well as men, are born. His idea of a union with the cosmos meant the restoration of man's divinity. The old cosmos, he says in *Apocalypse*, was entirely religious and godless. There was no idea of "creation" or of "separateness" or of "God versus world." The cosmos was, is, and will be. It is *we* who have grown apart, insisted Lawrence. And it is in this growing apart that we have developed the extreme notions of the self, of the personality, and of God. The great sense of guilt which burdens man—and particularly the artist—springs from the deep realization that he is split off from the cosmos, that in a part of him he has made himself God and in another he has made himself human, all too human.

All this brings me to the present. We are facing an absolutely new condition of life, one that is almost unbearable, at least for a sensitive being. That such an antagonism always existed I have no doubt: the artist was always in conflict with the world, with the world in which he found himself. The fact that there *are* artists means that life is well-nigh insupportable. And yet, in the past there was always a thread of communication between the sensitive and the insensitive. There were forms and symbols, mythologies which served as alphabets and which enabled the uninitiated to decipher the divine script of the artist. Today the very thread—language—seems to have snapped. Powerless to communicate his vision, the artist loses his belief in himself, in his role or mission. Whereas before his escape from the pain of living was through art, today he has no escape except to deny his own validity. Today all the hierarchies have broken down: in every field of human endeavor we are faced with chaos. There is no choice, only surrender, surrender to the flux, to the drift towards a new and unthinkable order.

That Lawrence understood, that he revealed the trend, and that he offered a solution is what I wish to make clear. But to understand this it is necessary to recognize the peculiar nature of his temperament and the relation of such a temperament to

the times. The problem of an immediate and personal solution
to the all-besetting difficulties of the times may then be seen to
resolve itself into a much broader and much more human
problem of *destiny*. That we have a destiny, each of us and all of
us, seems more important right now than the question of an
immediate solution of life's problems. For it is in the very
establishment of a relation between oneself and the cosmos
that a new quality of hope will arise, and with hope, faith. We
must ask ourselves how it is that faced with a crushing destiny
there are some of us who, instead of shrinking or cowering, leap
forward to embrace it. There are some of us, in short, who in
assuming a definite attitude towards the world seek neither to
deny, nor to escape, nor to alter it, but simply to live it out.
Some more consciously than others. Some as though they saw
it written in the stars, as though it were tattooed on their
bodies.

There exists today all over the world a number of modern
spirits who are anything but modern. They are thoroughly out
of joint with the times, and yet they reflect the age more truly,
more authentically, that those who are swimming with the
current. In the very heart of the modern spirit there is a schism.
The egg is breaking, the chromosomes are splitting to emerge
with a new pattern of life. Something is germinating, and those
of us who seem most alien, most split, most divorced from the
current of life, are the ones who are going forward to create the
life as yet inchoate.

When I speak of a hope and a faith I ask myself what evi-
dences are there, what justification for such language? I think
again of the Renaissance and how Lawrence was obsessed with
that period. I see how we ourselves stand before the future,
divided between hope and fear. But at least we know that there
is a future, that the moment is momentous. We stand now as
we do sometimes in our own individual hum-drum lives,
thrilled by the thought of the morrow, the morrow which will
be utterly unlike today, or yesterday. Only the rare few are
privileged to regard the future with certainty, with hope and
with courage. They are the ones who are already living into the
future: they experience a posthumous joy. And this joy is no
doubt tinged with cruelty. In bringing about the death of an old

order a sort of sadistic pleasure is awakened. Another way of putting it would be to say that the heroic spirit is rekindled. The so-called moderns are the old and weary who see in a new collective order the gentle release of death. For them any change is welcome. It is the end which they are looking forward to. But there is another kind of modern who enters the conflict blindly, to establish that for which as yet there is no name. It is to this order of men that Lawrence addressed himself. The Apollonian show is over. The Dionysian dance has begun. The Orphic artists to come are the musicians of the new order, the seed-bearers, the *tragic* spirits.

It is of the utmost importance also to realize that the process of dissolution is accelerating. Every day the difference between the few and the many becomes sharper. A great yawning fissure divides the old from the new. There is still time perhaps to make the jump, but each day the hurdle becomes more perilous. The tendency so marked in Lawrence's work—to divide the world into black and white—becomes more and more actualized. It was one of the great distinguishing features of Dante's work. It was inevitable. It marks the great split in the mind, the angel's superhuman effort, as it were, to discover the soul of the new. During this process, which is nothing short of a crisis of consciousness, the spirit flames anew. Whatever is valuable, whatever is creative, must now reveal the pure and flaming spirit. The poet is bound to be oracular and prophetic. As the night comes on man looks out towards the stars; he no longer identifies himself with the world of day which is crumbling, but gives himself to the silent, ordained future. Abandoning the cunning instruments of the mind with which he had vainly hoped to pierce the mystery, he now stands before the veil of creation naked and awe-struck. He divines what is in store for him. Everything becomes personal in a new sense. He becomes himself a new person.

The world of Lawrence now seems to me like a strange island on which for a number of years I was stranded. Had I made my way back to the known, familiar world I should perhaps talk differently about my adventure, but that world is gone for me, and the island on which I was marooned serves as the sole remaining link, a memory which binds me to the past. This then will serve as a log of my strange adventure—if my memory does not fail me.

* * *

To his agent, J. B. Pinker, sending him the final batch of manuscript of *The Rainbow*, Lawrence wrote: "My beloved book, I am sorry to give it to you to be printed. I could weep tears in my heart, when I read these pages. If I had my way, I would put off the publishing yet awhile." In one of his most touching and most beautiful utterances Lawrence reveals the genuine artist-feeling for his offspring. This poor devil had to write to earn his way, yet he would put publication off for a while, because once the book is set adrift it is like a child that is laid on some doorstep, forgotten, denied. This great love of one's work can come only from the great pain it costs to bear it, to beget it. What a moving letter. How many authors have written such letters? Don't tell me that this man was a money-grubber, an opportunist. Don't call him a sentimentalist either. It wasn't a softy who wrote that letter: it was a genuine man, an earnest, sensitive spirit who truly valued his work and who had the greatest reverence for it.

Over the years during which I have written on Lawrence I have changed somewhat, and so have my ideas. If I had gone ahead with this book as I had originally planned it, I should have had only the satisfaction of finishing a task which was begun. It would have been an artificial success, or realization. I think it would have been a very bad book. So I went on with the book, in a totally different manner, and perhaps it is a worse book, but I believe it is better.

I have not scrapped what I have done in order to make a harmonious or symmetrical piece of art. I do not renounce what I said earlier any more than I would renounce my own past. But if today or tomorrow I decide to change my way of living, well... that brings about a whole new set of circumstances, a new expression, a new technique, as it were.

Over those years when I was not writing this book I naturally thought about the subject from time to time. It was a silent thinking which took place usually when I hit the pillow. Often too I wasted whole evenings discussing the subject with others and I was always infuriated with myself that I did not put this time to better advantage. Latterly I have refused to be drawn into any discussion of Lawrence and his work. I am becoming wise.

I had always desired this book to be an *uncritical* study of Lawrence, to be an impassioned and prejudiced thing. I have only the greatest contempt and disdain for such a solid, rounded critic as Middleton Murry. In fact, I heartily despise him and his whole tribe! Strike out right and left, I say to myself, and let the devil take the hindmost.

Such a method does not make for clarity and precision. Many people are going to be baffled and bewildered. But they would be baffled and bewildered anyway. So I say—to hell with them! And anyway, who have I written this for? For myself primarily. I have tried to make it clear to myself what I think and feel about Lawrence, so that he won't bother me any more. Perhaps everything I have to say could be put in a small paragraph, a sentence even. If I were a great enough individual I should be able to let it go at that and rest content. But apparently I am not. If I were very great I should be able to forget the whole thing and remain silent. But I am neither great nor sensible. It gives me tremendous satisfaction and pleasure to have gone into this thing in such great detail. Perhaps it will prove a pain in the ass for a lot of people, but that doesn't worry me. So long as it doesn't give me a pain in the ass, all right.

To have gone as far as I have in this task required an enormous amount of labor and patience. I don't think that I assumed such a burden thoughtlessly. There is something in me which must come out, must be said, and until it is said I shall not be easy in my mind. Then too, when one puts such a tremendous amount of material into the hopper something must be done about it. It doesn't just die inside of you. It moves about, it ferments, it changes position and stress, it leaves you always uncomfortable. It wants to be digested and spewed out, in short. And if it is held in too long one can die of constipation . . . .

One of the things that came to my mind, as I started writing afresh, is a phrase which I seem to have encountered repeatedly in Lawrence's writings—"what I am *trying* to do." It is very reminiscent of Cézanne who was always trying to *realize* something. It is a phrase which touches me deeply, for the reason, most likely, that I am in the same boat. This *trying* seems to be the creation itself. And it is this effort to go beyond oneself, to surpass, to say, and do the impossible, which makes certain men a subject of eternal debate. It mars everything they do, makes them "failures," as the smooth-tongued critics would say. And yet it seems to me that it is only these men who count, who really affect us and influence us. They strive to go beyond "art" into life again. They come through the other side of art into a world of reality which is too much for them—not simply because they find themselves isolated, but because they are in deep and unknown waters. There are no rules, laws or conventions to guide them. There is only conscience, and this conscience is sadly troubled. They speak two tongues, and one tongue contradicts the other. They are themselves baffled and bewildered. In the vernacular they can make themselves understood, and though they want very much to be understood, yet they are unable to employ this common language where they are deeply concerned. What they most deeply wish to convey to the world is rendered then in a hermeneutic language which estranges them. They are marked out as anomalies, sports, freaks, anti-social, incommunicative beings. And these, by the irony of fate, are the very men who have a supreme desire to communicate with others. It is the saddest plight into which any man can fall. Lawrence was such a man *par excellence*.

It seems to me absolutely hopeless, useless, to tackle him as one would the ordinary distinguished artist. Whichever way you grasp hold of him he eludes you, wriggles out of your clutches. Why try to grasp him at all? Why not let him be, let him be there in the midst of his creation, and walk around him, surveying him now from this angle, now from that, but always remembering that he is a man, a very human creature of flesh and blood, surrounded by his creation. Why not pull his beard once in a while, to make sure that it is real and not a part of his creation? Why not give him a boot in the ass once in a while, when he is obstinate and unyielding? Why not cajole him and wheedle him and flatter him and praise him? He was a human being like all of us, and he was susceptible to all the things to which we ourselves are susceptible. He made foolish errors, he conducted himself unwisely, he contradicted himself, he diminished himself, he was a bad friend now and then, and a bad husband and lover too. He wrote some bad books, he wrote atrocious nonsense too. He whined and complained, like Job. But all the time he was *trying*, trying harder almost than any man you can think of, and if he failed to *realize* all that he was attempting, he nevertheless succeeded in trying, and that seems to me to be the most inportant thing about him.

Lawrence was the very incarnation of struggle, the Promethean type so dear to the Aryan race. And though he wandered about a great deal, almost all over the earth, when you look back on his life, when you think of him as pure spirit, you are obliged inevitably to think of that other mythological figure who was forever chained to the cliff, his bowels forever eaten away by a vulture. Lawrence was consumed by the passion to surpass himself, by the passion to become a man who would be rid of the pursuit of the ideal. At times he becomes truly god-like, truly quiet and knowing and calm in his absolute self-possession. Then nobody is comparable to him. He is there in the quick of the absolute and no one can dislodge him. But there is a penalty to pay for this transgression of the human path. It is the penalty of crucifixion. And it is not the world that crucified Lawrence, but he himself, or the god in him. Man and God do not marry. As long as there is anything remotely corresponding to the idea of God, man is a victim. To surpass himself man does not, or should not, become God, but more a man, more Man.

Towards the end Lawrence caught on to this, but then it was too late. The books written on his death-bed are a paean to the earthly life of man, the life he had forsaken in his quest of a beyond. But this earthly life, though he himself was not to experience it, was a transfigured life which is open to all of us to know and to enjoy. It is as impressive to me now, when I contemplate Lawrence, as it was to the disciples when they contemplated Christ. It is the desire at the bottom of every man's heart when he is truly alone with his own soul.

Notes to Introduction

p. 12   "I am almost...." Henry Miller, *Letters to Anaïs Nin*, edited and
with an introduction by Gunther Stuhlmann (New York: G.P.
Putnam's Sons, 1965), p. 43. Hereafter referred to as *LAN*.

p. 12   "book of the century...." *LAN*, p.65.

p. 12   "fever...." *LAN*, p. 66.

p. 12   "I want to say...." *LAN*, p. 66.

p. 13   "as I said...." *LAN*, p. 67.

p. 13   "Henry has buried himself...." Anaïs Nin, *The Diary of Anaïs Nin*,
193-1934, edited and with an introduction by Gunther Stuhlmann
(New York: The Swallow Press & Harcourt, Brace and World, Inc.,
1966), p. 143.

p. 13   "with these four divisions...." *LAN* p. 67.

p. 13   "The Brochure keeps expanding...." *LAN*, p. 68.

p. 13   "a veritable...." *LAN*, p. 68.

p. 13   "All these pages...." *LAN*, p. 69.

p. 14   "Big Macrocosmic Connections." *LAN*, p. 69.

p. 14   "The notes pile up...." *LAN*, p. 69.

p. 14   "knocking the shit..." Quoted by Jay Martin in his *Always Merry
and Bright: The Life of Henry Miller* (Santa Barbara: Capra Press,
1978), p. 286.

p. 14   "I want more...." *LAN*, p. 90.

p. 14   "I feel I have...." *LAN*, p. 91.

p. 15   "a little runt...." *LAN*, p. 43.

p. 15   "remark the sickly letters...." *LAN*, pp. 44-45.

p. 15   "The language is matchless...." *LAN*, p. 90.

p. 15   "I am amazed...." *LAN*, p. 91.

p. 16   "I realize suddenly...." A hitherto unpublished letter from Henry
Miller's papers.

p. 20   "My head's bursting...." *LAN*, p. 116.

p. 20   "Epoch-making days...." *LAN*, p. 117.

p. 20   "It may seem unusual...." From the manuscripts, hitherto unpublished.

p. 22   "The great need...." *LAN*, p. 118.

p. 22   "after the Lawrence book...." *LAN*, p. 253.

p. 22   "The fact remains...." Henry Miller, "The Universe of Death," in
The Henry Miller Reader, Edited by Lawrence Durrell (New York:
New Directions, 1959), p. 205. Hereafter referred to as *Reader*.

p. 24   "There is evidence...." *Reader*, p. 204.

p. 24   "*embraced* everything" *LAN*, p. 117.

Notes to Chapter I

p. 27 "I am rather..." *The Collected Letters of D. H. Lawrence*. Edited with an Introduction by Harry T. Moore (New York: The Viking Press, 1962), p. 269. Hereafter referred to as *Letters*.

p. 29 "written in..." *Letters*, p. 259.

p. 29 "I have no longer..." *Letters*, pp. 263-64 (emphasis Miller's).

p. 29 "You know how..." *Letters*, p. 273.

p. 30 "We ought to..." *Apocalypse* (1932; rptd. New York: The Viking Press, 1966), p. 200.

p. 31 "Let the Horse..." *Letters*, p. 768.

p. 31 "Man, as yet... " "Reflections on the Death of a Porcupine," in *Phoenix II: Uncollected, Unpublished, and Other Prose Works by D. H. Lawrence*. Collected and Edited with an Introduction and notes by Warren Roberts and Harry T. Moore (New York: The Viking Press, 1970), p. 471. Hereafter referred to as "Reflections."

p. 32 "a savage enough pilgrimage" *Letters*, p. 736.

p. 32 to Garnett] *Letters*, p. 272.

p. 32 "There isn't a soul... " *Letters*, p. 275 (emphasis Miller's).

p. 32 "complete, but limited" Mabel Dodge Luhan. *Lorenzo in Taos* (New York: Alfred A. Knopf, 1932), p. 37. Hereafter referred to as Luhan.

p. 33 "her ugly-beautiful mouth" D. H. Lawrence. *The Rainbow* (1915; rptd. New York: The Viking Press, 1965), p. 43.

p. 33 "that which is physic... " *Letters*, p. 281.

p. 33 "They will progress... " *Letters*, p. 280.

p. 33 Nietzsche... against Socrates] Friedrich Nietzsche. "The Twilight of the Idols," in *The Portable Nietzsche*, Selected and Translated, with an Introduction, Prefaces, and Notes, by Walter Kaufman (New York: The Viking Press, 1969), p. 473.

p. 34 "I don't so much care... " *Letters*, p. 282.

p. 34 "the source of all life... " *Letters*, p. 280.

p. 34-5 "Yes, the paralysis... " *Letters*, p. 1194.

p. 35 "What man... " *Apocalypse*, p. 199.

p. 37 "sex-crucified" J. Middleton Murry. *D.H. Lawrence: Son of Woman* (1931; rptd. New York: Krause Reprint Corp., 1972), pp. 19-58.

p. 37 as Frieda said] Dorothy Brett. *Lawrence and Brett: A Friendship* (Philadelphia: J. B. Lippincott, 1933), p. 31, pp. 256-57.

p. 38 one of the great novels] *Mastro-don Gesualdo* by Giovanni Verga. See *Phoenix: The Posthumous Papers of D. H. Lawrence*. Edited and with an Introduction by Edward D. McDonald (New York: The Viking Press, 1936; rptd. 1968), pp. 223-31. See also *Letters*, pp. 668, 691.

p. 38   an introduction] D. H. Lawrence. "Introduction to these Paintings," in *Phoenix*, pp. 551-84.

p. 38   Richard Aldington] *D. H. Lawrence* (London: Chatto & Windus, 1930), p. 30. Hereafter referred to as Aldington.

p. 39   "You tell me I am wrong" Aldington, epigraph and pp. 10-11.

p. 40   the Holy Ghost] "Reflections," in *Phoenix II*, pp. 470-71.

p. 41   "Love can be terribly obscene . . ." D. H. Lawrence. *Studies In Classic American Literature* (1923; rptd. New York: The Viking Press, 1971), p. 68. Hereafter referred to as *Studies*.

p. 41   "It seemed to me . . ." Luhan, pp. 128-29.

p. 42   The Carswell woman] Catherine Carswell, author of *The Savage Pilgrimage: A Narrative of D. H. Lawrence* (New York: Harcourt, Brace and Co., 1932).

p. 42   "out of a pattern" *Studies*, p. 2.

p. 42   "old rampers" D. H. Lawrence. *Lady Chatterley's Lover* (1928; rptd. New York: New American Library, 1962), p. 189.

p. 44   "Death is no . . ." *The Letters of D. H. Lawrence*. Edited and with an Introduction by Aldous Huxley (London: William Heinemann Ltd., 1932), p. 379. This letter to Lady Cynthia Asquith is not in the Moore collection.

p. 45   "There never was . . . " D. H. Lawrence. *Fantasia of the Unconscious* (1922; rptd. New York: The Viking Press, 1960), p. 181. Hereafter referred to as *Fantasia*.

p. 45   "At length . . . " *Fantasia*, p. 182.

p. 45   "Will the bird . . . " *Letters*, p. 765.

p. 45   "This is a winter . . ." *Letters*, p. 468.

p. 46   "failed artist" See Otto Rank, "The Artist's Flight with Art," in *Art and Artist* (1932). *Art and Artist* is reprinted in Otto Rank, *The Myth of the Birth of the Hero and Other Writings*, edited by Philip Freund (New York: Vintage Books, 1964). See esp. pp. 184-210.

p. 47   "More life! . . . " D. H. Lawrence. "Aristocracy," in *Phoenix II*, p. 483.

p. 47   "A *deathly* book . . ." Murry, p. 143.

p. 48   "The only thing . . ." *Letters*, p. 424.

p. 48   *The Plumed Serpent* (1926; rptd. London: Penguin Books, 1961), p. 445. Hereafter referred to as *Serpent*.

p. 48   "People are . . ." Aldington, p. 41.

p. 49   "a *mystic*" *Studies*, p. 143 (emphasis Miller's).

p. 49   the finest lines] *Studies*, pp. 145-61.

p. 50   "Don't think . . ." *Letters*, p. 326.

p. 50   "One thing . . ." *Letters*, p. 395.

p. 50   "The *Grenzeleute* . . ." *Letters*, pp. 663-64.

p. 50   *Memoirs of the Foreign Legion*] by Maurice Magnus with an Introduction by D. H. Lawrence (1924; rptd. in *Phoenix II*, pp. 303-61).

p. 50   "And so..." *Phoenix II*, p. 359.

p. 51   "It is the..." Murry, p. 190.

p. 53   the union] *The Rainbow*, p. 479.

p. 53   "animality" Murry, p. 90.

Notes to Chapter II

p. 57   "He was looking..." *Serpent*, p. 207.

p. 61   "Our story..." D. H. Lawrence. *Aaron's Rod* (1922; rptd. New York: The Viking Press, 1950), p. 34. Hereafter referred to as *AR*.

p. 61   "His father..." *AR*, p. 60.

p. 62   "I'm damned..." *AR*, p. 61.

p. 62   "What I should..." *AR*, p. 62.

p. 63   "I reckon..." *AR*, p. 71.

p. 63   "Don't you think..." *AR*, p. 71.

p. 63   "Oh yes..." *AR*, p. 72.

p. 63   "The finest thing..." *AR*, p. 72.

p. 63   "He's a profound..." *AR*, p. 72.

p. 64   "I only live..." *AR*, p. 74.

p. 64   "It isn't that..." *AR*, p. 78.

p. 64   "I like the man..." *AR*, p. 78.

p. 65   "But he..." *AR*, pp. 79-80.

p. 65   "I had..." *AR*, p. 67.

p. 66   "I hate..." *AR*, p. 85.

p. 66   "Morning Star" *Serpent*, p. 404 and *passim*.

p. 66   "Then why not..." Murry, p. 321.

p. 67   "Tanny's the same..." *AR*, p. 91.

p. 68   The leader] Murry, p. 219.

p. 68   "make a criminal..." *AR*, p. 95.

p. 68   "And can you..." *AR*, p. 96.

p. 68   "It is a man's..." *Fantasia*, p. 135.

p. 69   "The feminine..." Oswald Spengler, *The Decline of the West* (New York: Alfred A. Knopf, 1928, 2 vols; rptd. 1957), II, 327. Hereafter referred to as *Decline*.

p. 70   "Why, you're..." *AR*, pp. 97-98.

p. 71   "And you're..." *AR*, p. 100.

p. 71   "The two men..." *AR*, p. 100.

p. 71   "There isn't..." *AR*, pp. 101-02.

p. 72   "men are..." *AR*, p. 102.

p. 73   "only killing time" *AR*, p. 98.

p. 73   his flute] *AR*, p. 103.

p. 73　"Aaron's rod..." *AR*, p. 102.

p. 73　"scarlet runners" *AR*, p. 103.

p. 73　Leo Frobenius] author of *The Voice of Africa, being an account of the travels of the German Inner African Exploration Expedition in the Years 1910-1912* (1913; rptd. New York: Benjamin Blom, Inc., 1968, 2 vols.).

p. 73　"And no sooner..." *AR*, p. 104.

p. 74　"Save for..." *AR*, p. 105 (emphasis Miller's).

p. 74　"He walked quickly..." *AR*, p. 106.

p. 74　"It was a fact..." *AR*, p. 113.

p. 75　"The Germans..." *AR*, p. 114.

p. 76　"All I want..." *AR*, p. 114.

p. 76　"I'm *not* going..." *AR*, p. 115.

p. 76　"A brave ant..." *AR*, pp. 115-16.

p. 76　Lowenfels] Walter Lowenfels, an American poet, was the author of *USA With Music* and *Apollinaire: An Elegy*. "When Miller met Lowenfels in April, 1931, he was working on an elegy for D. H. Lawrence" to which Miller refers below. See Jay Martin, *Always Merry and Bright: The Life of Henry Miller* (Santa Barbara: Capra Press, 1978), pp. 222ff.

p. 76　Fraenkel] Michael Fraenkel, author of *Werther's Younger Brother* whose Carrefour Editions had published Lowenfels' *USA*, was a wealthy retired American business man in Paris devoting himself to literature and philosophy when he and Miller met through Lowenfels. See Jay Martin, pp. 223ff.

p. 77　"He knew..." *AR*, p. 116 (emphasis Miller's)

p. 79　"Heaven is..." "Reflections," in *Phoenix II*, p. 472.

Notes to Chapter III

p. 85　"Every soul..." *Decline*, I: 358.

p. 86　"It is this..." *Decline*, I: 359.

p. 86　Petrie] William Matthew Flinders Petrie, author of *The Revelations of Civilization* (London: Harper & Bros., 1911), cited below.

p. 86　"I appended..." Friedrich Nietzsche, "The Birth of Tragedy," in *Basic Writings of Nietzsche*, trans. Walter Kaufmann (New York: The Modern Library, 1968), p. 24.

p. 87　Keyserling] Hermann Keyserling, author of *America Set Free* (New York: Harper & Brothers, 1929), cited below.

p. 87　"History..." James Joyce, *Ulysses* (1922; rptd. New York: The Modern Library, 1946), p. 35. Hereafter referred to as *Ulysses*.

p. 93　"something solid like a city" Edmund Wilson, *Axel's Castle* (1931; rptd. New York: Charles Scribner's Sons, 1943), p. 210. Hereafter referred to as Wilson.

p. 94　"possess Dublin..." Wilson, p. 211.

p. 94 "In such manner . . ." Louis Gillet, "James Joyce and His New Novel," in *Claybook for James Joyce,* Translation and Introduction by Georges Markow-Totevy, with a Preface by Leon Edel and an Article by André Gide (1931; rptd. London: Abelard-Schuman, 1958), p. 52. Hereafter referred to as Gillet.

p. 95 "a panorama . . ." Gillet, p. 52.

p. 98 memorable treatise on art] Marcel Proust, "The Past Recaptured," in *Remembrance of Things Past,* trans. Frederick A. Blossom (New York: Random House, 1932), pp. 983-1124. Hereafter referred to as *Remembrance.*

p. 100 "When Albertine . . ." *Wilson,* p. 182.

p. 101 the discussion] Proust, "The Captive," in *Remembrance,* pp. 644ff.

p. 102 "Being alive . . ." D. H. Lawrence, "Aristocracy," in *Phoenix II,* p. 483.

p. 104 "obtained from . . ." Proust, "The Past Recaptured," in *Remembrance,* pp. 1006-07.

p. 107 "So rich . . ." Wyndham Lewis, "An Analysis of the Mind of James Joyce," in *Time and Western Man* (London: Chatto and Windus, 1927), p. 109.

p. 108 the famous section] *Ulysses,* pp. 650-722.

p. 109 "to forge . . ." James Joyce, *A Portrait of the Artist as a Young Man* (1916; rptd. Harmondsworth: Penguin Books, 1977), p. 253.

p. 109 "No, mother . . ." *Ulysses,* p. 12.

p. 112 Ludwig Lewisohn] *The Story of American Literature* (New York: Harper & Brothers, 1932). Hereafter referred to as Lewisohn.

p. 114 "The metaphysical comfort . . ." *The Birth of Tragedy,* p. 59.

p. 117 "We, dear reader . . ." "Introduction to these Paintings," in *Phoenix,* pp. 569-70.

p. 117 *New Heaven and Earth]* "Look! We Have Come Through," in *The Complete Poems of D. H. Lawrence,* Vivian de Sola Pinto and Warren Roberts, eds. (1917; rptd. New York: The Viking Press, 1971), pp. 256-61. Hereafter referred to as *Poems.*

Notes to Chapter IV

p. 119 I was a lover . . . "New Heaven and Earth," in *Poems,* p. 257.

p. 119 "the painted fungus of rottenness" D. H. Lawrence, *The White Peacock* (1911; rptd. London: J. M. Dent & Sons, Ltd., 1935), p. 162.

p. 119 the dead womb] "The Crown," in *Phoenix II,* p. 367.

p. 121 "Dark, ruddy pillar . . ." *Poems,* p. 40.

p. 123 "devil-creator"] Anaïs Nin, *D. H. Lawrence: An Unprofessional Study* (1932; rptd. Chicago: The Swallow Press, 1964), p. 95. Hereafter referred to as Nin.

p. 123 "Well, all right then . . ." D. H. Lawrence, *Kangaroo* (1923; rptd. London: William Heinemann Ltd., 1939), p. 183.

p. 125 "They are all . . ." *Letters,* p. 459.

p. 125 tells us] Carswell, p. 30.

p. 129 "Why not?..." *Serpent*, p. 249.

p. 131 "Whatever single act..." "The Crown" in *Phoenix II*, p. 392.

p. 131 "I believe..." Luhan, p. 19

p. 133 "He was the Son..." Luhan, p. 170.

p. 133 "He was entombed..." Luhan, p. 193.

p. 135 "This was..." D. H. Lawrence, *Twilight in Italy* (1916; rptd. New York: The Viking Press, 1967), p. 35.

p. 135 "not for a second..." *Fantasia*, p. 173.

p. 136 "You've got to..." *Letters*, p. 470.

p. 137 "He who gets..." "Aristocracy," in *Phoenix II*, p. 483.

p. 137 "He was born..." *Studies*, p. 138.

p. 138 "Why pin..." *Studies*, p. 140.

p. 138 "It is one's..." *Studies*, p. 136.

p. 141 "Don't think..." *Letters*, p. 775.

p. 142 Rank tells] "The Artist's Fight With Art," cited above.

p. 142 "Death is..." "The Crown," in *Phoenix II*, p. 374.

p. 144 "Let's wipe..." *Letters*, p. 830.

p. 145 "If I am..." *Letters*, p. 1154.

Notes to Chapter V

p. 147 "I was the God..." *Poems*, p. 257.

p. 147 "I was so weary..." *Poems*, p. 256.

p. 147 "Living..." Nin, pp. 102-03.

p. 153 Lilly massages] *AR*, p. 91.

p. 153 "I want..." *Kangaroo*, p. 72.

p. 154 "as a man..." D. H. Lawrence, *The Ladybird*, in *The Short Novels*, Vol. I (1921); rptd. London: Heinemann, 1965), p. 49.

p. 154 "My great religion..." *Letters*, p.180.

p. 155 "It has been..." *Letters*, pp. 378-79.

p. 158 "Men are free..." *Studies*, p. 6.

p. 160 he wrote appreciatively] *Letters*, pp. 517-18.

p. 160 "long green dragon" *Apocalypse*, p. 146.

p. 161 "Perhaps..." *Letters*, p. 723.

p. 161 as Murry says] Murry, p. 29.

p. 161 another title] *Letters*, p. 1043.

p. 161 *Tenderness*] *Letters*, p. 1030.

p. 162 "Horoscopy..." *Apocalypse*, p. 174.

p. 162 "When I hear..." *Apocalypse*, p. 47.

p. 162 "By the time..." *Apocalypse*, pp. 45-46.

p. 163 "Only now..." *Apocalypse,* p. 90.

p. 163 says Spengler] *Decline,* I: 45-46.

p. 163 "There are no..." *Decline,* I: 41.

p. 163 "my own philosophy..." *Decline,* I: 46.

p. 164 Havelock Ellis] *The Dance of Life* (Boston: Houghton Mifflin Company, 1923), p. 309, n2.

p. 164 *"Pessimissimus?"* in Oswald Spengler, *Reden und Aufsätze* (1921; rptd. München: C. H. Beck'sche Verlagsbuchhandlung, 1951), pp. 63-79.

p. 166 "I feel myself..." quoted from *Decline,* I: 144.

p. 167 "early science..." *Apocalypse,* p. 161.

p. 167 "the very ancient..." *Apocalypse,* pp. 159-65.

p. 171 "Lawrence was..." Murry, p. 46.

p. 172 "Second Religiousness" *Decline,* II: 310-15.

p. 174 "People are..." Aldington, p. 41.

p. 174 "If anyone asks..." Luhan, p. 171.

p. 174 "He was..." Luhan, p. 170.

Notes to Chapter VI

p. 177 "I don't intend..." *Fantasia,* p. 53.

p. 178 "little warm flame" *Letters,* p. 828.

p. 178 "a real kindliness" *Letters,* p. 829.

p. 179 "moral critic..." *Decline,* I: 346.

p. 179 "Art..." Nietzsche, p. 31.

p. 181 "if sex..." *Fantasia,* p. 220.

p. 185 "The great goal..." *Fantasia,* p. 214.

p. 186 "And in France?..." Phoenix, p. 562.

p. 191 "railed against dancing..." Luhan, p. 189.

p. 191 dancing he spoke of] *Letters,* p. 796.

p. 192 "If there is..." Samuel Putnam, *The New Review* (Paris, 1930). For Miller's relationship with Putnam see Jay Martin, pp. 233-34.

p. 193 "All Lawrence's philosophy..." Frederick Carter, *D. H. Lawrence and the Body Mystical* (London; Denis Archer, 1932), pp. 17-18, 56.

p. 193 "What we want..." *Apocalypse,* p. 200.

p. 196 "It is an old fear..." *Phoenix,* pp. 551-52.

p. 196 "The appearance..." *Phoenix,* p. 555.

p. 197 "Now we know..." *Phoenix,* p. 556.

p. 198 "Man dies..." Murry, p. 48.

p. 200 "I don't feel it *here.*" Quoted by Aldous Huxley in the Introduction to his *Letters,* p. xv.

Notes to Chapter VII

p. 205 "When you are . . ." *Letters*, p. 899.

p. 207 "only youth . . ." *Decline*, I: 152.

p. 208 "These sly . . ." *The Rainbow*, p. 201.

p. 209 "They are dead . . ." "Cypresses," in *Poems*, p. 297.

p. 210 "The carrion birds . . ." "The Crown," in *Phoenix II*, p. 406.

p. 210 "The vulture . . ." *Phoenix II*, p. 409.

p. 211 *"To me . . ."* Note to "The Crown," in *Phoenix II*, p. 364.

p. 213 what Spengler means] *Decline*, I: 356-63.

p. 223 "greatest" "radiant . . ." Murry, pp. 171, 186.

p. 224 "But he was not . . ." Murry, p. 174.

p. 225 "The artist needs . . ." Murry, pp. 172-74 (emphasis Miller's).

p. 227 "The 'I' . . ." Murry, p. 318.

p. 227 "from the beginning . . ." Murry, p. 319.

p. 228 "Lawrence's last . . ." Murry, p. 318.

p. 228 "The old courage . . ." Murry, p. 320.

p. 228 "The moment comes . . ." Murry, p. 321.

p. 230 "The fact remains . . ." Luhan, pp. 292-94.

p. 231 "no man . . ." Murry, p. 323.

p. 231 "Jesus . . ." Murry, p. 322.

Notes to Chapter VIII

p. 233 "But there is . . ." Murry, p. 55

p. 234 "if Lawrence's . . ." Murry, p. 191.

p. 234 "straightway they . . ." Murry, p. 197.

p. 234 "by that knowledge . . ." Murry, p. 198.

p. 236 "The most interesting . . ." *Phoenix*, p. 571.

p. 237 "Cézanne's . . ." *Phoenix*, p. 567.

p. 237 "Poor Cézanne . . ." *Phoenix*, p. 568.

p. 238 "Men live . . ." *Fantasia*, p. 57.

p. 239 "nothing will ever . . ." *Fantasia*, p. 56.

p. 243 *"We are Hamlet . . ."* *Letters*, p. 180 (emphasis Miller's).

p. 244 "freedom to do . . ." *Decline*, I: 39.

p. 246 "the important thing . . ." *History of Art*, trans. Walter Pach (New York: Harper and Brothers, 1921-30; 5 vols).

p. 248 "If only we . . ." Huxley *Letters*, p. 279 (not in Moore).

p. 255 "The world . . ." *Letters*, pp. 445-46.

p. 260 "My beloved book . . ." *Letters*, p. 347.

Finis.